The 14-HOUR WAR

The 14-HOUR
WAR

Valor on Koh Tang and
the Recapture of the
SS *Mayaguez*

James E. Wise Jr. and Scott Baron

NAVAL INSTITUTE PRESS
Annapolis, Maryland

Naval Institute Press
291 Wood Road
Annapolis, MD 21402

Library of Congress Cataloging-in-Publication Data
Wise, James E.
  The 14-hour war : valor on Koh Tang and the recapture of the SS Mayaguez /
James E. Wise Jr. and Scott Baron.
      p. cm.
  Includes bibliographical references and index.
  ISBN 978-1-59114-974-3 (hardcover)
  1. Mayagüez incident, 1975. 2. Mayagüez (Ship) I. Baron, Scott, date. II.
Title. III. Title: Fourteen-hour war.
  E865.W57 2011
  972.95'6—dc22

                                                        2011009044

Printed in the United States of America.

19 18 17 16 15 14 13 12 11   9 8 7 6 5 4 3 2 1
First printing

Dedicated to the lion-hearted American airmen, sailors, and Marines who fought a combat-hardened enemy on Koh Tang, a small island located in the Gulf of Thailand, in May 1975.

Few today know of their valor in fighting the last battle of the Vietnam War.

Contents

Preface

This book is about piracy, American military heroics, and human tragedy. During the twentieth century there were only two incidents of piracy of American ships: the USS *Pueblo* (1968) and the SS *Mayaguez* (1975). Both ships were hijacked and their crews removed from their vessels. The *Pueblo* was on a U.S. Navy intelligence patrol off North Korea, and the *Mayaguez*, an American container ship, was plying the waters of the Gulf of Thailand. The *Pueblo* was captured by North Korean military forces, the *Mayaguez* by members of the revolutionary government (Khmer Rouge) of Cambodia. Both ships were in international waters. The stories of these incidents are fading into history. While both stories are important parts of our history, the seizure of the American-flagged container ship *Mayaguez*, though remembered by few, is worth recounting because of the current, almost unstoppable, hijacking of foreign merchant ships transiting the Gulf of Aden and waters as far south as off the coast of Kenya in the Indian Ocean.

The emergence of Somali hijacking of foreign freighters and tankers in the Gulf of Aden has become front-page news. In 2008 some forty successful hijackings occurred; in the first half of 2009, another thirty-one ships were seized. More than twenty thousand merchant vessels pass through the Gulf every year—all are inviting targets for Somali pirates. At any given time, some twenty to thirty captured foreign ships are being held for ransom in Somali ports. Two attacks were made on an American merchant ship, the *Maersk Alabama*. On 12 April 2009 U.S. Navy Sea, Air, and Land (SEAL) snipers killed three pirates that were holding the captain of the ship (Capt. Richard Phillips) hostage. A second attack was made on the same ship in November 2009. However, on this second occasion the pirates were fended off by an onboard private security group using gunfire, a long-range acoustical device painful to the human ear, and evasive maneuvers. On Monday 28 December 2009, Somali pirates seized two ships "at once" a thousand miles apart: A British-flagged chemical tanker was captured in the Gulf of Aden. Three hours later, a Panamanian-flagged carrier managed by Greece was seized in the Indian Ocean.

Although hijackings continued in 2010, naval cooperation among NATO forces, China, Russia, and other countries with shipping interests in the Gulf of Aden has decreased the number of attacks on foreign freighters off the coast of Somalia. Some twenty-two countries have formed an international naval force that regularly patrols the troubled Gulf waters. On Thursday 9 September 2010, U.S. Marines stormed on board a pirate-held cargo ship off Somalia's coast and reclaimed control of the vessel without firing a shot, in the first such boarding raid by the international antipiracy flotilla. Just before dawn that day, the U.S. team from the 15th Marine Expeditionary Unit's Maritime Raid Force launched the assault from on board the USS *Dubuque*, an amphibious transport ship. However, attacks in the southern part of the Somali Basin (which is twice as large as the Gulf of Aden) have little international antipiracy naval coverage. Additional manned or unmanned surveillance assets are being planned, but as of 14 January 2011 Somali pirates were holding twenty-eight ships with 660 foreign crewmen.

The 14 Hour War: Valor on Koh Tang Island and the Recapture of the SS Mayaguez includes a comprehensive account of the battle to recapture the *Mayaguez* and free its crew; the strategy that evolved during four days of intense discussions between President Gerald Ford and his National Security Council; the perils of directing a war halfway around the world; the casualties incurred on those who heroically rushed into battle; and most importantly numerous first-person accounts by Marine, Navy, Air Force, and Coast Guard personnel relating where they were and what they did during the fierce engagement on Koh Tang Island. Also included is the latest information regarding the fate of the three Marines who were left behind, as recounted in 1999 by the enemy battalion commander who was in charge of Khmer Rouge forces on the island.

Finally, this book looks at the initial U.S. government cover-up of an operation where everything that could have gone wrong went wrong!

Map 1. **Southeast Asia**

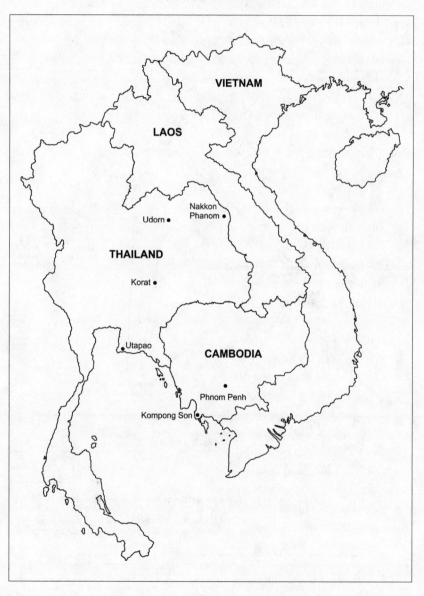

Map 2. The *SS Mayaguez* Incident

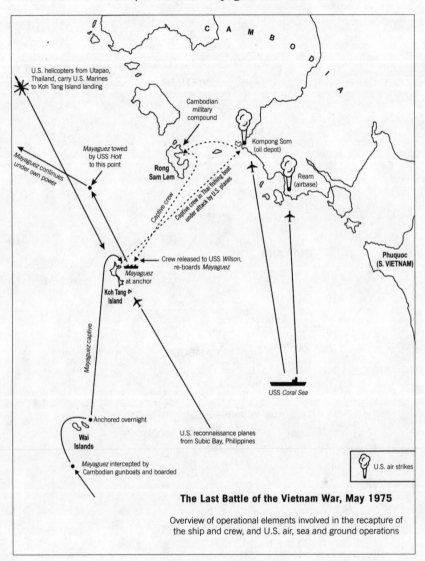

U.S. helicopters from Utapao, Thailand, carry U.S. Marines to Koh Tang Island landing

Cambodian military compound

Kompong Som (oil depot)

Mayaguez towed by USS *Holt* to this point

Mayaguez continues under own power

Rong Sam Lem

Ream (airbase)

Captive crew

Captive crew in Thai fishing boat under attack by U.S. planes

Crew released to USS *Wilson*, re-boards *Mayaguez*

Mayaguez at anchor

Koh Tang Island

Phuquoc (S. VIETNAM)

Mayaguez captive

USS *Coral Sea*

Anchored overnight

Wai Islands

U.S. reconnaissance planes from Subic Bay, Philippines

Mayaguez intercepted by Cambodian gunboats and boarded

U.S. air strikes

The Last Battle of the Vietnam War, May 1975

Overview of operational elements involved in the recapture of the ship and crew, and U.S. air, sea and ground operations

Map 3. **Koh Tang Island**

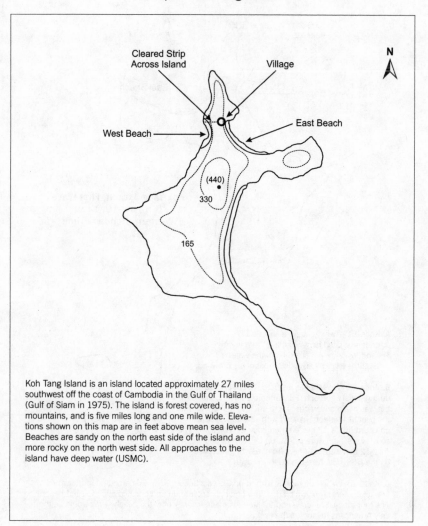

N

Cleared Strip
Across Island

Village

West Beach

East Beach

(440)

330

165

Koh Tang Island is an island located approximately 27 miles southwest off the coast of Cambodia in the Gulf of Thailand (Gulf of Siam in 1975). The island is forest covered, has no mountains, and is five miles long and one mile wide. Elevations shown on this map are in feet above mean sea level. Beaches are sandy on the north east side of the island and more rocky on the north west side. All approaches to the island have deep water (USMC).

Map 4. **Insertion Assault Operations**

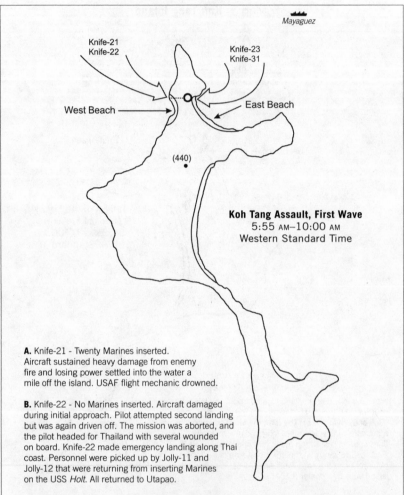

Mayaguez

Knife-21
Knife-22

Knife-23
Knife-31

West Beach

East Beach

(440)

Koh Tang Assault, First Wave
5:55 AM–10:00 AM
Western Standard Time

A. Knife-21 - Twenty Marines inserted. Aircraft sustained heavy damage from enemy fire and losing power settled into the water a mile off the island. USAF flight mechanic drowned.

B. Knife-22 - No Marines inserted. Aircraft damaged during initial approach. Pilot attempted second landing but was again driven off. The mission was aborted, and the pilot headed for Thailand with several wounded on board. Knife-22 made emergency landing along Thai coast. Personnel were picked up by Jolly-11 and Jolly-12 that were returning from inserting Marines on the USS *Holt*. All returned to Utapao.

C. Knife-23 - While attempting to land on the east beach, Knife-23 came under intense enemy fire. Its tail section blown off, the hovering helicopter spun and crashed into the sand beach. The four-men USAF crew and 20 Marines made it safely onto the beach. They would be the only Americans to land on the east beach.

D. Knife-31 came under the same fierce fire as Knife-23. Its port fuel tank was struck by gunfire and exploded. This was followed by an RPG hit that blew away a large portion of the front section of the aircraft. Knife-31 crashed in surf waters 15 to 30 meters from the eastern shoreline. Ten Marines, two Navy corpsmen, and the USAF copilot were killed. The surviving 13 crewmen and Marines swam out to sea and floated until rescued by the USS *Henry B. Wilson*.

Note: Knife & Jolly were radio call signs

Map 5. **Insertion Assault Operations**

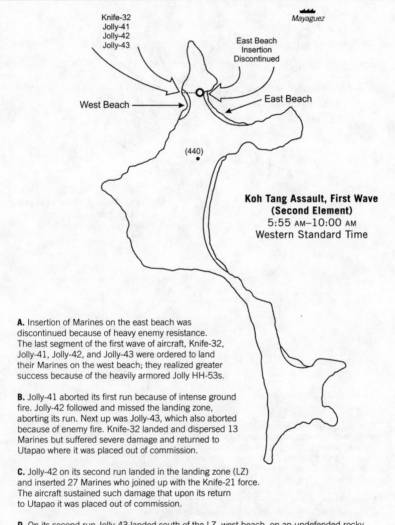

Knife-32
Jolly-41
Jolly-42
Jolly-43

Mayaguez

East Beach
Insertion
Discontinued

West Beach

East Beach

(440)

**Koh Tang Assault, First Wave
(Second Element)**
5:55 AM–10:00 AM
Western Standard Time

A. Insertion of Marines on the east beach was discontinued because of heavy enemy resistance. The last segment of the first wave of aircraft, Knife-32, Jolly-41, Jolly-42, and Jolly-43 were ordered to land their Marines on the west beach; they realized greater success because of the heavily armored Jolly HH-53s.

B. Jolly-41 aborted its first run because of intense ground fire. Jolly-42 followed and missed the landing zone, aborting its run. Next up was Jolly-43, which also aborted because of enemy fire. Knife-32 landed and dispersed 13 Marines but suffered severe damage and returned to Utapao where it was placed out of commission.

C. Jolly-42 on its second run landed in the landing zone (LZ) and inserted 27 Marines who joined up with the Knife-21 force. The aircraft sustained such damage that upon its return to Utapao it was placed out of commission.

D. On its second run Jolly-43 landed south of the LZ, west beach, on an undefended rocky outcropping and unloaded 29 Marines.

E. Jolly-41 landed on the west beach after four aborted attempts and inserted 22 Marines. Because of damage to its fuel tanks and rotors, it was later grounded for the remainder of the mission.

F. 131 Marines and four USAF crewmen were on the island awaiting the second wave of troop-carrying aircraft.

Map 6. **Insertion Assault Operations**

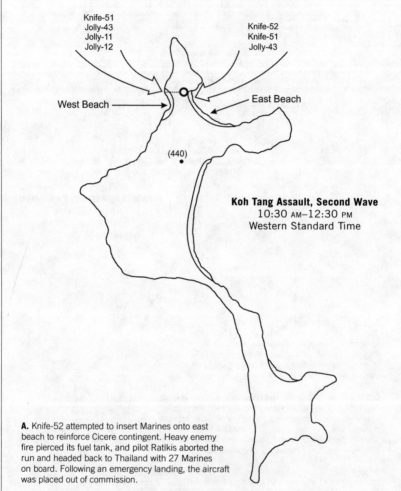

Knife-51
Jolly-43
Jolly-11
Jolly-12

Knife-52
Knife-51
Jolly-43

West Beach

East Beach

(440)

Koh Tang Assault, Second Wave
10:30 AM–12:30 PM
Western Standard Time

A. Knife-52 attempted to insert Marines onto east beach to reinforce Cicere contingent. Heavy enemy fire pierced its fuel tank, and pilot Ratlkis aborted the run and headed back to Thailand with 27 Marines on board. Following an emergency landing, the aircraft was placed out of commission.

B. Knife-51 and Jolly-43 aborted their runs on the east beach due to fierce enemy fire. The remaining four helicopters were diverted to the west beach.

C. Knife-51 landed 19 Marines, then Jolly-43 inserted 28 more. At noon Jolly-11 brought in 27 Marines, followed by Jolly-12, which landed another 26, all on the west beach.

D. The addition of 100 more Marines brought the total west beach force to 221 Marines.

E. That afternoon Jolly-43 again attempted to extract the Marines isolated on the east beach. The aircraft was driven away by intense machine-gun fire. Pilot Purser flew to the aircraft carrier *Coral Sea* and was safely recovered.

Map 7. **Extraction Operations**

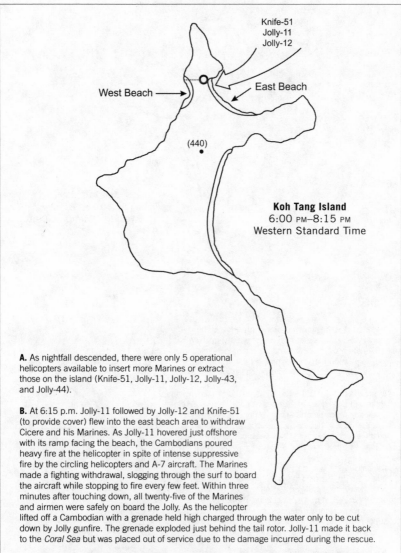

Knife-51
Jolly-11
Jolly-12

West Beach

East Beach

(440)

Koh Tang Island
6:00 PM–8:15 PM
Western Standard Time

A. As nightfall descended, there were only 5 operational helicopters available to insert more Marines or extract those on the island (Knife-51, Jolly-11, Jolly-12, Jolly-43, and Jolly-44).

B. At 6:15 p.m. Jolly-11 followed by Jolly-12 and Knife-51 (to provide cover) flew into the east beach area to withdraw Cicere and his Marines. As Jolly-11 hovered just offshore with its ramp facing the beach, the Cambodians poured heavy fire at the helicopter in spite of intense suppressive fire by the circling helicopters and A-7 aircraft. The Marines made a fighting withdrawal, slogging through the surf to board the aircraft while stopping to fire every few feet. Within three minutes after touching down, all twenty-five of the Marines and airmen were safely into board the Jolly. As the helicopter lifted off a Cambodian with a grenade held high charged through the water only to be cut down by Jolly gunfire. The grenade exploded just behind the tail rotor. Jolly-11 made it back to the *Coral Sea* but was placed out of service due to the damage incurred during the rescue.

C. As Jolly-11 departed for the *Coral Sea*, Jolly-12 and Knife-51 were directed to stay in the area and search for a reported Marine who had taken refuge in the wreckage of Knife-31. Jolly-12 hovered over the remains of the helicopter and lowered a rescue device while Knife-51 provided cover. There was no response from within the wreckage and the aircraft was heavily damaged by Cambodian fire. Jolly-12 limped back to the *Coral Sea* and was placed out of service. That left just three helicopters to extract the 200 Marines on the west beach.

Map 8. **Extraction Operations**

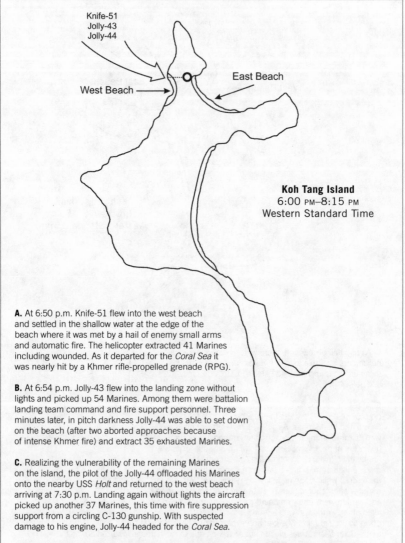

Knife-51
Jolly-43
Jolly-44

West Beach

East Beach

Koh Tang Island
6:00 PM–8:15 PM
Western Standard Time

A. At 6:50 p.m. Knife-51 flew into the west beach and settled in the shallow water at the edge of the beach where it was met by a hail of enemy small arms and automatic fire. The helicopter extracted 41 Marines including wounded. As it departed for the *Coral Sea* it was nearly hit by a Khmer rifle-propelled grenade (RPG).

B. At 6:54 p.m. Jolly-43 flew into the landing zone without lights and picked up 54 Marines. Among them were battalion landing team command and fire support personnel. Three minutes later, in pitch darkness Jolly-44 was able to set down on the beach (after two aborted approaches because of intense Khmer fire) and extract 35 exhausted Marines.

C. Realizing the vulnerability of the remaining Marines on the island, the pilot of the Jolly-44 offloaded his Marines onto the nearby USS *Holt* and returned to the west beach arriving at 7:30 p.m. Landing again without lights the aircraft picked up another 37 Marines, this time with fire suppression support from a circling C-130 gunship. With suspected damage to his engine, Jolly-44 headed for the *Coral Sea*.

D. Knife-51 returned from the *Coral Sea* and made three aborted attempts in the darkness. On the fourth attempt the aircraft was landed safely with all lights turned on, drawing a massive barrage of fire from the Cambodians. Knife-51 gunners opened fire with their miniguns while a C-130 peppered the enemy positions with 20-mm and 40-mm fire. Knife-51 remained on the ground for ten minutes while taking on board 29 Marines (thought to be the last Marines on the island at the time). Before lift-off crew members and Marines surveyed the beach area looking for any stray Marines. Finding none the helicopter and supporting aircraft departed the area.

All maps created by Dominic Chiappetta

PART ONE

Introduction

If you walk along the Vietnam Veterans Memorial in Washington, DC, make your way to the panel just west of the center of the wall, and scan panel 01W (West), lines 124 through 131, you'll find the names of the last forty-one servicemen killed in combat in the Vietnam War. What is unusual is that these airmen, sailors, and Marines were killed in May 1975 in Cambodia, nearly two weeks after the fall of Saigon and more than two years after the U.S. military withdrawal from Vietnam.

Early in 1975 the United States was suffering from a lack of prestige. Richard Nixon had resigned the presidency the previous August rather than risk impeachment, making his successor, Vice President Gerald Ford, the first person to hold the office of president of the United States without being elected as president or vice president. At that same time, the Communists were gaining momentum in Southeast Asia.

On 12 April 1975 the United States evacuated its embassy at Phnom Penh, Cambodia, in the aftermath of the Khmer Rouge victory. On 25 April the U.S. Embassy in Saigon was likewise evacuated, with the city capitulating to North Vietnamese forces on 30 April. The U.S. government had no diplomatic relations with the new governments of either country.

PART TWO

The Capture of the
SS *Mayaguez*

O n 12 May 1975 the SS *Mayaguez*, a 500-foot cargo ship of U.S. reg-istry, was steaming off the coast of Cambodia, en route from Hong Kong to the port of Sattahip on the coast of Thailand, when it was approached by gunboats of the Khmer Rouge navy.

The ship's master, Capt. Charles T. Miller, recorded the following in the *Mayaguez*'s logbook: "On 12 May 1975 at approximately 1410 hours the vessel was challenged by Cambodian gunboat P128. At 1420 hours reduced to maneuvering speed and gunboat fires antiaircraft machine guns across starboard bow. 1421 hours Engines stop . . . 1425 hours gunboat P128 comes along side . . . 1435 hours boarded by seven armed men."[1]

As crew member Jared "Jerry" Myregard later recalled, "When I got outside, I saw these Khmer Rouge soldiers coming on board with black pajamas, bandoliers, automatic weapons, rocket launchers and I knew what was happening." The *Mayaguez* had been seized in international waters, and its thirty-nine crew members taken captive.[2]

At 0718 hours local time on 12 May, Mr. John Neal of the Delta Exploration Company in Jakarta, Indonesia, received the following May-day message from the *Mayaguez*: "Have been fired upon and boarded by Cambodian armed forces at 9 degrees, 48 minutes North/ 102 degrees 53 minutes East. Ship is being towed to unknown Cambodian port."

The commander in chief-Pacific (CINCPAC) was notified of the event by the U.S. Embassy in Jakarta, and copies of the radio message were sent to the White House, National Security Agency (NSA), Central Intelligence

The SS Mayaguez. National Archives and Records Administration

Agency (CIA), Defense Intelligence Agency (DIA), and the National Military Command Center (NMCC) at the Pentagon.[3]

In Washington, DC, National Security Adviser Brent Scowcroft woke President Gerald Ford with the news that an American merchant ship had been seized in international waters off Cambodia. Ford ordered a meeting of the NSC for 1000 hours.

There was a feeling among Ford's advisers that it was imperative that action be taken rapidly. The seizure of the USS *Pueblo* in 1968 served as a reminder that the United States had to act before the *Mayaguez* crew was taken to the mainland, where mounting an operation to rescue them would be near to impossible.[4]

The fact that the United States had no diplomatic relations with the new government in Cambodia greatly complicated negotiating the ship's release; overtures to the People's Republic of China to mediate proved unsuccessful, so Ford was left with no option but military action. As then–secretary of state Henry Kissinger noted, "Having just evacuated Indochina, we could not graduate to the point where American ships could be captured on the high seas."[5]

President Ford meeting with members of the NSC in the cabinet room on Monday 12 May 1975. National Archives and Records Administration

In the interim, the president had placed American forces in the Western Pacific (WESTPAC) on alert and ordered continuous monitoring of the *Mayaguez* by U.S. Navy P-3 Orion reconnaissance aircraft out of the Royal Thai Air Force Base (RTAFB) at Utapao, Thailand. Unfortunately, it was three hours before the order to monitor the ship's movement was issued, and another two hours before the order was implemented, creating a five-hour darkened window between the seizure and the commencement of the surveillance.[6]

This surveillance on the morning of 13 May revealed that the *Mayaguez* had been moved in the early morning from the vicinity of Paulo Wei Island, where it had been seized, to Koh Tang Island, a three-mile by two-mile crescent-shaped island twenty-seven miles off the southwest coast of the Cambodian port of Kompong Som. The Cambodians had intended for the *Mayaguez* to dock at Kompong Som, but Captain Miller claimed that the radar was inoperable, and that it would be impossible to dock safely without it. The *Mayaguez* was diverted to Koh Tang Island, and she dropped anchor at about noon.[7]

Meanwhile, in Washington, where the eleven-hour time difference made it 1350 hours on 12 May, the White House announced the seizure of the *Mayaguez* to the press. Following a meeting of the NSC, a naval force consisting of the aircraft carrier USS *Coral Sea* (CVA-43), destroyer escort USS *Harold E. Holt* (DE-1074), the guided missile destroyer USS *Henry B. Wilson* (DDG-7), and the amphibious carrier USS *Hancock* (CV-19), all of which were in port at Subic Bay in the Philippines, was ordered into the area. By chance, the commander of Destroyer Squadron 23 (ComDesRon-23), Capt. D. P. Roane, was on board the *Holt*.

Following a second meeting of the NSC at 1030 hours the following day, Marines of the III MAF (Marine Amphibious Force)—primarily made up of Battalion Landing Team 2d Battalion 9th Marine Regiment (BLT 2/9), which was formed from 2d Battalion 9th Marine Regiment (2/9) on Okinawa, Japan, and D Company 1st Battalion 4th Marine Regiment (1/4) at Subic Bay in the Philippines—were ordered to prepare for deployment to Thailand. Flown in by Air Force C-141s, both elements were in place in Utapao by late morning of 14 May, late evening of 13 May in Washington, just fifteen hours after the deployment order was given in Okinawa.[8]

Concurrently, the Air Force was tasked with monitoring the *Mayaguez* and preventing the further movement of the ship and crew, including stopping water-borne traffic between the mainland and Koh Tang. It was the Air Force that suffered the first casualties of the operation when a helicopter carrying a contingent of USAF security police (SP) went down in a remote section of northwest Thailand.

PART THREE

First Casualties

The men, members of the 56th Security Police Squadron (SPS), were assigned to the 56th Special Operations Wing at Nakhon Phanom, Thailand, and were en route to Utapao, on the southeastern coast of Thailand, as part of a 125-man SP component to be utilized as helicopter landing zone (LZ) security. It was a stop-gap measure as commanders scrambled to get assets in place before the *Mayaguez* crew could be moved to the mainland, and was a subject of heated debate between Marine and Air Force commanders. As Seventh Fleet commander Adm. George P. Steele later stated, "The idea that we could use U.S. Air Force air police and Air Force helicopters as an assault force appears as ridiculous today as it did then."[1]

At 2230 hours on the evening of 13 May, three CH-53 Sea Stallion helicopters, code-named Knives, departed Nakhon Phanom RTAFB carrying fifty-one SP of the 56th SPS. While flying at an altitude of nine thousand feet, one of the helicopters, Knife-13, disappeared from the airfield's departure radar, and crashed thirty to forty miles west of the airfield in an area close to the Thai-Laotian border, the same area where another aircraft had been shot down two months earlier, killing all four crew members. All eighteen SP officers and the five-man crew of Knife-13 were killed in the crash.[2]

The U.S. government initially stated that these troops "were not involved with the U.S. military reaction to the seizure of the container ship *Mayaguez*," a statement intended either to fool the Thai government that had expressly forbidden the use of American troops from Thailand or to minimize and hide the extent of the losses in the operation from the American public.[3]

Early on the morning of 14 May, at about 0600 hours, an A-7D Corsair of the 388th Tactical Fighter Wing (TFW) flying over the *Mayaguez* reported that a Thai fishing boat and three Cambodian patrol boats had departed Koh Tang Island and were headed toward the port of Kompong Som on the mainland. In Washington it was 1900 hours on 13 May; when President Ford was advised of the development, he called a third meeting of the NSC, which was still dealing with the earlier loss of the twenty-three airmen of Knife-13. They were advised of this new urgent development. The pilot of the aircraft was patched through directly to the NSC meeting. He reported that he had observed Caucasians on board the fishing boat.[4]

This event highlights the two shortcomings of the operation that influenced all subsequent decisions: lack of reliable intelligence regarding the location of the crew of the *Mayaguez* and the confusing, convoluted, and overlapping chain of command.

It is fair to say that the location of the crew was the preeminent concern of planners on all levels, especially in the later stages as deadlines approached. If the crew were moved to the mainland, an invasion of Koh Tang Island would be unnecessary. But intelligence could provide no definitive information as to whether any, part, or all of the crew was on board the fishing boat, on Koh Tang, on neither, or on both.

Additionally, the command and control element of this joint service operation was at best cumbersome. The president and the NSC; the JCS; the NMCC in Washington, DC; Air Force Lt. Gen. John J. Burns, theater commander headquartered at Nakhon Phanom, Thailand; and Adm. Noel Gayler, CINCPAC in Honolulu, Hawai'i, all monitored events and could give input in real time. Unfortunately, inquiries for information from a myriad of sources often tied up communication channels at critical times, obstructing tactical operations. The Marine Weapons Platoon commander, 2nd Lt. Dan Hoffman, who later landed on the west side of Koh Tang Island, recalls how, while under fire, the executive officer (XO) of G Company, 1st Lt. Richard "Dick" Keith, was distracted by requests for information by higher headquarters. "I remember Keith on three radios, trying to communicate with multiple commanders simultaneously."[5]

This communication clutter extended to the highest levels, as Admiral Steele later recalled: "We requested permission to fly reconnaissance flights . . . specifically over the island of Koh Tang. Despite repeated requests, it was denied until so late that the flight's photographic results could not be processed in advance of the actual assault on the island. I think that this is another example of a disastrous attempt to micromanage from distant headquarters with inadequately trained staff large operations in which communications plays so great a part."[6]

In Washington, Ford was faced with two options. If he allowed the fishing boat to proceed to the mainland and the crew was on board, the odds of getting them back were nil. But if he told the pilot to strafe the boats, Americans could be killed. While the NSC debated the options, the pilot circled overhead and the boats drew nearer to Kompong Som. Finally, at approximately 2300 hours, Ford made the decision to sink the patrol boats and use only chemical agents on the fishing trawler.[7]

Accounts differ in how many Cambodian gunboats were sunk or damaged, with most placing the figure at three sunk, four damaged, but all accounts agree that despite firing warning shots across the bow, deploying chemical agents, and the wishes of the Thai crew who were "persuaded" through their armed guards' threats, the fishing trawler proceeded to Kompong Som. Air assets followed the fishing boat to within twelve miles of the coast, where the rules of engagement prohibited further pursuit, at which point the pilots lost track of the ship in the haze.[8]

One *Mayaguez* crew member, Raymond Friedler, later recalled, "They shot the gun boats leading us, they shot those out of the water right away. There were two that turned around and went on either side of us and as I turned around I could see them blowing them out of the water so there was only us left."[9]

Captain Miller later recalled being impressed with the precision of the USAF pilots: "We were bombed a hundred times by our jets. Ten feet forward of our bow, they fired rockets and machine guns. You have to give our pilots credit. They can thread the eye of a needle from a mile away.

They did everything that was possible without blowing us out of the water to try to get this boat to turn around and take us back to the ship."[10]

Despite everyone's expectations, and undetected by U.S. intelligence, the crew was not unloaded at Kompong Som, but was again moved on board the Thai fishing trawler to the nearby island of Rong Som Lem.

PART FOUR

President Ford Orders Military Action

F inally out of options, at 1645 hours on 14 May (0345 hours on 15 May in Cambodia) Ford approved military action to recapture the *Mayaguez* and rescue her crew. The final operational order included a two-phase assault to begin at sunrise on 15 May local time:

- Using eight USAF CH/HH-53 helicopters, execute a combat assault on Koh Tang Island, with 175 Marines in the initial wave and a subsequent buildup to 625 Marines, and rescue members of the SS *Mayaguez* that may be found on the island.
- Using three USAF helicopters, insert forty-eight Marines, twelve USN/MSC (Military Sealift Command) personnel, an explosive ordnance demolition (EOD) team, and a Cambodian linguist on the USS *Holt*, close with the *Mayaguez*, and board and secure her.
- Provide close air support and area coverage against all Cambodian small craft with USAF and USN tactical air. Make naval gunfire support available and direct B-52 strikes and naval tactical air against possible reinforcing mainland Cambodian targets.[1]

The eleven helicopters designated for the initial assault were made up of six USAF HH-53 Jolly Green Giant helicopters of the 40th Aerospace Rescue and Recovery Squadron (40th ARRS) and five CH-53 Sea Stallion helicopters of the 21st Special Operations Squadron (SOS). The HH-53s, code-named Jollys, were capable of in-flight refueling and thus

11

could remain on station, while the CH-53s depended on external fuel tanks to boost range, a critical consideration when assigning assets. All five CH-53s as well as three of the HH-53s were assigned to carry the Marine assault force to Koh Tang Island, with the remaining three CH-53s transporting the Marines to recapture the *Mayaguez*.[2]

Maj. Gen. Carl W. Hoffman, the III MAF commander, selected his assistant chief of staff (Operations & Plans) G-3, Col. John M. Johnson, to command Task Group 79.9 with the Koh Tang element, Lt. Col. Randall W. Austin to command BLT 2/9 with its integral rifle companies, Capt. Mykle Stahl to command E Company, Capt. Michael McCarty to command F Company, Capt. James Davis to command G Company, and Capt. John Gutter to command H Company (designated 79.9.1), and Capt. Walter Wood to command the *Mayaguez* element, composed of D Company 1/4 Marines (designated 79.9.2). Accompanying Wood's Marines would be a headquarters element consisting of the battalion XO, Maj. Raymond E. Porter, and the assistant operations officer, Capt. J. P. Feltner.[3]

As Wood later recalled, "We first learned of the Cambodian seizure of an American vessel on 12 May. Information concerning the ship's capture was rather sparse and it wasn't until the next morning that things began to pick up. My battalion commander, Lt. Col. C. E. Hester, ordered me to organize two platoons and a headquarters element, total force size to be 120 men, and be ready to move out at 2300." At 0110 hours Wood and his men boarded Air Force C-141s for the four-hour flight to Utapao.[4]

As forces moved into place, AC-130s of the 16th SOS were tasked with maintaining surveillance and halting waterborne traffic through the night. Flight time from the mainland to Koh Tang Island was more than an hour, which meant that the AC-130s could remain on station a maximum of four hours before returning to Thailand to refuel, since none of the aircraft was configured with external fuel tanks for in-flight refueling. Complex scheduling of resources was necessary to maintain constant surveillance.

When Captain Wood and his Marines landed at Utapao at 0505 hours on 14 May, they were accompanied by six U.S. Navy sailors and six civilian volunteers from the USNS *Greenville Victory*, an MSC cargo ship. The sailors were to board the recaptured *Mayaguez* and get her under way. Infrared photos had shown that the power plant on board the *Mayaguez* had been shut down. "The vessel could not move on her own power for some three hours due to boiler light off time and the like. The one question that constantly troubled us was the location of the crew. Since the crew could still be on board, fire discipline in the actual assault was stressed."[5]

Once the Marines arrived at Utapao, they remained on and off alert throughout the day as planners worked out details of the assault and waited for approval from higher headquarters. Wood remembers,

> *We were informed that approximately thirty Cambodians were on board the vessel, armed with automatic and antitank weapons. This information had been gleaned from photos taken by P-3 aircraft, which were constantly on station above the vessel and Koh Tang. The launch [of the assault] had been postponed until 0910, then again until 1230, and in our discussions we decided we could not effectively launch after 1415. The helicopter flight would have to cover some 270 miles from Utapao to the* Mayaguez *and would take approximately two hours. Keeping in mind that evening nautical twilight would occur at approximately 1915, it was understandable why we had to launch by 1415.*

GySgt. Francis McGowin, who served as the BLT intelligence officer, later recalled that the 2d Battalion on Okinawa was called in from training, and that he was originally briefed for a mission in Laos involving seized students. He did not learn until arriving at Utapao that their mission was in Cambodia. "When we arrived, we were told hard intelligence numbered the opposition at sixty to eighty. Later, after we returned to Okinawa, a subsequent intelligence summary stated that there were approximately eight hundred Khmer Rouge soldiers on the island equipped with automatic weapons and light artillery. It was all because of a dispute between Cambodia and Vietnam over ownership of the island and its oil."[6] Estimates of the opposing force vary widely, depending on source. Lieutenant Colonel Austin recalls a subsequent intelligence summary estimating the number of enemy combatants as between 250 to 300. In either case, the Marines were significantly outnumbered.

It illustrates the lack of credible intelligence on this operation that there were no aerial photos or maps of Koh Tang Island available for review by the Marine commanders. "The only photo we had of the island was a 1:100,000 scale map, with Koh Tang a green speck on a sea of blue," McGowin later recalled. To fill this gap, an Army U-21 Ute, the military version of a Beechcraft King Air A90, was sent aloft to fly over the island. On board was Brig. Gen. Walter H. Baxter representing General Burns and the Thirteenth Air Force; Col. Lloyd Anders, the Seventh Air Force helicopter mission commander; Colonel Johnson; Lieutenant Colonel Austin; Major Hendricks; and Captain Davis. Also on board were the battalion's two forward air controllers (FACs), 1st Lt. John J. Martinoli and 1st Lt. Terry Tonkin; and McGowin. They took off at 1500 hours, and flew 195 miles from Utapao to Koh Tang. Although restricted to an altitude of six thousand feet due to hostile fire, the plane descended to forty-five hundred feet and Davis snapped photos using his Minolta 35-mm camera.

The photos revealed an island about a mile wide that was shaped like a cross at its southern end, with a narrow middle and a northern end often described as shaped like a pork chop. There were four beaches. The two beaches on the southeast end were of little interest: the crew was believed to be held on the northern end. There was a narrow path connecting the beaches on the western and eastern sides. Little detail could be seen from the photos. The *Mayaguez* rested at anchor about one mile north. The decision was later to be made to assault the two northern beaches of the island.

A closer inspection, had it been possible, would have revealed a more formidable target. Em Son, the twenty-three-year-old battalion commander of the Khmer Rouge, had evacuated the small fishing village to the mainland and fortified the island, hacking away the shrubbery to provide overlapping fields of fire on the beaches. There were rock-fortified fighting positions connected by shallow trenches, and munitions bunkers strategically sited to provide rapid access. Heavy and light machine guns, mostly U.S. Army ordnance captured from the defeated Lon Nol government, were mounted for utilization as both antiaircraft and beach defense.

PART FIVE

Operation Plan

A planning session with General Burns' staff at Nakhon Phanom at 1900 hours on 14 May was attended by Johnson and Austin; a final operational plan was finalized. The plan was to begin at 0542 local time on 15 May, four minutes before sunrise. It was hoped that coming in just before sunrise in reduced visibility would afford the Marines the element of surprise, and allow the operation to take place in the morning light, essential for locating, identifying, and rescuing the hostages. They knew that the break of dawn would occur twenty-six minutes prior to sunrise and that good ground visibility would exist before the sun rose, but, as Lieutenant Colonel Austin later recalled, "It [the danger] was both known and considered. There were not any other reasonable options. Landing the helicopters in complete darkness earlier seemed to carry more risk than the option selected, especially considering the estimated level of potential enemy resistance based on available intelligence."[1]

The finalized plan called for two assaults to occur simultaneously. Three of the heavily armored HH-53s would carry fifty-nine D Company 1/4 Marines, who would be lowered by rope ladders onto the deck of the *Mayaguez*. The Marines would be accompanied by eleven volunteers (six MSC mariners, two Navy corpsmen, two USAF EOD sergeants, and an Army Intelligence officer who was fluent in Cambodian).

At 2300 hours, just four hours prior to the helicopters' scheduled departure, updated information regarding the arrival of the USS *Holt* in the area caused a change of plans. The decision was made to offload the

15

Marines onto the destroyer, which would transport them alongside the
Mayaguez so they could board and capture her. "When we learned that
we would receive the Marine support for the operation," later recalled
Cdr. Robert A. Peterson, captain of the USS *Holt*, "we decided to take
the *Holt* alongside the *Mayaguez* rather than use small boats. Aircraft
patrolling the area reported several hostile gunboats in the vicinity of the
Mayaguez and we'd expected to have to fight our way in. [By not using
boats] all fire-team personnel could be devoted to topside positions on
board in support of installed weapons systems: one 5-inch gun forward
and our basic point defense missile system aft."[2]

Since it was assumed there would be armed Cambodians on board,
USAF A-7s would spray the *Mayaguez* with chemical agents ten minutes
prior to the boarding, necessitating Wood's Marines to make the assault in
unwieldy chemical, bacteriological, radiological (CBR) masks.

The Koh Tang air element would consist of the remaining eight helicopters (five Knives, three Jollys) in four flights of two. The BLT command
group and Davis' G Company would go in first, with Stahl's E Company
coming in on the second wave after a four-hour round trip to Utapao to
pick up and insert those Marines. The first two helicopters would deposit
Davis and part of G Company on the west beach as a blocking force to
prevent enemy escape from that side of the island, and would deposit the
majority of G Company and Austin's BLT command group, 81-mm mortars, and the forward air control party on the wider, eastern beach. The
main force under Austin would move west along a cleared strip that ran
across the northern neck of the island, and link up with Davis' blocking
force. Once combined, the force would then clear the northern part of the
island, then drive south and sweep the island. Meanwhile, the helicopters
would recycle twice, inserting E Company onto the island in a second
wave and the remainder of 2/9 in a third wave. Because of the uncertainty
of the location of the hostages, there would be no supporting naval gunfire or close air support strikes.

Davis and GySgt. Lester A. McNemar organized G Company into
helicopter teams according to the number of seats available on each helicopter, trying to keep platoons, squads, and fire teams intact when possible. Both men had previous experience from the Vietnam War.

Staff and officers of G Company 2/9 Marines, Camp Schwab, Okinawa 1975.
U.S. Marine Corps

To provide air cover and support for the helicopters, F-4 Phantoms, A-7 Corsairs, F-111 Aardvarks, and AC-130 gunships would fly in from Thailand and coordinate their actions with the Airborne Command and Control Center (ABCCC) aircraft, an orbiting EC-130 code-named Cricket. On board the USS *Coral Sea,* located 350 miles to the southeast of Koh Tang, pilots and crews of ten A-6 Intruders of Attack Squadron VA-95 armed with five hundred–pound laser-guided bombs, and twenty-four A-7E Corsairs from VA-22 and VA-94 armed with a dozen standard five hundred–pounders, prepared to take off. Protected from MiGs by F-4N Phantom fighters from VF-51 and VF-111, the dive-bombers would launch and divide into four waves, assigned targets of ships at anchor in Kompong Som Harbor, runways and hangars at Ream Airfield, ships at Ream Naval Base, and Kompong Som port facilities. The planned strikes were estimated to last four hours.

Although the original time of takeoff was scheduled for 0405 local time, the first helicopters took to the air at 0414 on 15 May as three HH-53s—Jolly-11 (1st Lt. Donald Backlund), Jolly-12 (Capt. Paul Jacobs), and Jolly-13 (1st Lt. Charles Greer)—carried D Company Marines to the rendezvous with the *Holt*, now located twelve miles southwest of Koh Tang. They were delayed awaiting the "Go" order from the president, possibly in order to give President Ford time to brief congressional leaders as required by the War Powers Act of 1973.

The helicopter landing platform on board the *Holt* was too small to accommodate the entire size and weight of the HH-53s, necessitating the pilots to hover, one at a time, with their forward landing gear touching the pad as the Marines exited the starboard side door. "At first light on 15 May," Peterson recalled, "three Air Force Jolly Greens arrived and offloaded fifty-nine Marines, a six-man MSC nucleus crew and EOD personnel. As soon as we had our passengers, we stationed general quarters and started for the *Mayaguez*, which lay at anchor about fifteen miles to the east." The Jollys then headed back to Thailand.

The *Holt*'s skipper, Commander Peterson, and his XO, Lt. Cdr. John Todd, met with Major Porter and Captain Wood, and Peterson decided that he would bring the *Holt* alongside the *Mayaguez* on the side away from the island to use the ship to shield the Marines from potential hostile fire. He estimated that, once alongside the *Mayaguez*, the 01 deck of the *Holt* (above the main deck) would match the main deck of the *Mayaguez*.

The boarding party of 1/4 Marines readied themselves for action. It would be the first time Marines would make a ship-to-ship boarding of a hostile vessel since 10 September 1861 when Marines and sailors of the USS *Pawnee*, under the command of Cdr. S. C. Rowan and while part of the Atlantic Blockading Squadron, boarded the West Indies schooner *Susan Jane* during the Civil War.[3]

As the *Holt* neared the *Mayaguez*, Wood met with Cpl. Carl R. Coker; Coker's squad would be first across to race up to the bridge while Sgt. William Owen's squad would follow and descend below deck to take control of the engine room. Wood later recalled, "We recognized that we had to seize as quickly as possible four critical areas—the bridge, the engine room, and the main decks fore and aft. Once these areas were seized, the ship could then be cautiously and thoroughly searched." As Navy gun teams set up machine guns on deck, the Marines checked their loads and

A Marine and an Air Force pararescueman of the 40th Aerospace Rescue and Recovery Squadron run to board an Air Force HH-53 Jolly Green helicopter during Koh Tang Island assault operations. Department of Defense

fitted on their gas masks. Those on board could see black smoke rising from Koh Tang Island and helicopters buzzing along the north end of the island as they pondered their upcoming fight to take back the *Mayaguez*. Surveillance overflights had observed armed Cambodians on board the *Mayaguez*.

At 0710 hours, two A-7s swooped down to lay a cloud of chemical agents over the stationary ship as Peterson and others scanned the *Mayaguez* for movement or the flash of gunfire, but nothing broke the stillness. As the *Holt* neared the *Mayaguez*, it became obvious that both main decks were on the same level, and Marines scrambled down the ladder to arrive at the bow just as the two ships came abeam. In a remarkable piece of seamanship, Peterson pulled alongside without damage to either ship. As the two decks came together at 0725, Lieutenant Commander Todd gave the order "Marines over the side."

Corporal Coker was the first across, followed closely by Captain Wood. Coker raced up an exterior ladder, and, as Wood later recalled, "I proceeded aft [and] turned to my rear to view the progress of Coker's squad and the rest of the boarding party who were supposed to secure

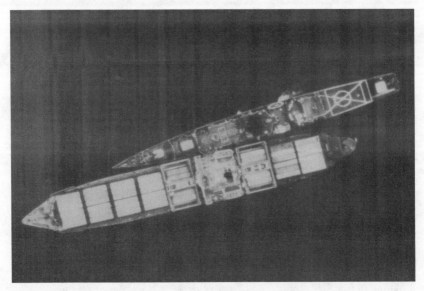

USS Holt *alongside the SS* Mayaguez. Department of Defense

Marines board the Mayaguez. Department of Defense

Major Porter raises colors over recaptured Mayaguez. Department of Defense

the lines. . . . Much to my surprise, I discovered that Coker and I were the only Marines on board." The backwash from coming alongside had pushed the two ships apart and now a distance of twenty-five feet separated the two vessels. Wood lifted his mask, Coker later recalled, and the two worked feverishly to make fast the lines tossed over by sailors on board the *Holt*.[4]

The rest of the boarding party crossed over and moved purposefully to preassigned objectives, cautiously scanning for hostile forces while encumbered by gas masks. Two USAF EOD sergeants, SMSgt. Joe Moore and Sgt. Harold Young, scanned the areas for explosive booby traps while the medics prepared to treat potential casualties and Clinton J. Harriman, first officer of the USNS *Greenville Victory*, waited with five other civilian mariners for the engine room to be secured before restarting the ship's power plant. Surprisingly, the Marines found the *Mayaguez* deserted and undefended, and the ship was declared secure at 0822 hours. Three minutes later, as all present came to attention, Major Porter raised the colors over the *Mayaguez*.[5]

The *Holt*'s deck force sailors hurriedly prepared the *Mayaguez* to be towed, since her engineering plant was found to be in a completely cold state. Once the towing hawser was made fast, they got under way. Peterson later recalled, "Not long after we were under way with the *Mayaguez* in tow, we learned that the *Henry B. Wilson* had retrieved the captured *Mayaguez* crew. She returned to our vicinity and sent the Master, Charles Miller, and his crew back to their vessel on a small boat. Soon after he was back on board, Captain Miller called me by bridge-to-bridge radio, offered me his thanks and a round of beer for my crew, and said he would soon have steam up and be ready to proceed on his own power." Later in the afternoon, the *Mayaguez* proceeding under her own power, the *Holt* was ordered to return to Koh Tang to assist with the extraction of the Marines on the island.[6]

PART SIX

Marine "Boots on the Ground" on Koh Tang

A t 0420 hours, six minutes after the three Jolly Green helicopters took off for the *Holt*, four CH-53 helicopters took off for Koh Tang Island (Knife-21 and Knife-22 headed for the west beach while Knife-23 and Knife-31 flew toward the east beach), followed five minutes later by the remaining CH-53 (Knife-32) and three HH-53s (Jolly-41, Jolly-42, and Jolly-43). The island assault force, 180 of the planned 250 Marines, was already twenty minutes behind schedule.

Moments before takeoff, a noncommissioned officer (NCO) had handed an envelope to Captain Davis. Inside were large, glossy photographs of Koh Tang Island. As they studied the photos by flashlight, the unidentified NCO pointed out barracks, bunkers positioned to defend the beaches, and, worst of all, antiaircraft positions. With no time to rework the plan, Davis and McNemar debated whether to share the information with the troops. Deciding that revealing the information would have a detrimental effect, Davis pocketed the photos and passed the word to expect enemy fire.

Knife-21 would be the first chopper in, dismounting its Marines on the west beach as part of the aforementioned blocking force. It was piloted by Lt. Col. John Denham, commander of the 21st SOS. He and his crew, copilot 1st Lt. Karl Poulsen and flight mechanics TSgt. Robert Boissonnault and SSgt. Elwood "Woody" Rumbaugh, had flown together through some difficult times. "We had been through the Saigon and Phnom Penh

23

[evacuations] together, the same crew; we pretty well knew what each man would do. We didn't have much to discuss going in to the island."[1]

On board Knife-21, twenty Marines of 1st Platoon G Company, under the command of 2nd Lt. James McDaniel, tensely prepared their gear for the insertion. They would be the first onto the beach, much like Marines in other wars. McDaniel gave the order "lock and load," and the interior of the cabin echoed with the sound of charging handles of M-16s sliding home.

Few of the younger Marines had combat experience, and some had only recently arrived, like Pfc. Fred B. Morris, a nineteen-year-old from Evansdale, Iowa:

> We'd been in Oki [Okinawa] about a week, before we went on alert for the Mayaguez rescue. The company had just stood down from being on alert because of the evacuation of Saigon, Operation Frequent Wind. The afternoon I arrived at Camp Schwab to join Golf 2/9, they were training in the field. They had us throw our gear in lockers, issued us combat/field gear, and trucked us out to join our unit. The next day, they put us on alert, trucked us back to Schwab, geared us up, and shipped us down to Kadena Air Force Base (AFB) where we were loaded aboard C-141s and flown to Thailand.[2]

Following behind 1st Platoon G Company was Knife-22 (piloted by Capt. Terry Ohlemeier and 2nd Lt. David W. Greer, with SSgt. Michael Wilson and Sgt. Paul Norman as flight engineers). They carried Captain Davis, Gunny Sergeant McNemar, and more of G Company. Only Davis among the officers, McNemar, and eight NCOs had combat experience. Some of the 2/9 Marines had not yet even "battle-sighted" their weapons. They would be inserted onto the west beach behind Knife-21.

In Thailand, it had seemed like a game. "The collective wisdom of our squad and platoon leaders was . . . just another alert," Morris later recalled. "It was posturing to get someone's attention . . . most didn't think we'd actually go in." Now on board helicopters skimming low over the water in darkness, it was becoming real.[3]

Sitting in the tail of Knife-21 was Pfc. Allen Bailey of College Park, Maryland, a nineteen-year-old rifleman in 1st Platoon G Company. "I was in the first chopper going in. Like most of the guys, I was fresh out of boot camp and I'd never seen combat."[4]

It was approximately 0555 as Knife-21 and Knife-22 approached the western LZ, unopposed by any enemy fire. As McDaniel later recalled, "The sun was just starting to creep over the horizon. . . . It was black and then all of a sudden the sun [came] up and everything was blazing in light."[5]

As Knife-21 came in for a landing, the Cambodians opened up with automatic weapons, mortars, and rifle-propelled grenade (RPG)–7s. Ohle-meier, Knife-22's pilot, hovered five hundred feet behind. He later recalled looking at the bright lights twinkling in the dark green foliage and thinking of a Christmas tree. There had been a mass mission briefing at Utapao for the Ground Security Force (GSF) and helicopter crews that included weather, call signs, frequencies, and intelligence on the opposing forces. Morris remembers, "We were briefed that there was a platoon-sized force of fisherman militia types defending the island . . . [and] they did not expect heavy resistance." Such did not turn out to be the case.[6]

What they found instead was a force of battle-trained Khmer Rouge veterans entrenched in extensive fortified positions that ringed the beaches, comprising machine-gun (MG) pits and bunkers that were connected by interlocking trenches. Unbeknownst to the Americans, Cambodia had reinforced the island during a dispute with Vietnam over sovereignty of the island.

Denham brought Knife-21 to a low hover and swung his craft around so that the ramp faced the tree line, unlike Marine pilots who were trained to go in nose-first so that the craft would provide cover for the dismounting Marines. As Bailey later recalled, "Before we could even land the chopper, there were rounds already going through the chopper. You could see daylight coming through. It made a funny noise going through, sort of like an ice pick stabbed through cardboard, very sharp, and a few of us got hit. Before you knew it, the chopper swung around and we were on the beach."[7]

McDaniel's memories are similar: "I couldn't hear the gunshots, but bullets punching through the light helo skin sounded like BBs thrown against sheet metal. The bullets flew slowly from one side to the other between my men and created shafts of light, like pathways to eternity."

As twenty Marines of the 1st Platoon charged onto the beach into intense enemy fire, both choppers took numerous hits from ground fire. One of Knife-21's T-64 engines sustained terminal damage, and Knife-22 aborted her approach after taking major damage. Knife-21 tried to lift off but failed with serious transmission damage. Jettisoning the external fuel tanks, Denham powered up and barely lifted off toward the sea, literally skipping across the water as he dumped fuel to lighten the load. Knife-22 made a second run at the island, guns blazing to divert attention from the crippled aircraft, then followed Knife-21 out over the water.[8]

Knife-21 continued to lose power and settled into the water about a mile out, rotors snapping off as water rushed into the downed craft as it rolled onto its side. Boissonnault, Rumbaugh, and Denham were able to escape, but Poulson was trapped inside, unable to release his safety harness. When Rumbaugh surfaced and noticed the missing copilot, he returned to free the trapped Poulson and dragged him to the surface. As others made efforts to revive Poulson, Rumbaugh disappeared below the surface, the first casualty of the day.

Knife-22, damaged and losing fuel, saw Knife-32 and Jolly-41 approaching and turned over rescue efforts to them as Ohlemeier turned the craft for one more attempt at landing his Marines on the west beach. He again encountered heavy fire: slugs ripped apart the aircraft, damaging an engine and rupturing a fuel tank. With several wounded on board, including the assault company commander, Captain Davis, Ohlemeier aborted his attempt to insert the Marines and headed for Thailand, eventually making an emergency landing along the Thai coast, approximately eighty-five miles east of Utapao. Picked up by Jolly-11 and Jolly-12, who were returning from dropping their Marines on board the *Holt*, the crew and Marines were transported back to Utapao. For his efforts, Ohlemeier was later awarded the Silver Star.

Back on the west beach, the Marines were getting hammered by enemy fire. As Bailey later recalled,

The first one on the beach was Staff Sergeant Bernal, who'd served two tours in Nam. He stood on the beach with rounds going through that chopper, with all of us on the floor, and he was standing in the

open on the beach hollering, "Get out of the chopper! Fire and shoot! Fire and shoot!" He was waving his .45 in the air. . . . We got off the beach and into the jungle line as fast as we could, but that was about as far as we could get.

I had a LAW [light antitank weapon] on my back, my M-16 slung over, and I was carrying two boxes of ammo. I was the first off behind [Bernal]. Fifty feet in the bluffs, there were two [Cambodians] shooting down on us. I walked my rounds up to their position, killing one and wounding the other. Fred Morris came up alongside me. He fired one round, and his rifle jammed. I was standing and he was prone, and we were firing not realizing that we were being fired down on from all sides.[9]

As bad as things were, they were worse on the east beach. Knife-23 (piloted by two first lieutenants, John Schramm and John Lucas) led the way. It was trailed on the left by Knife-31 (piloted by Maj. Al Corson and 2nd Lt. Richard Vandegeer). Both Knives had heard the call "Hot LZ" go out over the radio. As they approached the LZ, they came under intense enemy fire.

On board Knife-31, flight engineers SSgt. Jon Harston and Sgt. Randy Hoffmaster returned fire with their miniguns; even the copilot, Vandegeer, returned fire by sticking his M-16 rifle out the left window. The port fuel tank was struck by gunfire; it exploded, causing a huge fireball that quickly spread to inside the cargo bay. This was almost immediately followed by an RPG hit that blew away a large portion of the front of the cockpit, instantly killing Vandegeer and stunning Corson. The aircraft crashed into the surf fifteen to twenty meters from the eastern shoreline, directly in front of a Khmer Rouge gun position, which raked the downed aircraft with automatic fire.[10]

Harston exited the aircraft via the starboard cabin door as the aircraft burst into flames, but surfaced to find himself under fire from the shore. He returned to the aircraft to retrieve his AR-15 (semiautomatic rifle). Despite a wound to his leg, he swam underwater to reenter the burning helicopter through the right door. The aft section was already submerged; amid the fires and exploding ammunition, Harston found three Marines disoriented and trying to break out the windows. He led them out of the craft, and then returned to the front of the still-burning hull to find that the front of the craft had been blown away. He assisted Corson in extracting himself into the water.

Already in the water was 1st Lt. Michael Eustis, the artillery liaison officer. Wounded when blown out of the exploding aircraft, he nonetheless assisted Corson in moving seaward from the burning wreckage. With only two life preservers available, Eustis made a flotation device from his trousers, and helped the others do the same, assisting them in staying afloat in the water. For his "daring actions, resolute determination, and inspiring leadership," Eustis later was awarded the Silver Star.[11]

Harston swam to the other side to assist Vandegeer, but the fire was too intense. "I could see that he was already gone," Harston later recalled. He had swum out when he saw a wounded Marine by the craft and swam back to assist him, at which point he saw another Marine. He helped the two stay afloat until their rescue almost three hours later. For his actions, Harston was presented the Air Force Cross on 14 July 1975.[12]

In the water the battalion FAC, 1st Lt. Terry Tonkin, dog paddled, assisting Corson to stay afloat. Having lost his own radio, he asked to borrow Corson's survival radio; he used the emergency channel to call for an air strike. Around him, Marines began shedding gear: helmets, boots, web gear, and vests were discarded. LCpl. M. Gaston, Sgt. Victor Salinas, Pfc. James Maxwell, and Pfc. Timothy Trebil, the last Marine out from the burning hulk, all floated in a group as rounds from the shore kicked up water around them. Salinas was burned and blinded. Maxwell was shot in the back of the head; Trebil tried to help, but Maxwell died and sank under the waves. Realizing that the reflection from the antenna was attracting enemy fire, Tonkin swam away from the group and continued to call for an air strike.

Three A7-D Corsairs from the 388th TFW at Korat RTAFB (Royal Thai Air Force Base), led by USAF Capt. Scott Ralston, were flying overhead, monitoring Tonkin's Mayday call, but it would take precious minutes to sort out the situation, locate friendly forces, and identify enemy targets. Tonkin remained on the air with Cricket. Tonkin directed incoming air strikes as best he could, actions for which he was later awarded the Silver Star.

During the same time, Knife-23 attempted to land on the east beach, taking such devastating fire that the entire tail section was blown away. Without the tail rotor, the helicopter began a violent spin to the right and crashed into the sand only feet below where they'd been hovering, allowing all of the crew and the twenty Marines on board to safely exit onto the beach. As 2nd Lt. Michael Cicere, the leader of 3d Platoon, directed his Marines in setting up a defensive perimeter, Lucas got on his survival radio and began calling in air strikes. Cicere, his Marines, and the crew of Knife-23 would be the only Americans to land on the east beach. An effort to extract the isolated force was attempted by Jolly-13 (lieutenants Greer and Brown) between 0825 and 0830 hours, but this attempt was unsuccessful. The damage it incurred during the attempt was so severe that Jolly-13 barely made it back to Utapao, and was out of action for the rest of the mission. As Cicere later recalled, "With one helicopter [Knife-31] burning out in the water and the carcass of what [was] left of our helicopter [Knife-23] sitting fouling the LZ, it became apparent very quickly that no one else was going to land there." Isolated and under fire, they remained pinned down for the next ten hours. For his attempt to land and for his later actions, Greer received the Silver Star.[13]

And his effort wasn't without value. The location of Knife-23's survivors was confirmed and an A-7 overhead identified enemy positions and, acting as FAC, Greer directed a flight of F-4s in to engage targets on the eastern side of the island.

Five Marines, two Navy corpsmen—HM1 Bernard Gause and HN Ronald J. Manning—and the copilot, Lieutenant Vandegeer, died on board the downed Knife-31. Staff Sergeant Rumbaugh drowned when Knife-21 went down. LCpl. Gregory S. Copenhaver and two other Marines were killed charging the island. One Marine died of his wounds clinging to debris, and one drowned, for a total of fourteen killed. The remaining thirteen Marines and aircrew swam farther out to sea and stayed afloat until the USS *Henry B. Wilson* rescued them more than two hours later.[14]

Only minutes into the landings, four of the eight helicopters were damaged or destroyed, two small groups of Marines were isolated on two separate beaches, and fourteen Marines, sailors, and airmen were dead.

On board the circling ABCCC aircraft, communication channels were jammed with messages—requesting information, directions, and assistance.

The remainder of the first wave of helicopters (Knife-32 and Jolly-41, -42, and -43) arrived; seeing the wreckage, Jolly-42 (1st Lt. Phillip Pacini) and Jolly-43 (Capt. Roland Wayne Purser) radioed for instructions on inserting their Marines. They were initially cleared for the designated LZs on the east beach. In Knife-32, 1st Lt. Michael Lackey, who had recovered the three surviving crew of Knife-21, looked down on the flaming wreckage and sought clarification: "Cricket, do you want me to insert my Marines in the same LZ where Knife-23 and 31 have gone down?" He was diverted to the western LZ. When the Jollys radioed for clarification, the decision was made to close the east beach to further insertions and divert the remaining aircraft to the west beach.[15]

The second flight of four helicopters experienced slightly greater success inserting their Marines into the western LZ, due in part to the fact that three of the four were the more heavily armored Jolly HH-53s, which also had a 7.62-mm minigun in the tail of the cargo bay. Additionally, their foam-filled external fuel tanks made catastrophic explosions less likely.

Jolly-41 (1st Lt. Thomas D. Cooper) was farthest to the west, and was the first to attempt the insertion onto the west beach, but ground fire damaged the right fuel tank and ramp area, and Cooper aborted his run. Jolly-42 was next, but missed the LZ and also pulled away. Jolly-43 was met with intense ground fire and also aborted.[16]

This left the already damaged Knife-32 to be first in. It initiated a steep descent as bullets tore into the fuselage and mortar rounds exploded in the surf. The Marines and recovered Knife-21 aircrew fired their weapons as the craft skimmed onto the beach. USAF SSgt. Nick Morales was seriously wounded by a gunshot to the chest as he worked the door gun. It collapsed his lung and severed an artery. Two of the Marines were also wounded, but all thirteen Marines charged off the helicopter into the firefight; an Army interpreter refused to dismount the aircraft and returned with it to Utapao. With extensive damage, including seventy-five holes in the fuselage, Knife-32 was placed out of commission on its return to Thailand.[17]

Lieutenant Pacini brought Jolly-42 around for another run, hovering in the area where Knife-32 had unloaded. His rear gun provided covering fire as twenty-seven Marines charged down the ramp onto the beach and united with Lieutenant McDaniel's twenty Marines, strengthening the perimeter. Among them was 1st Lt. Richard Keith, G Company XO, who as senior officer assumed command. Pacini lifted off, also sustaining major battle damage, and returned to Thailand where Jolly-42 was placed out of commission with nineteen holes in the fuselage.

Captain Purser in Jolly-43 was south of the LZ when he located a rocky outcropping that was undefended; he unloaded his complement of twenty-nine Marines along the beach, south of the main force. The Jolly-43 inserted Marines, led by Lieutenant Colonel Austin: Austin's battalion staff and command element and an 81-mm mortar section. The group was armed primarily with .45 automatic pistols, and had only four M-16 rifles among them. Austin was aware of their vulnerability, and knew they were well separated from the other Marines farther north.

As the battalion operations officer, Maj. John B. Hendricks, remembers, "The first order of business on the ground was to reorganize. After a quick appraisal of the situation, Lieutenant Colonel Austin decided to get supporting air strikes going, and then establish a link-up of the forces on the western side of the island, which were then some 1,200 meters of rugged rock and jungle away. The battalion air liaison officer, Capt. Barry Cassidy, commenced coordinating air strikes of the Air Force A-7s and AC-130 gunship. The lack of gridded maps hampered all fire coordination efforts."[18]

In fact, almost a mile separated the two forces, and Austin ordered his Marines to cautiously advance north up the beach in hopes of linking up with the main force before the Khmers became aware of their presence.

Cooper, in Jolly-41, finally muscled his craft onto the beach after four previous attempts and inserted twenty-two of the twenty-nine Marines of 2nd Lt. Richard Zales' second platoon onto the west beach. His success was facilitated by Spectre-61, an AC-130 gunship that provided the first effective air support to the assault force. Accounts vary as to the time of this insertion, with Marine Corps records citing the time as 1010 hours local time.[19]

As Jolly-41 made its way back to Thailand where the damage to its fuel tanks and rotors and fifteen holes in the fuselage would ground it for the remainder of the mission, 131 Marines and 5 airmen in three widely separated groups dug in to await the second wave. As they huddled under fire in makeshift defensive positions facing a numerically superior and well-armed veteran force, the Marines were unaware that their mission objective had already been accomplished.

Unknown to the Marines on the ground or to much of the chain of command, the crew of the *Mayaguez* had been held overnight on Rong Som Lem Island and interrogated, then released on the morning of 15 May.

At 0607 hours a Cambodian radio broadcast by Khmer Rouge propaganda minister Hu Nim announced a willingness to release the *Mayaguez*. At 0630 hours the crew was released, and within an hour it had boarded the Thai fishing trawler *Sinvari*. There they joined that craft's Thai crew of five, which had been held captive for almost six months, and four Cambodian guards. They headed out to sea, followed by a second boat carrying more guards, which was a concern to Captain Miller. A short time later, the guards on board the *Sinvari* transferred to the second boat. The crew was set free and set course for Koh Tang Island and the *Mayaguez*, worried both about being gunned down by the Cambodians or being sunk by Air Force jets by mistake. They had no information regarding the current condition of the *Mayaguez*, nor did they know if the Cambodians were still on board.[20]

Across the Gulf of Thailand, Cdr. Mike Rodgers stood on the bridge of the *Wilson*, watching as sailors worked on the bow of the *Holt* to rig a bridle to tow the *Mayaguez* out to sea. Rodgers and the *Wilson* were returning to Cambodia, after having been stationed off Kompong Som during the evacuation of Phnom Penh from 25 March to 17 April. They had proceeded to Vietnam's Vung Tao peninsula during the evacuation of Saigon and had fired the *Wilson*'s 5-inch guns in defense of fleeing refugees; these possibly were the last shots fired by a U.S. Navy vessel in the Vietnam War. On 12 May the *Wilson* had been ordered back toward Kompong Som.

The *Wilson* had arrived in the area of Koh Tang Island shortly after daybreak, her 5-inch guns anxious for a fire mission. At about 0720–0730 hours, as Rodgers scanned the hulks of two helicopters, one still burning, a lookout reported seeing heads bobbing in the water off the port bow. Unintentionally, the *Wilson* had located the survivors of Knife-31.

"As we closed the northeastern tip of the island to a thousand yards, one of the lookouts shouted down to the bridge that he saw people in the water," Rodgers later recalled. "Soon, we had located three groups of men in the sea." Ignoring MG fire from shore, Rodgers brought the *Wilson* to a stop. "The ship's gig [a fast light motorboat], under the command of Lt. (jg) Fred H. Naeve, was ordered launched and armed with machine gunners to suppress hostile fire from shore."[21]

One of the sailors manning the gig was Tom Noble, a twenty-eight-year-old radarman first class from Jamestown, Kentucky, a place "so far back in the hills," as he puts it, "they had to pipe in daylight." A ten-year veteran of the Navy, he'd served a tour in Vietnam on board riverboats, and had attended Vietnamese language school before being assigned to the *Wilson*.[22]

Under the command of an ensign, Noble, his buddy Alvin "John" Ellis, and five others maneuvered the gig to pull thirteen wounded and burned Marines and aircrew on board, even as enemy fire from shore kicked up geysers of water around them. Noble and Ellis returned fire with M-60 machine guns brought along on the unarmed gig as they rescued the lucky thirteen, one by one.

The rescued men were taken to sick bay; the gig had been secured when, at approximately 0923 hours, a P-3 Orion reported observing a Cambodian gunboat approaching the *Mayaguez* from the east, about twenty nautical miles distant. The naval task force commander on board the *Holt* ordered the *Wilson* to intercept the gunboat. Earlier, during Operation Eagle Pull, which was the evacuation of U.S. nationals from Cambodia, small craft approaching the *Holt* had been a concern. As the captain, Commander Rodgers, later explained, "There is a fairly wide area around a destroyer that is inside the minimum depression angle of the main gun battery and the minimum firing range of the missile system. Hostile small craft, lightly armed, can operate within this area and 'out-gun' a large warship. . . . During [Operation] Frequent Wind we were constantly surrounded by hundreds of small craft, including gunboats, and occasionally [we] were the target of hostile fire."[23]

To prepare for this eventuality, the *Wilson*'s executive and weapons officers had organized a close-in defense team made up of veteran sailors armed with 7.62-mm M-60 machine guns and hand grenades, positioning them along the deck with interlocking fields of fire. Command and control was maintained from the bridge via the ship's general announcing system. They mustered on deck as the ship approached.

Jim Beck, a second class petty officer on board the *Wilson*, later recalled,

> *During the Vietnam War, destroyers like the* Wilson *had 50-caliber machine guns installed, in place of the torpedo tubes, to combat swift boats. The* Wilson *was not outfitted with them and thus had no way to defend against the reported swift boats. To do so, the captain ordered the sonar gang to go on deck and defend the ship. We had M-1 rifles, M-60 machine guns, and concussion grenades to defend the ship. When the fishing boat approached the* Wilson *we were told a swift boat was approaching. We stood ready with our small arms. Had anyone on that fishing boat moved wrong I'm sure we, myself included, would have fired on them. The sonar gang who defended the* Wilson *during this engagement received Combat Action ribbons. We were the only ones on the ship to receive them and I'm sure they were the last Combat Action ribbons issued to any Navy personnel during the Vietnam War.*[24]

As the *Wilson* closed on the vessel, its gun and missile radars locked on the target; Rodgers watched for hostile intent. A revised report by the P-3 identified the vessel as a pleasure craft with twenty-five to thirty Caucasians on board, waving white flags. The *Wilson* pulled alongside at 0949 hours and Rodgers hailed them over the topside loudspeaker: "Are you the crew of the *Mayaguez?*" Yes! They shouted back. "Are you all there?" Again they responded, Yes. "Then lay alongside. You are safe now," they were told. At 1007 hours, Captain Miller led his crew up the ladder to the deck as the *Wilson*'s XO, Jim Hall, advised Washington by radio that all crew members were safe.[25]

It was 2308 hours in Washington, DC, when President Ford received word that the crew was safe, but because the P-3 had initially reported "twenty-five to thirty Caucasians" on board the fishing trawler, and there was a concern that some of the crew remained on Koh Tang Island, it was not until 2315 hours that Ford was advised that the entire crew had

Fishing trawler carrying the entire Mayaguez *crew.* U.S. Naval Institute Photo Archive

been recovered. Ford then ordered Secretary of Defense James Schlesinger to cease all offensive actions against Cambodia; this was interpreted to mean that the second wave of Marines en route to Koh Tang should be recalled.

Despite Captain Miller's efforts to honor his promise to the Cambodians to get the United States to cease the bombings, A-6 Intruder and A-7 Corsair fighter-bombers from the USS *Coral Sea* proceeded to bomb Ream Airfield, destroying seventeen aircraft and damaging the runway and several hangars. At 2330 hours, as Ford returned to his residence to prepare for a television appearance, a second air strike attacked the oil storage facility at Kompong Som Harbor.

At 1227 hours President Ford went on live TV to address the nation:

> *At my direction, the United States forces tonight boarded the American merchant ship SS* Mayaguez *and landed at the island of Koh Tang for the purpose of rescuing the crew and the ship, which had been illegally seized by Cambodian forces. They also conducted supporting strikes against nearby military installations.*

The rescued crew transfers to the USS Wilson. U.S. Naval Institute Photo Archive

> *I have now received information that the vessel has been recovered intact and the entire crew has been rescued. The forces that have successfully accomplished this mission are still under hostile fire but are preparing to disengage.*[26]

Ford made no mention of the fact that the Cambodians had voluntarily released the *Mayaguez* crew, instead permitting the erroneous perception that the crew had been rescued rather than released.

Meanwhile, intense lobbying by the commanders on the scene got the high command to countermand the order recalling the second wave, which was desperately needed to secure the extraction of Marines already on the ground, but not before precious time was lost and the insertion of reinforcements delayed. Lieutenant Colonel Austin later recalled, "I am not sure who else 'lobbied' for the second wave, but through the ABCCC I strongly urged that the second wave was absolutely necessary. I did so not because we were contemplating extraction, but rather, not knowing the crew had been recovered, because additional Marines were required to push to the south, defeat the enemy forces, and recover the crew. In other words, [it was needed] to continue the assigned mission."

Also complicating the insertion of the second wave was the lack of air resources. Of the eight helicopters assigned to the assault on Koh Tang, only Jolly-43, under the command of Captain Purser, was still operational. Three had been destroyed, and four others had been damaged so severely that they were no longer operational.

Although the three helicopters used to insert Marines onto the *Holt* had emerged undamaged, Jolly-13 sustained extensive damage attempting to rescue those on board Knife-23, knocking it out of service and leaving only Jolly-11 and Jolly-12 available. Even if the two SAR helicopters, Knife-51 and Knife-52, were used, only five helicopters were available to deliver reinforcements to the island. Despite this, there were two positive developments: The *Coral Sea* had an updated estimated arrival time of midafternoon and could be used as an offloading platform for the withdrawal if it became necessary, which would shorten the turnaround time for the helicopters. And, with the *Mayaguez* crew reported safe, air cover could be intensified without fear of harm to civilians.

The situation on the ground was not much better. Small isolated groups of Marines were scattered over three separate areas facing a well-armed, entrenched veteran force that outnumbered them. On the east beach, Lieutenant Cicere with twenty Marines of 3d Platoon and the five crew members of Knife-23 remained pinned down, while on the west beach the command element under Lieutenant Colonel Austin, with another twenty-nine Marines, was located a mile south of where the main force of eighty-two Marines under Lieutenant Keith was dug in. The planned insertion force of 180 had been reduced to 131.[27]

McDaniel's 1st Platoon had been the first ashore on the west beach and had moved inland about fifty meters into the tree line to set up a perimeter while coming under unexpectedly heavy fire. McDaniel later recalled, "I had given the pilot my radio frequency before landing and he relayed it to some other plane or chopper that was monitoring the tactical radio net. . . . I had good commo with tactical air. . . . There was a platoon of forty or so Communists surrounding us, giving us a little sniper fire, but mainly concentrating on the helos."[28]

For the next hour, until Knife-32 unloaded an additional thirteen Marines at 0640 hours, McDaniel's Marines were the only force on the west beach. "I kept tactical ground net advised of our situation and called for more reinforcements. A chopper made several passes within the next hour, but kept being driven off [by] enemy fire. Finally, it got in, and we got more Marines and the company XO [executive officer], First Lieutenant Keith."[29]

Marines on the beach that morning have their own recollections. Al Bailey later recalled, "It was dark when we came in at about 0556, but when we landed, that sun was shining bright as hell. They were ready for us when we came in. We got up into the jungle a little way, and we were pinned down, I would say for every bit of two and a half to three hours. They said another chopper came in after an hour and fifteen minutes. I'll be damned if I remember that; I just remember we were pinned down for three hours." Fred Morris agrees: "I don't know what the time span actually was but it seemed hours went by before we got any help. . . . I was pinned down there [on the west beach] all morning."

The Marines tried to expand the perimeter to create an LZ for the helicopters, but numbers and terrain worked to their disadvantage. As Bailey later recalled, "You couldn't see them. They were on a bluff, maybe fifteen feet above us. There was no way you could see them. But we knew they were there and they knew we were there, but we had no way to know in what number. We were a bunch of nineteen-year-old kids."[30]

The next senior officer, First Lieutenant Keith, assumed command and began trying to coordinate events, calling in air support and updating higher command, while trying to link up with the isolated units and consolidate the command. After making radio contact with Austin and the command element and being apprised of their lack of firepower, Keith ordered McDaniel to take a patrol south to attempt a link-up.

James McDaniel, a twenty-three-year-old native of Virginia Beach, Virginia, was the son of a career Marine aviator. He earned his commission through the NROTC program at Marquette University; command of the 1st Platoon G Company was his first assignment out of The Basic School (TBS) of the Marine Corps. Like most of the men he commanded, he had never been in combat. "I recall that Lieutenant Keith wanted me to accomplish two missions: link up with Lieutenant Colonel Austin's group and escort them back to our lines, and find and neutralize a machine gun that was driving off our helicopters."

Choosing ten Marines, including Bailey, McDaniel led his men south into the dense foliage, inside the tree line along the beach. "I remember the jungle was so thick we could only see a few feet in front of us, so controlling my men was very difficult. Although I started in a disbursed formation, I was fearful of someone getting lost, so I formed a single file."[31]

Bailey remembers, "The jungle was dense as shit. They knew where we were at but we really didn't know where they were at. We made a right envelopment, and we started to move around to link up, but when we moved, I was in the back. All of a sudden, grenades started going off. A grenade came down and blew the hell out of me; [it] hit the other side of the tree and knocked me out. I caught some shrapnel from the grenade, and the concussion had me disoriented."[32]

LCpl. Ashton Loney was at point, followed by Pfc. Mark Dick, with McDaniel third in file as they hacked their way through the vines and underbrush. They had penetrated only thirty to forty yards when suddenly the ground was rocked as several grenades exploded and automatic rifle fire raked the men from the front and both flanks, killing Loney instantly and wounding several others, including Dick and the Marine behind McDaniel, but oddly leaving McDaniel himself unscathed. "Grenades rained down on us at the start, and continued for what seemed like five minutes. Automatic rifle fire was very thick, and looked like a chain-link fence with interlocking bullet paths stretched about one to two feet over our heads. I could clearly see the paths from the leaves clipped off from the bullets' wake just above my head while I lay prone."

McDaniel was on the ground when a grenade landed beside him. "There was a tree in front of me, and as I heard a grenade land close to me, I scrambled around to the other side of the tree, using it as a barrier to the blast. I circled the tree several times, felt shock waves momentarily knock me unconscious, and observed sap running from the tree from thousands of shrapnel cuts surrounding the tree." McDaniel suffered several painful shrapnel wounds, but was otherwise unhurt. He decided to have his men execute a tactical withdrawal. The men hit the dirt as more grenades landed among them. As McDaniel later recalled,

> *After a space in time, there was silence, and I recall the enemy laughing in derision all around me. I felt they would soon walk through us in tight formation and kill us all, and that we had to discourage them from doing so. I shot back and encouraged my men to do likewise, but our response was sporadic, not united, and drew concentrated return fire from the enemy. I changed tactics and threw four or five hand grenades beyond our perimeter in each of the three directions facing us, and that seemed to discourage the enemy from advancing or continuing to fire upon us. I crawled to the front of the line to the second Marine in the file, Private First Class Dick, removed his backpack, and covered him while he crawled back to the rest of my patrol. I whispered out, but could not see or hear Lance Corporal Loney, and presumed he was dead.[33]*

The ambush was effective as the Marines took fire from three directions. Toward the rear of the file, Bailey later recalled, "They were lobbing grenades down on us. We were all shooting and throwing grenades. And when we stopped, they stopped. And it was like a death waltz. Then grenades began again. My head was messed up and I lost track of time, but there were several small battles. They had the advantage because we had to throw uphill, and they could throw down on us."[34]

As McDaniel later recalled,

> *Based on the number of laughing voices and volume of fire, I felt we were outnumbered by a strong and organized force. I did not think*

our men could break through the enemy line to Lieutenant Colonel Austin's group, so I ordered my patrol to low-crawl back to our lines. I intended to be the last man out to ensure no one was left behind. After a short time of crawling, the patrol halted because the lead Marine thought he saw enemy soldiers closing off our path back to our lines. I instructed the next-highest-ranking Marine to be the last Marine out, and ensure no one was left behind, and then I took the lead in low-crawling back to our lines.[35]

Bailey also remembers, "The lieutenant decided we had to get the hell out of there. We couldn't go forward, so we had to go back. Several Marines got hit with grenades and shrapnel as we were under heavy fire. We never made contact with Colonel Austin." As they low-crawled back to their perimeter, they came to a clearing. McDaniel remembers,

There was a large open area between the jungle where we were and a tree line where our lines were formed. As we crossed the open space, we were fired upon, and the Marines carrying three severely wounded Marines were forced to drop their wounded comrades to reach our lines. When I heard about the wounded Marines still lying in the open area between the two lines of jungle, I led the effort to pick them up and bring them back. Enemy bullets landed close to us each time as we brought back the wounded."[36]

Awarded the Navy Cross for his actions, McDaniel's citation states, "Although in pain from multiple fragmentation wounds and under intense enemy fire, he personally carried two wounded Marines back to friendly lines." Nor was he alone in his efforts as other Marines scrambled to recover their comrades. Bailey later recalled, "I carried one guy out, then I went back and got another. I don't know how many times I went in. I only remember that my buddies were up there and they needed me." Bailey's Navy Achievement Medal with Combat Distinguishing Device credits his "bold and aggressive actions as instrumental in returning the wounded safely to the defensive perimeter."

Staff Sergeant Bernal also demonstrated bravery when he led a group of Marines from secure positions, across open terrain under fire, to provide cover for McDaniel's withdrawal. When he learned that there were still wounded Marines exposed and outside the perimeter, he raced across open terrain to recover Private First Class Dick and carry him to safety. All of the wounded were returned to the perimeter without any additional casualties.[37]

In the interim, at about 1010 hours, Jolly-41 inserted an additional twenty-two Marines under Lieutenant Zales onto the west beach; these were the last Marines of the initial insertion. Keith placed them on the southern perimeter and was finally able to establish contact with the tactical air coordinator (airborne) (TAC[A]) and call in close air support. Because the two opposing forces were so close, Air Force jets could not use bombs and were limited to cannon fire to hold back the Cambodians.

Austin and the command group, isolated south of the main body, again made radio contact with Keith. With Zales' additional Marines, the main force was strong enough to attempt another link-up. Lieutenant Hoffman obtained Lieutenant Keith's permission for another attempt, and grabbed the first eleven volunteers he could find, including First Sergeant Funk and Staff Sergeant Bernal. He and those volunteers left the perimeter to press south as Austin, in a creatively tactical improvisation, used his 81-mm mortars to support his group's advance north. The leader of the Mortar Platoon, 2nd Lt. Joseph McMenamin, acted as a forward observer, taking a position on a rise to call down accurate fire on Khmer Rouge positions.

As Hoffman's patrol drove a wedge between the Cambodians, McMenamin observed Cambodians moving to attack Hoffman's exposed flank. Taking two lance corporals, Larry T. Branson and Robert Shekon, they attacked the surprised Cambodians and drove them into the jungle.

As Hoffman later recalled,

We couldn't go through the woods, so we returned to the beach and proceeded along the rocky shoreline until we came upon a log bunker, defended by several Cambodians. We charged, and took out the bunker, killing three of the enemy. Inside, we found lots of captured U.S. ordnance, and, strangely enough, a PRC-44 radio turned to our frequency, as well as ammunition, grenades, and two 81-mm [mortar] tubes. While we were still at the bunker, McMenamin emerged from the jungle, followed by Austin and the rest of his group.

For his actions, Hoffman was later awarded a Bronze Star.[38]

Keith coordinated air support, no easy task considering the FAC, Lieutenant Tonkin, and, more important, the UHF radios were on board Knife-31, which had been shot down earlier on the east beach. Keith and the battalion air liaison officer, Capt. Barry Cassidy, improvised a radio relay system whereby information was forwarded on the battalion's tactical frequency to the Airborne Mission Commander (AMC), who in turn relayed the information to the A-7s and F-4s flying close air support. Even more incredible was that Cassidy was with the command element while Keith was with the main force.

The link-up occurred at about noon, just prior to the arrival of reinforcements in the second wave. As McDaniel later recalled, "[We] managed to push down and link up [with the command element]. This relieved the fire on our right flank and we finally got the LZ secured. Two or three more choppers came in after the link-up and we got three tubes of the 81-mm mortars and another company, E Company. The Cambodians didn't want to screw around with this many people with air and mortars, so they left, and life quieted down for a while."[39]

PART SEVEN

Extraction

I n Thailand, Hawai`i, and Washington, it was decided that all effort would now be on disengaging, extracting, and recovering the U.S. military still on Koh Tang. But this force would have to be reinforced before it could be safely extracted. Priority was given to reinforcing Cicere's Marines and the crew of Knife-23 on the east beach.

But back on the island, the perceived need for reinforcements was significantly different, as Lieutenant Colonel Austin later recalled: "Maybe those not on the island thought reinforcements were needed so that extraction could be done successfully, but, on the island, I didn't know the crew had been recovered until our second wave arrived and at that point in time I needed the second (and maybe a third and fourth) wave to continue the mission. Our plan was to secure the LZs and beach coves on the northern end, then push south to defeat the enemy forces and continue the search for the crew."

As the five remaining helicopters comprising the second wave made their way toward Koh Tang with their Marines, they were initially recalled by higher command, who ordered the cessation of all offensive operations once the *Mayaguez* crew had been reported safely recovered. This prompted urgent protests from both Lieutenant Colonel Austin, the GSF commander on the ground, and Colonel Johnson, the task force commander isolated at Utapao who understood that reinforcements were critical for the survival of the Marines already on Koh Tang. In the helicopters of the second wave Marines muttered, "Bullshit! There are Marines down there. Who's going to take them off?" Similar queries made their way up the chain of command; within fifteen minutes the order was rescinded, and the helicopters turned back toward Koh Tang.[1]

Although the initial plan had provided for the insertion of 250 additional Marines in the second wave, the limited number of available helicopters had reduced the number to 127 men who were crowded into the five remaining helicopters. As they made the two-hour trip south, they saw the Spectre AC-130 gunship passing overhead, en route to Utapao for refueling. Without the AC-130 orbiting overhead to coordinate close air support, the helicopters would be inserting their Marines onto Koh Tang for the second time without any suppressive air cover except from the fast-moving fighter aircraft. Only the presence of Spectre-61 had allowed Jolly-41 (piloted by two first lieutenants, Thomas Cooper and David Keith) to insert its Marines earlier, and that only after four aborted attempts. For his efforts, Cooper was later awarded the Silver Star.

At approximately 1145 hours local time, the second wave arrived in the vicinity of Koh Tang; at 1150 hours Knife-52 (1st Lt. Robert E. Ratikis and 2nd Lt. David Lykens), low on fuel, made the first attempt to insert Marines onto the east beach to reinforce Cicere. Despite earlier air strikes, heavy enemy fire erupted skyward, piercing the chopper's fuel tank as it flew over the beach east to west after aborting the run. Concerned over lost fuel, and without the ability to refuel in flight, Knife-52 turned back toward Thailand, its twenty-seven Marines still on board. It made an emergency landing about eighty miles southeast of Utapao, and was placed out of action. After both Knife-51 (First Lieutenant Brims and 2nd Lt. Dennis L. Danielson) and Jolly-43 (Captain Purser and 1st Lt. Robert Gradle) aborted their runs on the east beach, the remaining four helicopters were diverted to the west beach.[2]

The air strikes on the west beach had apparently been more effective, and the Marines from G Company had established a small perimeter around the LZ. The hovering airships provided covering fire, as one by one they cycled onto the LZ. First in was Knife-51 at 1155 hours. Brims hovered above the surf, turning his tail toward the jungle as the ramp fell and nineteen Marines of Captain Stahl's E Company charged onto the beach even as G Company Marines carried five wounded on board.

Once loaded, Knife-51 lifted off and headed toward Utapao, to be quickly replaced by Jolly-43, which inserted twenty-eight Marines without taking significant damage. After lifting off, Purser flew to the HC-130 tanker, refueled in flight, and returned to the area of the east beach.

At noon, Jolly-11 (1st Lt. Donald Backlund and 1st Lt. Gary Weikel) and Jolly-12 (Capt. Paul L. Jacobs and Capt. Martin A. Nickerson) flew in and inserted twenty-seven and twenty-six Marines, respectively, onto the west beach. A total of one hundred additional Marines were inserted, bringing the total to 221 Marines on the west beach, with Cicere's twenty Marines and five USAF crew members isolated on the east beach. Both Backlund and Jacobs inserted their Marines without sustaining damage. Additionally, Jolly-12 picked up four additional wounded while hovering under fire and then picked up the grounded Marines from Knife-52 on the Thai coast before returning to Utapao and being subsequently relaunched.[3]

With his numbers increased, Austin continued to consolidate and expand his position, dividing his area into two areas, with the northern or left perimeter under the command of the just-arrived Captain Davis' G Company, and the southern or right perimeter under the control of Captain Stahl's E Company. Two three-man M-60 MG teams and other Marines from E Company headed south into the unsecured territory, one team comprising LCpl. Joseph N. Hargrove, Pfc. Gary L. Hall, and Pvt. Danny G. Marshall, and the other comprising LCpl. J. E. Taylor, Pfc. D. A. Ramierez, and Pvt. P. G. Mehrhof, with Hargrove's team taking the extreme right flank of the perimeter. The Marines dug in, not knowing if they would be extracted or remain overnight.

By 1430 hours Cambodian fire had significantly decreased. The Cambodian commander later said that he'd decided that, considering his casualties and the increased strength of his enemy, unless reinforcements arrived from the mainland, it would be best to withdraw and wait for nightfall. Additionally, his primary ammunition storage site was in the north, between the two American positions.[4]

With things relatively quiet in midafternoon, Austin considered an attempt to link up with Cicere, but it was clear that the enemy's strength was such that any attempt to push through to the east would result in heavy casualties. Meanwhile, there were plans being made for the Air Force to attempt to extract Cicere by helicopter. Both Jolly-11 and Jolly-43 were refueled by air and available.

At 1435 hours Jolly-43 attempted to extract the Marines isolated on the east beach. As a Spectre gunship and naval artillery provided covering fire along the east beach and A-7s dispersed tear gas, Purser began his approach. The gas was mistakenly deployed crosswind perpendicular to the helicopter's approach, however, rather than upwind and parallel, resulting in the helicopter being silhouetted by a white cloud of gas. As Purser hovered fifty yards from Cicere's position, his helicopter was engulfed in intense MG fire that severed the left engine's fuel line, causing it to lose power and spraying fuel inside the cabin. The left gunner attempted to return fire, but the minigun jammed, leaving the left side of the aircraft virtually defenseless. Shrapnel from mortars wounded Sgt. Thomas Bateson in the shoulder as he returned fire from the ramp minigun, which was the only one still operational. Bateson was later awarded the Silver Star for his actions.

With the Marines unable to run in the open through intense MG fire, and with his aircraft seriously damaged, Purser powered up and swung away from the island as Jolly-11 (Backlund and Weikel) provided covering fire. Purser flew to the *Coral Sea*, seventy miles south, and was safely recovered. The *Coral Sea*'s maintenance crew immediately began making repairs. Jolly-11 also landed and refueled. With the arrival of the *Coral Sea*, the two-hour trip to Utapao was unnecessary, saving precious time.

At approximately1600 hours two USAF OV-10 forward air control aircraft (Nail-68 and Nail-47) arrived in the area from Korat RTAFB. Nail-68 (Maj. Robert Undorf) assumed the duties of on-scene commander (OSC) in control of air support, and coordination between ground and air assets improved.[5] Nail-47 (Capt. Rick Roehrkasse) orbited in support of the west beach as Undorf concentrated on the task of extracting the isolated Marines who were on the east beach. Austin credits Undorf as a key factor in turning the tide. "Undorf unquestionably was the first aircraft on scene that seemed to sense what was going on, what had to be done, and how to coordinate with us on the ground to make it happen."[6]

Sometime between 1630 and 1700 hours, depending on accounts, Captain Rogers on board the *Wilson* (code-named Black Velvet) received permission to utilize his 5-inch guns to engage a Cambodian gunboat. With Undorf making corrections, Rogers zeroed in and fired twenty-one rounds, setting the gunboat afire and sinking it as a column of dense black smoke rose into the air. Meanwhile, Nail-47 called in air strikes by F-4 and A-7 aircraft, marking targets with smoke, to prevent the Cambodians from moving back into positions earlier vacated.[7]

Darkness was rapidly closing in, and the decision had to be made on whether to try to extract the Marines by helicopter or naval craft, or whether to remain on the island overnight. Austin believed the Marines on the west beach could defend their position overnight, but Cicere on the east beach had a tight perimeter for his twenty-five men and lacked heavy weapons. If the decision was made to extract, the Marines on the east beach would have to be extracted first. To do otherwise would sign their death warrant.

McDaniel later recalled, "[At] about 1700, we got the word we'd have to dig in and set up our perimeter. There were more than a couple of people ready to faint . . . but the holes were dug." The Marines had gone in ten hours earlier with only two canteens of water each, most of which had been consumed in the intense tropical heat. Apart from brief naps, most had not slept since being pulled from field exercises forty-eight hours earlier.

By 1800 hours General Burns at Seventh Air Force Headquarters in Nakhon Phanom concluded that Cicere's Marines could not survive overnight and gave the order for their extraction. That decision was complicated by a lack of available air transport resources. Even with Jolly-43 back in service after a jerry-rigged repair to its fuel line and the arrival of Jolly-44 (piloted by two first lieutenants, Robert D. Blough and Henry M. Mason) from Nakhon Phanom, there were only five available aircraft, not counting two unarmed SH-3 helicopters on board the *Coral Sea*.

Also supporting the eastern extraction would be A-7 and F-4 air strikes coordinated by Nail-68 overhead and Black Velvet-1, the captain's gig from the *Wilson*, now armed with four mounted M-60 machine guns to provide close-in ship-to-shore suppressive fire, draw fire away from the landing helicopters, and rescue any Marines making a dash for the water.

At approximately 1815 hours Jolly-11 (Backlund) followed by Jolly-12 (Capt. Barry R. Walls and 2nd Lt. Richard L. Comer), and with Knife-51

(1st Lt. Richard Brims and 2nd Lt. Dennis Danielson) providing cover, requested smoke and zoomed in toward the east beach from the north with both door guns, manned by TSgt. Harry Cash and MSgt. John Eldridge, opening up with enthusiasm. Since Backlund had been to the LZ previously, he had knowledge of the Marines' positions. The Marines popped smoke grenades as he approached the LZ.

Even with all the suppressive fire from the circling helicopters and A-7 aircraft, as well as from the Marines on the ground, the Cambodians poured heavy fire at Backlund as he made a low-level approach at high speed then hovered just off shore, ramp facing the beach. He then hovered back into the cove where the Marines were pinned down.

As Cicere's Marines made a fighting withdrawal, moving toward the helicopter's rear ramp and stopping to fire every few feet, they were pursued by Cambodians, some who came within grenade range, only to be cut down by Cash and Eldridge. Pararescuemen Sgt. Joseph Stanaland and A1C Brad Marx dismounted the craft under fire to assist the wounded Marines on board. A USAF photographer on board, 1st Lt. Ronald Rand, provided covering fire with his automatic rifle.

In the air overhead, Knife-51 laid down suppressive fire with its miniguns, while in the cabin, pararescuemen TSgt. Wayne L. Fisk and Sgt. Ronald A. Cooper knocked out two windows and returned fire with their GAU-5 rifles (short-barreled versions of the M-16).

Offshore, Black Velvet-1 had entered the cove. On board was Tom Noble on his second excursion on the gig. He remembers, "In midafternoon it was determined that a massive effort would be made to recover our forces from the island. After dark, it would be very difficult to direct fire from Navy and Air Force units. Captain Rogers made the decision to arm our gig and have it proceed as close as possible to the recovery area. Lt. (jg) Larry Hall was put in command and eight of us sailors were picked to man the gig because of our familiarity with small arms and our prior combat experience in Vietnam." After being cleared by Nail-68 (Undorf), Black Velvet-1 opened fire on Cambodian positions north of the Marines.[8]

As Cicere's Marines slogged through the surf to board Jolly-11, the Navy and Air Force laid down a devastating array of ordnance to keep the enemy under cover, but the Cambodians responded with heavy fire at their attackers. As Noble later recalled,

> *Fire from enemy machine guns and recoilless rifles in the jungle was extremely intense. I had been in my share of firefights in Vietnam, and this one was right up there. While this heavy fire was going on, Air Force Lt. Donald Backlund flew his helicopter to within fifty yards of the enemy fire and set it down to take the Marines on board. He then started taking even heavier fire from three directions. We opened up on the position to the west of the CH-53 and then two of the three enemy positions opened up on us.*[9]

Within three minutes of Jolly-11 touching down, SSgt. Joseph S. Stanaland signaled the pilot that all twenty-five Marines and airmen were on board; as the craft lifted off, a Cambodian with a grenade held high charged the helicopter, only to be cut down by Cash's door gun, the grenade exploding just behind the tail rotor. With crew tending to the wounded on board and clear of the island, Backlund headed for the *Coral Sea*, which was ten minutes away. Damage to the aft section and three holes in the aircraft placed Jolly-11 out of the fight. For their actions in inserting troops onto the *Holt* and the west beach, and their extraction under fire of the Marines on the east beach, Backlund received the Air Force Cross; and Weikel, Cash, Eldridge, Stanaland, and A1C Brad E. Marx all received the Silver Star.

Around the same time to the south, a C-130 deployed a BLU-82 daisy cutter, a fifteen thousand–pound bomb with 7.8 tons of high explosive, the largest bomb in the conventional arsenal. It was used in Vietnam, usually to clear a helicopter LZ. The Marines on the ground were not informed of its deployment on Koh Tang, and as the pallet it was on floated down by parachute they assumed it was a resupply drop gone wrong. McDaniel later recalled, "I was sitting on the ground within the perimeter [when] without warning I felt the ground suddenly drop six to twelve inches, leaving me suspended in midair for a few seconds before the ground came back up and I fell into it. It was startling and unexpected. Didn't know what it was at the time." Morris agreed: "When it went off, it was deafening, and it felt like an earthquake."

The fact that it was deployed way south of the Marines, in the center of the island, suggests that its intended effect was more psychological than practical. If so, it was unsuccessful. The Khmer Rouge moved closer to the Americans, knowing that the Air Force would be unable to accurately deploy the weapon for fear of friendly casualties. Others believe it was aimed at Cambodians massing in the area. In any event, all accounts recall that the detonation was followed by a period of little activity by the Khmer Rouge. Undorf, in the air overhead, observed that enemy traffic along foot paths was greatly reduced following the bomb's detonation, but noted that sniper activity increased throughout the afternoon.

Meanwhile, back on the east beach, in response to reports that a Marine might have taken shelter in the fuselage of one of the downed helicopters, Walls maneuvered Jolly-12 over the remains of Knife-31 as Brims circled Knife-51 overhead to provide cover. Jolly-12 lowered a rescue device called a jungle penetrator—a hoist at the end of a cable—but there was no response from within the wreckage. The only response was heavy ground fire from the Cambodians that wounded the flight mechanic, Sgt. Jesus DeJesus, in the left leg. Ignoring his wound, DeJesus remained in an exposed position operating the hoist, his head outside the door visually searching the area, looking for any survivors. Enemy fire riddled the hovering craft, resulting in major damage to the slider guide mast, tail rotor section, hydraulic lines, auxiliary fuel tanks, and rotors. Satisfied that there were no survivors, both helicopters withdrew.

Having sustained no significant damage, Knife-51 remained in the area while Jolly-12 limped back to the *Coral Sea*, to be placed out of service. Only three craft—Knife-51, Jolly-43 (with a repaired fuel line), and Jolly-44 (newly arrived)—remained in service to extract the two hundred Marines on the west beach as the sunset transitioned into a moonless night.

At this point, Undorf, overhead in his OV-10, considered the two options of either inserting Marines to reinforce the west beach or extracting the remaining Marines. Feeling confident that he could keep air assets overhead in either case, Undorf consulted with Austin; with no input from higher commands, they made a "local tactical decision" to extract the Marines in a phased withdrawal.[10]

On the ground, the wounded were gathered into a central area. A staggered withdrawal would allow the perimeter to contract without compromising the integrity of their defensive line as Marines were withdrawn and extracted. F-4s and A-7s, directed by a second flight of OV-10s that had just arrived on scene to replace the others now low on fuel, Nail-51 (Capt. William Carroll) and Nail-69 (Capt. Greg Wilson) would fly strafing runs to pin down the Cambodians. Wilson focused on getting the helicopters in and out, Carroll concentrated on directing fire support, and Black Velvet-1 moved to the west to provide offshore fire support.

Low on fuel, Nail-68 (Maj. Robert Undorf) and Nail-47 (Capt. Rick Roehrkasse) withdrew after three hours on station and returned to base, leaving Nail-69 as the new OSC. Undorf would later be awarded the Silver Star for his actions. As is common in the confusion of combat, memories differ as to the amount of enemy fire during the extraction, but all agree the Cambodians became more aggressive as the perimeter contracted and the Marines were withdrawn. Austin later recalled, "I was within twenty-five yards of the first helicopter when it landed and the volume of enemy fire and the Marines' suppressive fire in response to it was very, very heavy."

Because it was low on fuel after hovering to provide fire support during the east beach extraction, Knife-51 (Brims and Danielson) was the first helicopter into the west beach at 1850 hours; at that hour it was silhouetted against the twilight sky. Coming in fast, its appearance caught the Marines unprepared. As Major Hendricks later recalled, "There was just enough light to see westward when a lone CH-53 turned and came boring in toward the beach. When asked whether he was to resupply or extract [us] he replied that he was to extract and other aircraft were on the way. As he settled into the shallow water at the edge of the beach he was greeted by an almost unbelievable hail of small arms and automatic weapons fire from a ridge to our south and east."[11]

Austin had already met with captains Davis and Stahl and devised a plan of withdrawal. Since the majority of the incoming fire was from the south or right edge of the perimeter, the Marines in the north or left edge of the perimeter would be withdrawn first, with the Marines in the south, a mixture of E and G companies, boarding last. At the meeting, Davis told Austin, "You had the day shift. I'll take the night." Austin had come in on the first wave and had been in combat all day, so Davis volunteered to "close" the beach. Austin later recalled, "I didn't agree because I had been there all day, but rather because our plan was the best tactical way to effect the extraction. I understood that what was needed as the perimeter was reduced was more infantrymen from the rifle companies and not a BLT command group. I decided to take the command group out once the wounded had been extracted and the rest of the extraction operation was well under way. Stahl and Davis would then lead the extraction of their respective companies, with Davis as the closer."[12]

As Knife-51 (Brims) landed, it began taking fire and mortars from the south and east. The battalion surgeon, Lt. John Wilkins, herded the wounded on board and supervised the loading of the seriously wounded, all under fire. At the MG position on the extreme right flank, Hall opened up with his M-60, laying down suppressive fire with Marshall and Hargrove firing their M-16s. Fisk dismounted the aircraft to assist the Marines on board. The Marines emptied their weapons into the jungle before racing on board. Once the forty-one Marines had loaded, Brims lifted off, narrowly avoiding a Khmer RPG, and headed toward the *Coral Sea*. Because of the lack of air assets, all helicopters were loading numbers in excess of the safe maximum.

Stahl, seeing Brims depart, blew three blasts on his whistle signaling E Company's pullback to secondary positions closer to the LZ. As the perimeter collapsed, the question of whether Hargrove's MG team, low on ammo, ever heard the signal and withdrew is debated. Some accounts have them remaining in place, unaware of the withdrawal. Others are certain they withdrew, covered by Sgt. Carl Anderson and Pfc. Fernando Rios, to set up on the southern edge of the beach. What is clear is that after being advised by Captain Stahl that all his men were accounted for, neither Captain Davis nor Gunnery Sergeant McNemar believed that there were Marines still outside the perimeter.

It was nearly dark when Jolly-43 (Purser) came in next at 1854 without lights; through a miscommunication Jolly-44 (Blough) also began an approach without lights and the two aircraft almost collided. Fortunately, Gradle in the copilot's seat saw the shadow of Jolly-44 and turned on a searchlight, causing Blough to veer off and avoid a collision.

As Jolly-44 orbited overhead, fifty-four Marines, including the BLT command and fire support personnel, loaded onto Purser's aircraft as captains Davis and Stahl further collapsed their respective perimeters in accordance with the plan as the Cambodians "walked" mortar rounds into the LZ. Undorf in Nail-68 located the mortar position and marked it with smoke for a flight of A-7s, but they were unable to find the mark in the darkness. By now the Cambodians were low on ammunition and exhausted, and they were ordered to concentrate fire on the helicopters. Jolly-43 (Purser) lifted off, en route to the *Coral Sea*. For their actions in inserting Marines in the first wave, landing reinforcements, and extracting Marines at Koh Tang, Purser was awarded the Air Force Cross, and Gradle the Silver Star.

Three minutes later, at 1857, Jolly-44 (Blough) made its second approach. Heavy fire caused him to abort, and it was pitch dark as he made his third approach. Visual orientation was difficult, but he set down on the beach and thirty-five exhausted Marines rushed on board, encouraged by the shouts and curses of their platoon sergeant, Clark Hale. Realizing the increasing vulnerability of the remaining Marines, Blough elected to unload his Marines on board the *Holt*, which was back in the area after having escorted the *Mayaguez* into open waters. An extremely dangerous maneuver under the best of circumstances, it was an incredible act of airmanship performed at night without lights (both the aircraft's landing light and searchlight had been disabled by gunfire), and it took three attempts. Finally, as he landed on the undersized *Holt* landing deck, holding light as the wheels touched the deck, the Marines exited through the right front door onto the ship. This cut the turnaround time in half, and Blough's was the first helicopter back in the area.

At 1930 hours Blough (Jolly-44) landed for a second load of Marines, this time under heavy fire and taking numerous hits. He picked up another thirty-seven Marines as Spectre-21 flew overhead raining down 20-mm and 40-mm cannon fire on Cambodian positions. With suspected damage to his engine, a second landing on the *Holt* was not an option, so Blough headed for the *Coral Sea*. For his actions, Blough was awarded the Silver Star.[13]

On the ground, Davis radioed Nail-69 to advise that they were in danger of being overrun; Wilson asked how many Marines were left. Davis' answer illustrates the confusion inherent in a night-time withdrawal under fire: "I don't know who's gone and who's here. I'm just going to have to do the best I can." It would be precious minutes until Knife-51 (Brims), en route back to the island, would arrive.

At 2010 hours, Brims returned, but became disoriented in the total darkness and aborted three runs. On the fourth attempt, he went in using all his lights on—landing lights, spotlight, hoist light, and hover light. This facilitated a safe landing but drew intense enemy fire. Spectre-21 peppered the enemy positions with 20-mm and 40-mm fire as Brims' gunners opened up with their miniguns.

On the ground, Technical Sergeant Fisk dismounted and assisted Davis and McNemar in moving through the perimeter to get the remaining Marines loaded on board. Wanting to make certain that no one remained in the area, Fisk sought and was granted permission to again dismount. As he dismounted, McNemar followed to stand as backup. Moving along the beach, Fisk took fire from a Cambodian position and returned fire with his GAU-5 submachine gun, possibly the last ground combat of the Vietnam War. Whether the Cambodians were killed by Fisk or by Spectre-21's following strafing run is unknown. He made a survey along the abandoned perimeter but found nothing. Believing a green flare to be a signal for a Cambodian assault, he rushed back to the helicopter. As he saw Fisk approaching, McNemar remounted the aircraft, with Fisk right behind him. The helicopter had been on the ground for almost ten minutes.[14]

As Knife-51 lifted off, the ramp, which had been in a neutral or unlocked position, dropped, and Fisk fell onto his back and began sliding down the ramp. He was saved from falling free of the aircraft by the grasp of several Marines who pulled him back on board as the ramp was reengaged. There was some initial confusion as Marines stated that there were still Marines on the island, but once again Davis confirmed his belief that all the Marines were off the island; Brims and the other aircraft headed for home, the mission complete. Brims lifted off with twenty-nine Marines, believed to be the last living Marines on the island. For their actions, Brims would be awarded the Air Force Cross and Fisk would receive the Silver Star.

Because of the Marines being evacuated to the mainland and onto three different ships, a full accounting of all personnel was not completed until after 2300 hours, at which time Hargrove, Hall, and Marshall were listed as unaccounted for. On board the *Coral Sea*, Rear Adm. R. T. Coogan debated sending a fourteen-man SEAL team, commanded by Lt. (jg) R. T. Coulter, onto the island; Davis, Stahl, and McNemar, among others, volunteered to go back in, but Coogan, aware of the JCS order to cease offensive operations, wanted confirmation that the Marines were still alive before committing any forces to a rescue operation. None was forthcoming, and no rescue operation was ever mounted, although the *Wilson* did lay offshore the next morning broadcasting messages in English, French, and Khmer without seeing any indication that the three Marines were still alive. At 1000 hours, under orders from Admiral Gayler's headquarters in Hawai'i, the *Wilson* departed the area and sailed for Subic Bay.[15]

The following day, as Thailand protested the violation of its sovereignty, the United States celebrated a diplomatic and political triumph, but deliberately withheld casualty figures, downplaying the losses and publicly misstating that the twenty-three airmen killed in Thailand were not connected to the *Mayaguez* rescue operation. Why did the *New York Times* headline on 16 May 1975 read, "Copters Evacuate U.S. Marines and Ship Rescue Mission Ends; Toll Includes One Known Dead," when the actual figure was forty-one dead and fifty wounded?

Besides those awards already noted, Austin, Denham, and Corson also were awarded the Silver Star, the crew members of Black Velvet-1 all received Bronze Stars, and the four OV-10 pilots received Air Medals. Medals for valor are awarded using criteria that are sometimes confusing. For instance, why was Purser awarded an Air Force Cross and Gradle the Silver Star when they experienced the same hazard on board the same aircraft? McDaniel will be the first to modestly tell you he did nothing to merit a Navy Cross, and was only doing his duty. Austin and the Marine Corps disagree. As Austin pointed out, "The Marine Corps doesn't hand out the nation's second-highest award for valor without the fullest justification." As Al Bailey observed regarding their actions that day, "We were finely trained Marines. We just did our job!"

Thirty-six hours after the last Marine boots left Cambodian soil, the 21st and 40th received a teletypewriter message from Colonel Johnson, which no doubt had been delayed due to its nontactical nature:

SUBJECT: RECOGNITION AND APPRECIATION
1.   TO U.S., "SEMPER FIDELIS" EXTREMELY MEANINGFUL.
     YOUR ACTIONS MAYAGUEZ / KOH TANG AFFAIR EPIT-
     OMIZED THAT MEANING.
2.   WITH DEEPEST SINCERITY, TO THE "JOLLIES" AND
     "CHARLIES" WE'RE WITH YOU, ANYWHERE, ANYTIME,
     ANY MISSION. THANKS

Perhaps the best summation was provided by John Francis Guilmartin, author of the book *A Very Short War*, who observed, "The bedrock on which all rested was the ability of the Marines on the ground to quickly organize themselves to respond to an unanticipated tactical situation."[16]

PART EIGHT

The Fate of the Missing Marines

Of the eighteen American servicemen who made the ultimate sacrifice that day on Koh Tang Island, the loss of Marines LCpl. Joseph N. Hargrove, Pfc. Gary Hall, and Pvt. Danny G. Marshall has garnered the more interest, speculation, and controversy. The fact that they remained on the island after all the other Marines were extracted is beyond dispute, but the circumstances that resulted in their being left behind and their ultimate fate is the subject of debate and hot dispute among historians, authors, and the veterans themselves.

Hargrove, Hall, and Marshall made up an M-60 MG team assigned to Captain Stahl's E Company, and were inserted onto the west beach by the second wave of helicopters at around noon. Assigned to protect the extreme right flank at the southern end of the perimeter, they were involved in combat operations throughout the afternoon and would be credited with preventing the Khmer Rouge infiltration from the south. The defensive perimeter itself was 180 degrees and extended inland a maximum of three hundred meters from the beach.[1]

LCpl. Joseph Hargrove, the team leader, was celebrating his twenty-fourth birthday on the island. Born on 15 May 1951 in Mount Olive, North Carolina, into a large family of modest means, he had been married only thirty-three days when he received orders for Okinawa. One older brother, Lane, an Army private first class, had been killed at Quang Ngai, Vietnam, on 21 April 1968, when he stepped on a landmine while on

LCpl. Joseph N. Hargrove, USMC.
U.S. Marine Corps

Pvt. Danny G. Marshall, USMC.
U.S. Marine Corps

Pfc. Gary Hall, USMC.
U.S. Marine Corps

patrol. By all accounts, Hargrove was anxious to "go to Nam" and left school to enlist.[2]

Pfc. Gary Lee Hall, the gunner, was a six-foot two-inch eighteen-year-old from the working class community of Covington, Kentucky, where he was raised with four siblings. Approached by a Marine recruiter while attending Holmes High School, he enlisted in the Marines shortly after graduating, over the objections of his mother. After boot camp at Parris Island, North Carolina, he was sent to Okinawa. Raised as a Baptist, Hall is remembered as quiet and responsible, a guy who didn't smoke, drink, or swear.

Pvt. Danny Marshall, the assistant gunner, was born on 9 March 1957 in Waverly, West Virginia, one of eight children, according to official records. His brother Robert served in the Army, and his brother Joe in the Navy; after Danny was charged with attacking a police officer who was arresting his brother, he was given the choice of jail or the Marines. He was barely eighteen when he landed on Koh Tang, having celebrated his birthday two months before. By all accounts, he was a good Marine.[3]

The MG team was positioned about twenty-five meters inland from the beach, and about five meters forward of a position occupied by Sgt. Carl Anderson and Pfc. Fernando Rios of 3d Platoon. Between 1830 and 1900 hours, a prearranged signal—three blasts on a whistle—sounded, initiating the contraction of the perimeter as the extraction of the west beach began. Private First Class Rios heard the signal and shouted to the team to withdraw, then pulled back. He never saw them again.[4]

It has been suggested that it is possible that the team never heard the signal and remained in place. LCpl. Jeffery Kern recalls that they were still on the line when he withdrew. On an online Website, he wrote, "As the choppers approached to extract us off the island, we were ordered to pull back to the LZ. I pulled past Danny's gun crew position and yelled for them to pull back to the beach, but they were ordered to hold by the E Company commander, Captain Stahl, to cover our withdrawal. I then gave them all the remaining 7.62 ammo belts that I had and ran toward the LZ. I was on the third-to-the-last chopper out and landed on the carrier *Coral Sea*."

But LCpl. John Scott Standfast, a squad leader in 3d Platoon E Company, whose squad was assigned the right or southern edge of the perimeter, is unequivocal in his memories that the team heard the signal and withdrew to the extraction LZ.

About 1700, I had a meeting with Lieutenant Davis, my platoon commander, who tasked me with rear security when the perimeter pulled back into consolidated positions on the beach. I asked Sergeant Anderson if he would make sure all the people got off the line and back to the beach when the signal was given, and he said he would. About an hour after dark, the signal was given to pull back.[5]

After I heard the three whistle blasts, I had the MG team of Hall, Hargrove, and Marshall withdraw first, with Sergeant Anderson and Rios, who I'd assigned as security for the team. I moved from position to position from right to left, water to inland, directing each pair of men to withdraw, physically checking their positions and accounting for all my men. I followed the last team toward the extract LZ to the north. I then returned to the perimeter, and again checked each position from [the] water to my squad's extreme left position inland and back to be certain all my Marines had withdrawn. I went to the LZ, scurrying from man to man, directing fire as needed, and making sure they were all accounted for.

I am certain, I know, that none of my men, including the MG team, remained at the primary or original perimeter. In fact, I clearly recall that they [Marshall, Hargrove, and Hall] were on the beach to my right, three to five men down. We were in a tight 180-degree perimeter. I heard someone call "MG team to the left" and I heard people running behind me to the left.[6]

Pfc. Andrew Piechna also is certain that at least Hall withdrew to the secondary perimeter.

When the word came to pull back to the beach into a consolidated perimeter defense, I moved back and got down into a fighting position. Word was passed that all those to the left of a particular fighting

*hole were to get on the next helicopter. I was on the right side of the
hole. To my right was Lance Corporal Standfast and about one meter
to his right was Private First Class Hall. When the next helicopter
came in, the people to the left moved to board it. Somebody grabbed
my leg and told me to get on that helicopter. I got up and ran to it.
There were about five people in front of me when the helicopter lifted
off. . . . [We] moved back to the beach and took up fighting positions.*

*About ten minutes later, the last helicopter landed and everyone
got on. The last time I saw Private First Class Hall was just before I got
up to attempt to board the second-to-last helicopter. I do not know if
he attempted to board it. I [did] not know Hargrove or Marshall, and
did not see Hall after I boarded the helicopter.*[7]

Pfc. David Wagner and Pvt. Mario Guttierrez were dug in on the
beach, and were tasked with helping load the wounded Marines onto
the first helicopter in. Both recall seeing Private First Class Hall dug in
on the beach behind his M-60 machine gun. They recall he was assigned
to provide cover for the evacuation of the wounded. As they loaded the
wounded on board the first chopper, Wagner recalls hearing Hall yell for
ammo, and he gave Hall his ammo just before boarding the helicopter.
Neither saw Hall again after they boarded.[8]

In the years since the battle, controversy regarding the fate of the three
missing Marines has remained. Headquarters Marine Corps (HQMC) has
taken the position that the men were already dead prior to the last extraction lift-off, despite Marines swearing that they had seen them still alive.
Cambodian sources maintain that the men hid for several days before
being captured and executed.

It would be two decades before American recovery personnel would
set foot on the island to search for the remains of the fallen and learn
more about the missing Marines. Cambodian witnesses were interviewed
on several occasions and an account of the battle was given by the Khmer
Rouge battalion commander, Em Son, who had been in charge of the
Khmer Rouge soldiers on the island during the engagement. Following
the interviews with Em Son, U.S. personnel strongly suspected that he had
been involved in the fate of Hargrove, Hall, and Marshall.

PART NINE

After the Battle

On 15 May 1975 members of the NSC exulted in the recapture of the *Mayaguez*, the rescue of its crew, and the initial report of few casualties. However, when postoperational reports and the actual number of casualties—dead, wounded, and missing—became known, the assault on the island was judged a near disaster; by then, though, it was too late to slow down the media blitz. *Newsweek* called the *Mayaguez* rescue "a daring show of nerve and steel . . . swift and tough—and it worked." *New York Times* columnist Cyrus L. Sulzberger praised President Ford's "resolute and skillful leadership" in the crisis. Senator Barry Goldwater summed up the feelings of the broader American public, remarking, "It was wonderful. It shows we've still got balls in this country."[1] Ford himself would boast in his memoir, "All of a sudden, the gloomy national mood began to fade. Many people's faith in their country was restored and my standing in the polls shot up eleven points."[2] The president would later have the *Mayaguez*'s ship's bell placed on his Oval Office desk as a sign of American resolve.[3]

Some critics accused Ford of overreacting in order to show his tough mettle; some even charged that the whole incident had been staged to bolster American morale following America's abandonment of South Vietnam. Kissinger responded to such allegations at a press conference on 16 May, saying, "We were not looking for opportunities to prove our manhood, only that it was essential for America's global role in the wake

President Ford in the Oval Office with (clockwise) Brent Scowcroft, Bud McFarlane, Donald Rumsfeld, and Henry Kissinger, celebrating the news that the Mayaguez *crew was safe and the ship had been recaptured.* National Archives and Records Administration

of the fall of Saigon to establish that there are limits beyond which the United States could not be pushed."[4] Though there remained questions in President Ford's mind as to why the Pentagon apparently ignored some of his orders during the crisis, he decided not to delve deeper into such matters since the NSC objective had been achieved.

The Marines conducted their own investigations regarding the operation. One of those inquiries concerned the circumstances surrounding the MIA status in the case of Pfc. Gary C. Hall, USMC; LCpl. Joseph N. Hargrove, USMC; and Pvt. Danny G. Marshall, USMC. Statements were taken from seventeen Marines who had fought at Koh Tang by Maj. Peter C. Brown, USMC, head of the investigating team. His written report of findings dated 7 June 1975 included the following:

Preliminary Statement

1. In accordance with the Commanding General, 3d Marine Division appointing order of 24 May 1975, which appears as enclosure (1), a detailed investigation into the events surrounding the

missing in action status of those three Marines cited in the subject, above, and hereafter referred to as HALL, HARGROVE
and MARSHALL, was conducted. The results of this investigation are as set forth in the remainder of this investigation report.

2. This investigation required by reference (a) MARCOR-
    CASPROCMAN [Marine Corps Casualty Procedures Manual],
    par 7004, was necessitated by the disappearance and declara-
    tion as missing in action of HALL, HARGROVE and MAR-
    SHALL upon conclusion of combat operations on Koh Tang
    Island, Cambodia. Koh Tang Island center of mass is located at
    geographic coordinates 10° 16' 50"N, 103° 8' 00"E. These three
    Marines, members of Company E, Second Battalion, Ninth
    Marine Regiment, were part of the Marine force which made a
    helicopter-borne assault on Koh Tang Island during the morning
    of 15 May 1975.

3. Koh Tang Island is forest covered, has no mountains, is five
    miles long and one mile wide. Beaches are sandy on the North-
    east side of the island and more rocky on the Northwest side. All
    approaches to the island have deep water.

4. The area of Koh Tang Island in which Marine force operations
    took place was characterized by normal tropical foliage which
    included dense jungle forest broken by an area without trees but
    in which grass ranging from four to six feet in height was pres-
    ent. Visibility in the general area of operations where HALL,
    HARGROVE and MARSHALL were last seen was limited dur-
    ing daylight hours and nonexistent during darkness. The beach
    area from which all personnel were extracted was clear.

5. Combat operations against enemy forces continued throughout
    the daylight hours with extraction of Marine forces effected dur-
    ing the hours of darkness on 15 May 1975. HALL, HARGROVE
    and MARSHALL were present and participated in combat
    operations throughout the day, as indicated in the findings of
    fact, below. None of the three Marines were injured or wounded
    prior to their disappearance. None of the three were seen subse-

quent to the final extraction of the Marine force from Koh Tang Island, which occurred about 2200 hours on 15 May 1975.

6. The service and health records of HALL, HARGROVE and MARSHALL were reviewed in detail with a summary of personal history contained in enclosure (20).

7. The service records of HALL, HARGROVE and MARSHALL disclosed that HALL and HARGROVE were unqualified swimmers and that MARSHALL was a Third Class swimmer.

Findings of Fact

1. That HALL, HARGROVE and MARSHALL landed on Koh Tang Island, Cambodia, at about 1230 hours on 15 May 1975.

2. That HALL, HARGROVE and MARSHALL comprised an M-60 machine-gun team which was attached to the 3d Platoon Company E, 2nd Battalion, Ninth Marines.

3. That the machine-gun team formed by these three Marines was positioned on the extreme right flank of a 180-degree defensive perimeter, of which the right portion consisted of the 3d Platoon of Company E.

4. That the 180-degree defensive perimeter extended a maximum of three hundred meters from the beach at its farthest point inland.

5. That the machine-gun position occupied by HALL, HARGROVE and MARSHALL was located not more than twenty-five meters from the beach.

6. That HALL, HARGROVE and MARSHALL were located about five meters forward of a position co-occupied by Sgt. Carl C. ANDERSON, 3d Platoon right guide and Pfc. Fernando A. RIOS.

7. That during the daylight hours of 15 May 1975 HALL, HARGROVE and MARSHALL were observed in their defensive position by several members of Company E.

8. That between 1830 and 1900 hours a prearranged signal was sounded initiating withdrawal of the defensive perimeter toward the beach, to execute the extraction of all Marine forces from Koh Tang Island.

9. That prior to initiation of the preplanned withdrawal, HALL, HARGROVE and MARSHALL had been briefed on the sequence

of events which would culminate with the extraction of all Marine forces from Koh Tang Island.

10. That when the signal was sounded to begin withdrawing toward the beach area, Private RIOS, who was located about five meters from HALL, HARGROVE and MARSHALL, shouted to the three Marines telling them to pull back, whereupon RIOS withdrew and did not see the three men again.

11. That the first phase of the withdrawal was executed as planned and a perimeter defense was reestablished.

12. That darkness prevailed when the signal to commence withdrawal was sounded and the action executed.

13. That upon reestablishment of the perimeter defense, HALL, HARGROVE and MARSHALL were observed by Sergeant ANDERSON to be nervous and in a confused state. Furthermore, upon questioning the three men Sergeant ANDERSON determined their supply of machine-gun ammunition was completely expended.

14. That upon determining HALL, HARGROVE and MARSHALL were ineffective as a machine-gun team, Sergeant ANDERSON ordered them to move to a new position which was located to the left of the position occupied by Capt. James H. DAVIS, Commanding Officer, Company G, who was there in charge of all Marine forces remaining on Koh Tang Island, and then to board the next helicopter which was extracting Marines from the island.

15. That Sergeant ANDERSON was the last member of the Marine force to see HALL, HARGROVE and MARSHALL and that the time was about 2000 hours.

16. That Captain DAVIS' position was located about twenty-five meters from the point where Sergeant ANDERSON directed HALL, HARGROVE and MARSHALL to withdraw from the reestablished defensive perimeter.

17. That HALL, HARGROVE and MARSHALL did not report to Captain DAVIS.

18. That during the approximate time when HALL, HARGROVE and MARSHALL should have reported to Captain DAVIS, a state of confusion existed in and about the beach area.

19. That when the fifth of six helicopters landed, incoming enemy small arms fire was received as well as incoming enemy grenades and that the execution of a final protective fire was ordered by Captain DAVIS.

20. That after the fifth of six helicopters lifted off, a 30-40 minute period of quiet prevailed at the Koh Tang Island extraction site. At this time no sounds were heard outside the Marine defensive perimeter.

21. That about ten minutes after the fifth of six helicopters lifted off Koh Tang Island an aerial illumination flare was ignited which lighted the entire area in and around the Marine defensive perimeter. At this time no movement was observed outside the perimeter.

22. That before lift-off of the final helicopter a check of the beach area was made by Captain DAVIS, his gunnery sergeant and the Air Force helicopter crew chief, and that no personnel remained in the beach area.

23. That darkness prevailed when the last extraction of Marine force personnel was made from Koh Tang Island.

24. That subsequent to the extraction of Marine forces from Koh Tang Island a search for serialized equipment known to be in the possession of HALL, HARGROVE and MARSHALL was directed by Captain STAHL resulting in negative findings.

25. That a physical search of Koh Tang Island was not made after HALL, HARGROVE and MARSHALL were discovered missing as the conduct of such a search was not authorized.

Opinions

1. That all Marine force personnel exercising authority over HALL, HARGROVE and MARSHALL performed their duties in a satisfactory manner.

2. That HALL, HARGROVE and MARSHALL did not obey the order issued by Sergeant ANDERSON to report to Captain DAVIS' position and moved elsewhere.

3. That HALL, HARGROVE and MARSHALL were not in the helicopter landing site area after lift-off of the fifth of six extraction helicopters.

4. That HALL, HARGROVE and MARSHALL were not in the helicopter landing site area when the sixth and final extraction helicopter landed.

5. That if HALL, HARGROVE and MARSHALL had been in the general vicinity of the helicopter landing site area, they would have attempted to board either the fifth or sixth helicopter unless they were unconscious, incapacitated because of wounds, or dead.

6. That if HALL, HARGROVE and MARSHALL had been conscious, and/or wounded or separated from the Marines remaining in the helicopter landing site area, they would have called for help during the 30-40 minute period of quiet which prevailed after the fifth of six helicopters lifted off.

7. That HALL and HARGROVE would not have attempted to swim from Koh Tang Island because they were unqualified swimmers.

8. That MARSHALL could have attempted to swim to safety from Koh Tang Island.

9. That HALL, HARGROVE and MARSHALL could have been fatally wounded subsequent to the last time they were seen by Sergeant ANDERSON at about 2000 hours and the time when the final helicopter lifted off, since there was firing by both enemy forces and the Marines awaiting extraction from Koh Tang Island.

Recommendation

1. That the status of HALL, HARGROVE and MARSHALL be changed from missing in action to killed in action (body not recovered).

Peter C. Brown[5]

This report was the official summation of the inquiry despite Marines on board the last helicopter adamantly insisting that Marines were still on the island, statements that are confirmed by audio recordings of transmissions between the pilots of Knife-51.

* * *

JOINT POW/MIA ACCOUNTING COMMAND

In 1973 the Department of Defense (DOD) established the Central Identification Laboratory Thailand to coordinate POW/MIA recovery efforts in Southeast Asia. Three years later DOD established the Central Identification Laboratory–Hawaii (CILHI) to search for, recover, and identify missing Americans from all previous conflicts. In 1992 the Joint Task Force–Full Accounting (JTF-FA) was established to focus on achieving the fullest possible accounting of Americans missing from the Vietnam War. In 2002 DOD determined that POW/MIA recovery efforts would be best served by combining the two central identification laboratories and the Joint Task Force (JTF). In October 2003 the Joint POW/MIA Accounting Command (JPAC) was established under the auspices of the Commander, U.S. Pacific Command (PACOM). PACOM is located on the island of Oahu, Hawai`i.

> The mission of the Joint POW/MIA Accounting Command (JPAC) is to achieve the fullest possible accounting of all Americans missing as a result of the nation's past conflicts. The highest priority of the organization is the return of any living Americans that remain prisoners of war. To date, the U.S. government has not found any evidence that there are still American POWs in captivity from past U.S. conflicts.
>
> . . . Commanded by a flag officer, JPAC is manned by approximately four hundred handpicked soldiers, sailors, airmen, Marines, and Department of the Navy civilians. The laboratory portion of JPAC, referred to as the Central Identification Laboratory (CIL), is the largest forensic anthropology laboratory in the world.
>
> JPAC also maintains three permanent overseas detachments to assist with command and control, logistics, and in-country support during investigation and recovery operations. They are Detachment One located in Bangkok, Thailand; Detachment Two in Hanoi, Vietnam; and Detachment Three, in Vientiane, Laos. JPAC has a fourth detachment, Detachment Four, located at Pearl Harbor, Hawai`i, responsible for recovery team personnel when they are not deployed.[6]

PART TEN

Return to Koh Tang

I n writing this segment of the book, the authors used many sources. The principal reference was Ralph Wetterhahn's book, *The Last Battle: The* Mayaguez *Incident and the End of the Vietnam War*. His five-year journey of investigative work, together with work by JTF-FA personnel, relates a detailed account of the battle on Koh Tang. (It must be said, though, that some veterans take issue with Wetterhahn's perception of certain events.) In any case, his personal investigative research, assistance to the JTF-FA mission, interviews of key Cambodian witnesses, and analysis of the possible fate of the three missing Marines are invaluable. Whether the information he was told by the Cambodians was truthful will remain unknown until the remains gathered at the alleged burial sites of the three Marines have been scientifically identified by JPAC.[1]

When the Marines withdrew from Koh Tang Island on 15 May 1975, three wrecked helicopters were abandoned along with fifteen dead and possibly three living members of a MG crew, the latter of which were later listed as MIA. The first return to the island by Americans occurred in November 1995 when the USS *Brunswick* anchored there. On board the vessel were members of the JTF-FA from Hawai`i whose mission it was to search for the remains of U.S. servicemen lost during the battle and to investigate the reporting of the MIA Marines. At that time, Navy divers recovered 161 human bones, and personal effects and munitions, both live and exploded, from the wrecks of the helicopters. A search of the island revealed various unspent ordnance, including a 105-mm shell and a minigun. In 1996 an unclassified field report was issued that included interviews with two witnesses. Both said that they heard that one surviving American had been captured on the eastern side of the island a week or so after the assault, and that he had been executed when he was caught stealing food. Neither could provide information as to where the body was buried. One witness was told that the American was white and wore a mustache.

During a visit to the island in 1998, JTF-FA members interviewed a former Khmer Rouge medic who went to the island with the group. He related first-hand knowledge about the assault and captured Marines whose descriptions matched those of the MG fire team. A year later a JTF-FA team returned to the island and the mainland coastal area of Kompong Som to interview Khmer Rouge veterans, conduct diving operations of the shallow waters off the east beach, and direct archaeology digs at numerous sites. It was during this visit (March 1999) that Em Son, the commander of the unit that had defended Koh Tang in 1975, showed up unexpectedly. Son wore horrific battle scars. His face had been burned, a collarbone shattered, his left leg scarred by gunfire, and his right leg, lost when he stepped on a Vietnamese land mine, amputated at the hip. He had been wounded sixteen times prior to Koh Tang. He walked slowly, with a crutch. The JTF interpreter was able to conduct a full debriefing, a report of which author Wetterhahn was able to obtain upon his return to the States.

Wetterhahn was told that Em Son "just appeared" one day when he heard that some people were seeking information about Koh Tang.

USAF Maj. Joe Davis, Public Affairs officer from JTF-FA, using a platoon sergeant's notebook, was able to locate the site of the MG cave used by the three missing Marines. Excavation of the site revealed M-16 ammunition; the area was strewn with .50-caliber MG rounds that indicated that heavy fighting had occurred at their position.

Em Son later recalled the day of the battle. "We were driven south about noon, to the southern part of the island." (That would coincide with the arrival of the second wave of Marines who landed at that time.) He stated that near sunset it appeared that the Marines were planning to

*Em Son, commander
of the Khmer Rouge
military unit that
defended Koh Tang in
1975.* Larry Barnett
collection

withdraw, so Em Son pushed his soldiers forward. "We tried to turn the southern flank, but it was too dangerous. We were driven back. We continued to fire mortars into the area, but could not advance." At dawn his unit began another mortar attack, advancing until they reached the beach. "The Americans were gone, except for one body, wrapped in a poncho." (That would have been LCpl. Ashton Loney, whose body had been abandoned under heavy fire during the night helicopter evacuation.)

At the end of the battle Em Son had fewer than sixty men; he had lost thirteen during the assault and his medics were treating an additional fifteen wounded, some of whom would not survive. (Accounts vary regarding the original size of the Khmer Rouge force on the island; taking into account the statements by both Khmer Rouge and Marine veterans, the final number of enemy soldiers was approximated at between 250 and 300, depending on the source.) During the early morning hours of 16 May, he dispersed a patrol to the western part of the island, an area the

Khmer Rouge had not controlled during the fighting. As the troops moved forward toward the beach they were fired upon by what sounded like M-16 weapons, though some of the Cambodians also carried M-16s. The point man, Won, was wounded and later died. The men hit the dirt; as they returned fire a grenade suddenly exploded near them. One of the lead troops had seen a single muzzle flash from a foxhole near the beach. The incident was relayed back to Em Son at the unit's camp, and the commander ordered that the enemy be taken alive. Moving forward low to the ground they surrounded the foxhole, stood up, and ordered a dazed American to surrender. They seized his weapon and ordered him to stand. The American said nothing: he raised his hands and just lay in the shallow dugout. His captors noticed that the American had dried blood on his right trouser leg above the knee. He obviously had been wounded prior to the skirmish. As they helped carry him toward Em Son's headquarters, the commander joined the patrol; together with their prisoner they returned to the headquarters' compound.

The prisoner and his captors stared at each other in silence. The description of the American as told by Em Son in the 1999 interview matches that of LCpl. Joseph N. Hargrove (blond hair, six feet tall, 148 pounds). What possibly happened was that Hall, Hargrove, and Marshall had been cut off from reaching the sixth and final extraction helicopter by the fierce fire storm that erupted between the adversaries that night. Though Air Force Technical Sergeant Fisk was the last man to leave the beach, his search for any remaining Marines proved futile because of the general confusion, and the pitch darkness and whirling sands from the helicopter rotor blades that severely limited visibility. In addition, Fisk saw a green flare arc in the darkness above and thought that it might be a signal for the Khmers to make a final assault on the beach. He quickly had boarded the helicopter; the battle ended as it flew away.

Em Son and one of his platoon commanders (Soeun) faced the American prisoner. In the 1999 interview of a former Khmer Rouge soldier, a JTF-FA interpreter related what happened next.

The American did not attempt to run or resist because he was badly wounded in one leg. The cadre [either Em Son or Soeun; the word or words had been excised from the report] aimed a pistol at the Ameri-

can [who] held his hands over his head and yelled out 'too she' [possibly 'Don't shoot']. The cadre fired at the American but missed because he was very nervous and trembling. The cadre then called to another Khmer who was armed with an AK-47 rifle and this man shot the American in the thigh. The round to the thigh didn't kill the American, so he shot him again in the chest and the American died.

Since the now-dead Khmer, Won, was a favorite of Em Son, it is possible that Em Son fired the first shot that missed, as he and Soeun carried the only handguns in the unit. After the American was killed, Em Son ordered his men to dispose of the body. The remains were dragged to a nearby mango tree and buried. (Using witness reports, a JTF-FA team searched an area two hundred yards around the alleged burial site in 1995 with negative results.)

Em Son went on to explain the fate of two Marines whose descriptions closely matched the other members of the MG team. Khmer night patrols were sent out daily to reconnoiter the beaches, since Em Son still believed another attack would be made. An American destroyer (*Wilson*) had been seen patrolling offshore and aircraft continued to fly over the island at high altitudes. One night a returning patrolling soldier noticed that food was missing from the headquarters' kitchen area. When the theft occurred again, Em Son ordered a systematic search of the area. It was not long before one of the soldiers discovered two sets of footprints in a mud patch. They were large, and their cleat-like tread marks matched those of boots worn by the Americans. For the next several nights the Khmers positioned men in the brush around the compound. Within a few nights two Americans emerged and moved through the darkness toward the food area. The Cambodians quickly surrounded and captured the two: one was a six-foot tall brawny man with dark hair (possibly Pfc. Gary L. Hall), and the other had sandy blond hair, was about five-foot three-inches tall, and weighed around 130 pounds (possibly Pvt. Danny G. Marshall). Marshall carried an M-16, which he handed over to the Khmers. The capture of the Americans was reported to the Khmer Rouge 3rd Division headquarters in Kompong Som by radio, and division officials ordered that the prisoners be brought to Kompong Som the following morning.

The Americans were taken to Ti Nean Pagoda, a Buddhist temple that had been converted into a prison and killing site near Sihanoukville. (During the nearly five year [1975–1979] reign of the Khmer Rouge regime, hundreds of thousands of Cambodians were tortured and executed at such sites.) The Americans were stripped of their clothes, except for their skivvies and green T-shirts. Their ankles were shackled, and each was jailed in a separate windowless room. They were held there until their fate was determined in Phnom Penh. An order came down a week later: the Americans were to be executed and their bodies disposed of immediately. They were taken to the main temple room where they were beaten to death by a soldier using the barrel of a B-40 grenade launcher. The larger of the two was killed first and his body was buried in a shallow grave in a distant beach north of the Pagoda. Dirt was shoveled over the body; his feet still protruded when they had finished, however. These were covered with more dirt and rocks.

The smaller dead American was thrown into the surf to the south. His remains were eventually tied to a vine. A month later his bones were seen bleaching in the sun.

The mainland burial site of the larger American was identified by Em Son. After troweling the surface, American anthropologist Dr. John E. Byrd discovered a single burial pit: on the excavation floor was the darkened outline of a body the same size and shape as Gary Hall. No bones were found since the acidic soil had long since destroyed them. Dr. Byrd searched a down slope adjacent to the pit because a road grader had leveled the area years ago and might have pushed dirt and any bones down the hill. After an hour's search, Dr. Byrd found what he believed was a human fibula (lower leg bone); he also found a set of wire cable hand manacles. There were other small pieces of bone, none of which could provide an acceptable mitochondria DNA sample. The feeling among the JTF-FA team was that they had found the remains of Gary Hall, but proving it scientifically might be extremely difficult.

At the same time, three JTF members were searching the alcove where the remains of Danny Marshall might be; the small team included Cambodian workers who worked as a bucket brigade handing up sand and debris to a screening table. After endless hours of digging and searching, a bone—perhaps human—was found. Dr. Byrd studied it and declared that it might be a fractured humerus (upper arm bone). Khmers witnessing the beatings stated that the smaller American had raised his arm to ward off the hammering blows of the grenade launcher.

The bones were taken to the CIL in Hawai`i, where a determination was made with regard to DNA analysis. Dr. Byrd reported, "The bones are too small for a DNA test. . . . [W]e found several more small pieces at the site. . . . [W]e're hanging on to all of them in case some new science comes along that allows us to get a sequence with less bone matter."

Ralph Wetterhahn had joined the JTF-FA task force teams during their visits to Koh Tang; he actually met Em Son and interviewed him briefly in 1999 before a JTF interpreter had fully debriefed the former Khmer commander. Later, upon his return to the States, Wetterhahn was able to obtain the full JTF-FA debriefing report. When Em Son suddenly appeared in 1999, Wetterhahn went to Koh Tang with the JTF team accompanied by Em Son to learn more about the 1975 battle from Em Son's perspective. While on the island, Em Son pointed out the site where a Marine was buried, having been left for dead on the west beach.

The following year (October 2000) four Marine veterans visited the island. These Marines—retired Marine first sergeant Clark H. Hale, former lance corporal Larry Barnett, former privates first class Curtis D. Myrick and Alfred G. "Gale" Rogers—were the first 1975 battle veterans to return to Koh Tang. They visited the various bunkers, trenches, and pits, which were overgrown with jungle foliage but still recognizable. They scoured the beaches and located their fighting positions. As they collected M-16 shell casings and other remnants of the fierce fighting that had erupted on the small island some twenty-five years ago, each seemed to reminisce quietly about what had happened long ago. They met Em Son while on the island, and Gale Rogers asked him if his forces had found a body on the west beach. Em Son answered that they had and that they had wrapped the body in a poncho and buried it near the beach. He went on to repeat his recollection of the fate of the three missing Marines that he previously had given to the JTF-FA team.

Disappointed that the remains unearthed during the 1999 JTF-FA search had not provided positive scientific identification of the three

Marines, Wetterhahn decided to try a new approach. He would obtain photos of the three Marines and have Em Son identify each as to where they were when they met their deaths. He subsequently went to visit Hall's and Marshall's relatives in Covington, Kentucky, and Waverly, West Virginia. JTF-FA had already furnished him with a photo of Hargrove in uniform.

Wetterhahn returned to Cambodia in October 2000 where he once again interviewed Em Son. He showed the former commander several photographs of American Marines. Mixed in the photo set were shots of Hall, Marshall, and Hargrove. Em Son looked through the photos and paused when he saw the picture of Hall. Wetterhahn got the sense that the photo of Hall stirred his memory; passing on to the others, Em Son remained expressionless. He then spoke of the Marine killed on the island, stating that his body was buried on the west side of the island by the stump of a mango tree near his headquarters. This information had not been revealed by Em Son in previous interviews with JTF-FA recovery teams.

Wetterhahn passed this information on to JTF headquarters in Hawai`i, and another JTF search was scheduled for January 2001. Because of his work and continued interest in the Koh Tang recovery operation, he was permitted to join the JTF team that departed Hawai`i on 5 January. Initially, he understood that there would be two sites; however, upon arriving in Hawai`i prior to takeoff he was told that only one site east of the headquarters shack would be attended to. The JTF had decided to work that site because of the information given to them by a former low-ranking Khmer soldier. The information was hearsay, and Em Son had told Wetterhahn that the body was on the west side. For Wetterhahn the mission began on an onerous note.

Upon their arrival in Phnom Penh, Wetterhahn contacted the interpreter he had used on previous visits about a follow-up interview with Em Son. He was told that the situation had changed because tribunals were being arranged by Cambodian prime minister Hun Sen to try Khmer Rouge leaders for massive killings during the reign of the Khmer Rouge. Hun Sen was prime minister of the Cambodian People's Party (CCP), the coalition government's pro-Socialist, pro-Vietnam element. After the fall of Saigon, the Vietnamese moved into Cambodia and ousted the Khmer Rouge from power. Although the former Khmer Rouge leaders were still residing in the country in lavish style, there was great fear among their ranks that their former leaders would be tried in the tribunals. Em Son had been told to remain silent about his role in the Koh Tang battle. He feared that he could become a scapegoat for others on trial. If a meeting could be arranged, it would take place in private, since Em Son was staying in a safe house in Phnom Penh.

The morning following their arrival, Em Son agreed to talk with Wetterhahn at his hotel room. Wetterhahn asked the JTF-FA public affairs officer, U.S. Army Lt. Col. Franklin Childress, to join the meeting. Em Son and interpreter Noma Sarvong arrived at the hotel at 1830 hours. After pleasantries were exchanged and the group became relaxed, Em Son recounted his story. It was much the same as his previous accounts, but this time he stated emphatically that the three missing Marines had died from their wounds. His previous testimony that had included the word "execution" was never mentioned. When asked about the Marine shot on the island, Em Son became very agitated and repeated that the Marine had died from his wounds sustained in battle. Wetterhahn laid out a map and Em Son pointed to the burial site of the Marine that was west of the Khmer Rouge camp.

The following morning Em Son was in Wetterhahn's hotel lobby talking to JTF team members Richard Wills and Capt. Angel Velez through an interpreter when he saw Wetterhahn. In the following discussion regarding the Marine killed on the island, Em Son revealed some additional information. This time he admitted that the Marine had killed one of his best men, Won, and that after the Marine was captured he died of his wounds. Em Son was tense, realizing that perhaps he was being trapped by his own fabrications. He suddenly remembered where they had buried the body of Lance Corporal Loney. This was news to the JTF personnel. Wills took notes during the conversation and suggested that they return to the island with Em Son in tow so he could point out the burial sites. Although Wetterhahn had a photo of Loney's body on the beach that he had passed on to JTF the previous year, the photo had somehow been overlooked. Wetterhahn had been given the photo by Marine Gale Rogers and had subsequently scanned it into his laptop. He showed it to Wills and this new information was passed to JTF. There were now two sites to be searched on Koh Tang. On 12 January 2001 Em Son, Wetterhahn, JTF members MSgt. Joe Fraley, anthropologist Richard Wills, and Capt. Angel Velez returned to the island.

Em Son led the group from the west beach, pointing to where Loney's body had been found and taking them to where the body was buried. They next walked through the jungle where the Khmer base camp had been located. Before reaching the site, Em Son stopped and pointed to the ground with his crutch and told the group that the patch of earth was where the Marine was buried . . . next to the stump of a mango tree. Fraley was completely frustrated, saying that with each of the previous interviews, Em Son would change his story. Wills had photos of the three missing Marines and asked Em Son to look at them and identify where he encountered each following the Koh Tang battle. Wetterhahn had not seen the one of Hall before, and Em Son studied the photo intensely. He finally identified Hall as the Marine who had died of his wounds on the island. Either he had in his own mind mixed the two up (Hargrove and Hall), or he had purposely misidentified the Marine so as to confuse the group.

The JTF team staked out both burial sites (Loney's and Hargrove's) and then proceeded to the east beach as originally planned; nothing was found at that site, however. JTF in Hawai'i approved the two new digs on the west beach. In the meantime, Wetterhahn returned to California and awaited the results of the west beach digs. On 2 February 2001 he received word from Captain Velez that the team had found long human bones at the first burial site on the west beach that Em Son had accurately located. The remains of what was thought to be LCpl. Ashton Loney were placed in a flag-draped coffin and repatriated to America in January 2001. The mission ceased on 2 February without a dig at the second west beach site (Hargrove's site).

In an April 2009 article titled "Time to Bring Joseph Home" a staff writer for the *Jacksonville North Carolina Daily News* newspaper wrote about one of the three missing Koh Tang Marines, LCpl. Joseph Hargrove. His cousin, Commissioner Cary Turner of Duplin County, North Carolina, started a personal journey in April 2007 to seek information about Lance Corporal Hargrove's fate.[2]

After reading Ralph Wetterhahn's 2001 book, *The Last Battle*, and other related material, Commissioner Turner introduced a resolution that sought support in recovering Lance Corporal Hargrove's remains and returning him home. The resolution with the support of county and state officials eventually went before the North Carolina General Assembly, where it passed unanimously.

In February 2008 Turner joined a JPAC team as it returned to Koh Tang to search for Hargrove and excavate other sites. Nothing was uncovered. Turner journeyed to the island in February 2009 and again failed to unearth anything.[3]

In October 2008 JPAC had reportedly uncovered four sets of remains on Koh Tang, some thirty yards from where Em Son initially indicated Hargrove had been executed. Three sets of remains were identified as Asian, and one as Caucasian. JPAC has yet to make a positive identification of the Caucasian remains. Commissioner Turner, however, is convinced that Hargrove has at last been found.

Turner met with JPAC representatives in March 2009 to voice his concerns about the long delay in identifying the Caucasian remains. JPAC confirmed that in October 2008 four sets of remains were indeed discovered and that samples from the recovered remains were sent to the armed forces DNA identification laboratory for analysis. The results are still pending as of this writing.

While the wait continued for a report on Hargrove, Hall, and Marshall, the United States became more deeply entrenched in a decades-long Cold War with the communist countries of the world. This virtually stopped any research efforts for recovery of remains of Americans lost in previous wars. That search only restarted after the end of the Cold War and the easing of tensions between the Eastern and Western adversary nations. Many questions remain regarding the Koh Tang recovery efforts. Why did Em Son suddenly show up on the island in 1995 to tell his side of the 1975 Koh Tang battle? Could he have been feeling the heat of perhaps forthcoming tribunal trials, and so wanted to get his story out in order to avoid any connection with the brutalities of the Khmer Rouge regime?

How much is he to be believed, since over time his accounts have changed: he used the word "execution" to explain the killings of the three Marines during early interviews and then changed the cause of the Marines' deaths to "died of their wounds." Testimonies by other Cambodian witnesses were often hearsay and not deemed credible. Leaders of the Khmer Rouge still reside in Cambodia today. Several have been placed under house arrest, but only one has been convicted (Kaing Guck Eav— AKA Duch—has been sentenced to nineteen years of imprisonment) for his role in the so-called killing fields holocaust. In September 2010 the International Tribunal announced that four more former Khmer Rouge leaders would stand trial in 2011. Unless the remains of the three Marines can be identified through DNA and dental comparisons, we might never know what happened to these brave men. Perhaps in the case of these Marines the bone fragments recovered will have to await future technological advances before analysis can result in positive identification.

PART ELEVEN

Epilogue

However the issue of the three Marines is resolved, there is no doubt that, given the character of the men, they served with the same courage and bravery as those who fought the bitter battle on Koh Tang Island. Few Americans today know about this ill-fated incident, which cost so many American lives. World War II, the Korean War, the Vietnam War, and even Desert Storm are fast fading into history. Today, as our servicemen and servicewomen fight the war on terrorism around the world, American valor and self-sacrifice abound. Although their mission is difficult and often costly, they meet each day's challenges with courage and optimism. They are indeed making America and the world a safer place.

To paraphrase a speech British prime minister Winston Churchill made in the House of Commons as a tribute to the Royal Air Force (RAF) in August 1940 during the Battle of Britain, "Never was so much owed by so many to so few." This sentiment holds true today as our military men and women continue in harm's way.

PART TWELVE

Recollections:
The Vets Remember

MAJ. STEPHEN ALTICK, F-111 PILOT,
428TH TACTICAL FIGHTER SQUADRON

Stephen "Steve" F. Altick was born in Wilkes-Barre, Pennsylvania, on 17 November 1940, the youngest of three boys. Unlike his father and both brothers who served as Marines, Altick wanted to fly. Upon his graduation from Oregon State University as a distinguished graduate in Air Force ROTC, Altick was granted a regular commission as a second lieutenant in the U.S. Air Force. He entered flight training in 1962 and upon graduation chose to fly fighter aircraft. He was assigned to Luke AFB, Arizona, for gunnery school, flying F-100 C/D/F fighters.

Upon graduation from flight training, he reported to his first operational unit, the 474th TFW [Tactical Fighter Wing] at Cannon AFB, New Mexico, and was assigned to the 428th Tactical Fighter Squadron. Soon after he was certified combat-ready in 1964, the crisis in the Gulf of Tonkin escalated U.S. involvement in Vietnam. His squadron was deployed to Danang AFB, Vietnam, in November 1964, and he immediately began to fly combat missions, which he did for the next few months. In January 1965 the squadron moved to Thailand, and flew the first combat missions into Laos. In March 1965 he participated in the first air strikes into North Vietnam.

After completing several more assignments flying in South Vietnam in support of ground forces, Altick returned to Cannon AFB, New Mexico, as an instructor pilot in F-100 aircraft in the 27th TFW. The unit began to convert to the new F-111D Aardvark aircraft, and he spent the next few years upgrading to instructor pilot in the F-111. In the fall of 1973, Altick was selected to attend the Air Command and Staff College; after a year of study, he was assigned back to Southeast Asia.

In 1974 Altick joined the 347th TFW at Korat RTAB, Thailand, as the chief of safety on the wing staff. He became combat-ready in the F-111, flying with the 428th Tactical Fighter Squadron, the same unit with which he had flown the first missions in 1965. When the *Mayaguez* was taken, the Air Force ordered aerial searches to locate its position. Because of the range of the F-111, the 347th was tasked to take part in the search. It was one of the 347th's aircraft that found and took handheld pictures of the ship off Koh Tang Island.

Immediately after the ship was found, planning began and different units were alerted for a rescue operation. The initial planning called for USAF security police [SP] to be gathered from bases in Thailand and make a helicopter assault to retake the Mayaguez *with air cover. During the collection of the forces, a helicopter crash killed some of the planned assault force and a change was made to have Marines take over the ground portion of the mission.*

Our wing was alerted and aircrews identified for possible missions in the afternoon of 14 May. I recall saying to Maj. Dave Anderson, the operations officer of the 428th TFS [Target Facilities Squadron], who had also been at Danang AFB in 1965, that we needed to be on this mission, because it might be the "last one, after flying the first one, almost ten years earlier." He put the two of us, with our right seaters, on the schedule, and we were alerted for a mission that night.

Our aircraft were loaded with four two thousand–pound bombs each. We took off around 0330 hours on 15 May, with instructions to maintain radio silence with the Thailand air control system, and we flew to Koh Tang Island. My recollection is we checked in with the on-scene command ship [ABCCC] and went into an orbit pattern over the island.

There were F-4s, A-7s, and gunships in the area as well. The A-7s were carrying gas canisters, commonly used in search and rescue [SAR] missions. The F-4s were loaded with ordnance. However, both of these aircraft were running low on fuel. We were able to monitor the HF [high-frequency] transmissions [the F-111 had the high-frequency communications], and we were aware that the ABCCC bird was talking with command elements in the CONUS [continental United States] on HF, and discussing rules of engagement, location, and concern for the Mayaguez *crew, and what the various options were.*

At the time we arrived, I believe there was one or two helicopters that had been shot down, and Marines were engaged on the beach. The focus of our mission was to make sure no Cambodian boats left the island, there being a concern that the Mayaguez *crew might be taken to the mainland.*

At some point, several Cambodian boats were observed attempting to leave. I recall that the A-7s were cleared to expend their gas canisters, and we were then cleared to drop our bombs in front of the boats as a means of getting them to return to the island: a two thousand–pound bomb causes a big splash. We were cleared to attack by the airborne commander, and we dropped a line of bombs in front of the boats. The boats returned to the island. We then returned to Korat.

The wing launched other follow-up missions during the hours of the battle, but to my recollection we did not expend any more ordnance. Later, the boat was retaken, the crew rescued, and the Marines evacuated. Earlier, a C-130 aircraft had dropped a fifteen thousand–pound bomb. I believe that was the last bomb dropped in the war in Southeast Asia.

In a sense, Altick was the Wilber McLean of the Vietnam War, having been witness to both its beginning and its end.

Altick's squadron deployed home to Nellis AFB, Nevada, in May; shortly afterwards Altick was assigned back to F-100 fighters, as an adviser to the Air National Guard. His final assignment was as the Air Force Detachment Commander supporting the U.S. Army's High Technology Light Division test with the 9th Infantry Division at Fort Lewis, Washington, where he retired as a lieutenant colonel in 1985, after twenty-two years and six months of duty.

LT. COL. RANDALL W. AUSTIN, COMMANDING OFFICER, 2/9 MARINES

Randall W. Austin was born in June 1936 in Philadelphia, and grew up in Glenside, Pennsylvania. After graduation from Germantown Academy in 1954, he attended Dartmouth College on an NROTC scholarship. He graduated in 1958 with a bachelor's degree in mathematics, and was commissioned a second lieutenant in the U.S. Marine Corps.

After completing The Basic School at Quantico, Virginia, with an occupational specialty of infantry officer, he was assigned to the 1st Marine Division at Camp Pendleton, California. There, and on a unit deployment to the 3d Marine Division on Okinawa, he served as a Rifle Platoon leader, Weapons Platoon leader, and rifle company executive officer [XO].

After returning to the United States, he served at the Marine Corps Recruit Depot (MCRD) Parris Island as a training officer and company commander; and in Boston, where he recruited for the officer candidate program at New England area universities.

In 1967 he returned as a captain to the 3d Marine Division in Vietnam where he served in the Northern I Corps area as a rifle company commander. Later, following his promotion to major, he served as the operations officer for an infantry regiment.

In late 1974 Austin, now a lieutenant colonel, assumed command of an infantry battalion, 2d Battalion, 9th Marines, 3d Marine Division, which was based at Camp Schwab on Okinawa.

Although I didn't know it at the time, the Mayaguez *incident started at 1612 [hours, Gulf of Thailand time] on 12 May 1975. The National Military Command Center [NMCC] in Washington was notified by the [U.S.] Embassy in Jakarta that the merchant ship* Mayaguez *had been seized sixty miles off the Cambodian coast. Various reactions commenced—recon aircraft were launched, ships got under way, planning was started.*

At 2030 hours on 13 May, I had just returned to my BOQ [bachelor officers' quarters] room at Camp Schwab when my phone rang. I expected that it would be the battalion duty officer, informing me about some event that had taken place in the battalion. Instead, it was the 3d Marine Division G-3 operations officer, who gave the terse but unmistakably clear order: "Get the battalion to Kadena AFB [Air

Lt. Col. Randall Austin, Commanding Officer, 2/9 Marines. Randall Austin collection

Force Base] as soon as possible. Battalion Landing Team [BLT] attachments, ammo and supply blocks will meet you there."

The 2/9 was one of six infantry battalions of the 3d Marine Division home-based on Okinawa. While the entire division was always at a high state of readiness, at all times there were two infantry battalions and certain other units assigned "air alert," meaning that they were prepared for deployment by military airlift at the very shortest notice. In May, 2/9 was one of the Division's "air alert" battalions.

At that time, Marines in the 3d Division came to Okinawa for a thirteen-month tour. While there had been a few individual replacements from time to time, most of the Marines in 2/9 were at approximately the same stage of their tours. Thus, the battalion had been together and training for the last several months, anticipating an upcoming deployment with the Seventh Fleet. Because of the increased number of readiness alerts the previous couple months, culminating in the Frequent Wind (Vietnam) and Eagle Pull (Cambodia) operations, the battalion had been training at an increased tempo on tactics with extra live fire for individual and crew-served weapons.

At the moment the deployment order was received, a large percentage of the battalion was conducting small unit training in the central training area of Okinawa, ten miles to the south of Camp Schwab.

When I hung up the phone, I immediately called those in the field back to camp, specified who and what would go, set the order of march, etc. At 0145 hours, now 14 May and just five hours after the phone call, the first truck convoy left Schwab for Kadena airfield, approximately twenty miles south on narrow, winding, unlighted roads. By 0530 the entire battalion and other units that had been designated for deployment had assembled.

At 0600 the first USAF C-141s arrived and were quickly loaded and launched for Utapao. By this time 2/9 (consisting of four rifle companies, and a headquarters and services company containing an 81-mm mortar platoon and a 106 recoilless rifle platoon) had been reinforced with a 4.2-inch mortar battery, an engineer platoon, a shore party platoon, an explosive ordnance demolition [EOD] team, and certain other small attachments; it was now BLT 2/9. We had almost exactly a thousand officers and men.

I honestly don't recall exactly when and how I learned what the crisis was, what our destination was, and what our mission might be. My best call is that sometime while still at Kadena we learned about the seizure of the Mayaguez and our destination of Utapao, a logical place to marshal forces for subsequent actions. As we were leaving for Utapao, I don't think that the national command authorities had yet defined what those subsequent actions might be.

Just before they closed the door on the aircraft I was on, the assistant division commander, Brigadier General Coffman, stuck his head in, chatted for a minute, shook my hand, and wished us the best. Of course, he didn't know any more than anyone else at that time, and I can assure you that there was no secret packet, no high-level briefing, just "good luck." Little did I know how much we were going to need it!

At Utapao the first elements of the BLT arrived by late morning and all elements were in place by 1400. Ammunition blocks and certain supplies, all prepackaged for air alert units, arrived early that evening. Shortly after my arrival in Utapao that morning, I was greeted *by my boss for this operation, Colonel Johnson, the G-3 of III Marine Expeditionary Force [III MEF]. His small staff included Lt. Col. John Hopkins and three majors, all also from the III MEF staff. I knew each of the officers from our time together on Okinawa.*

Also present in Utapao were representatives of Lieutenant General Burns, commanding general 7th Air Force/USSAG [United States Support Activities Group]. To my knowledge there were no U.S. Navy representatives. Information about the situation on or near the ship and the probable whereabouts of the crew was very sketchy. A little later in the day we learned it had been ordered, presumably by the National Command Authority, that there would be a two-pronged effort to recover the crew by landing on and seizing Koh Tang, a small island in the Gulf of Thailand, while at essentially the same time boarding the Mayaguez. BLT 2/9 was to be the Koh Tang force, and Marines from BLT 1/4, under Maj. Ray Porter, would be the boarding party.

In midafternoon the BLT S-3, Maj. John Hendricks; the assault company commander, Capt. Jim Davis; the BLT air liaison officer, Capt. Barry Cassidy; a member of the 79.9 staff; and I made a recon flight down into the vicinity of Koh Tang in an Army U-21 twin engine Cessna. It was a 380-mile round trip.

We saw the Mayaguez dead in the water about one mile north of Koh Tang, an island that looked to be about five miles long, maybe one mile wide at the widest point. The island was heavily foliated, with two natural coves at the north end with a cleared cut connecting them.

The pilots had been ordered not to go below six thousand feet, and although we coaxed them down to 4,300 for a while, it was still very difficult to see the detail we wanted. With the exception of a small boat, which could have been a gunboat, we saw no activity of any kind.

On returning to Utapao, the key personnel again met to finalize the plan. It is my understanding that Lieutenant General Burns had been ordered to commence the operation at 0542, first light, on 15 May, less than twelve hours away, and only thirty-three hours after we went on alert back on Okinawa.

Time was a key factor as there wasn't much time to get more in-formation and not enough time to muster more helicopters. Currently available were eleven HH-53 and CH-53 USAF helicopters. The allo-cation of these got considerable discussion. If all eleven were given to the Koh Tang assault, then it would be four-plus hours before troops could board the ship since it was a two-hour one-way helicopter trip from Utapao to the objective area. Conversely, if five or six aircraft were devoted to the boarding party, the Koh Tang group might be too small to handle the situation it might encounter. It was decided on eight helicopters for Koh Tang and three for the boarding party.

Even this gave what I considered an unsatisfactory build-up ashore rate: 175 in the first wave, then a four-hour-plus wait for the second wave, but we couldn't see any way to do it faster.

The safety of the Mayaguez *crew was also a significant factor in the planning. I wanted assault aircraft prep fires in the landing zones [LZs] but that was denied somewhere up the line, I assume because of possible risks to the crew if they were, in fact, being held on the island. Likewise, clearing LZs elsewhere on the island with "daisy cutter" bombs and other ordnance also involved a risk to the crew. Time also dictated against that.*

Intelligence was almost nonexistent. Nobody at Utapao—neither USMC nor USAF staffs—seemed to know much about what had transpired since the seizure of the ship, where the crew might actually be, what enemy force levels might be on the island and the ship, etc. Of course, it later turned out that no one—even at the highest levels including the CIA, as Secretary of State Henry Kissinger found out—had much of a handle on that information. Furthermore, there was almost no aerial photography, no maps, etc.

During the day, someone at Utapao produced a former Cambo-dian naval officer, supposedly friendly, who was provided to me as an intelligence source on Koh Tang. We questioned him hard and he de-scribed the island as we had seen it, confirming that the coves near the north end were the center of all activity on the island. He said that the normal inhabitants of the island were twenty to thirty fishermen or irregular type forces, lightly armed; and that with families and part-

time visitors to the island there could be up to one hundred; he made no mention of it being a base for, or defended by, regular troops.

The USMC and USAF planners and the ground and helicopter operating forces at Utapao knew that there had been some gunboat activity in the area, that some aircraft had been fired on from somewhere in the vicinity, which was a reason our recon aircraft was limited to a six thousand–feet minimum. We did not know the extent of the fire received from the island. However, we also did not put much credence in what we had "learned" from the Cambodian officer. It just didn't jive with what little we knew at the time and the small pieces that we picked up as the day and night unfolded.

We knew that if the crew was being held on the island it would be difficult to recover them. Either way, there could be a fight and we prepared for it. Of course, as is well known now, there were intelligence reports that never reached the forces conducting the operation until days afterwards, reports that placed on the island as many as 250–300 Khmer regular forces, well armed, and with prepared fortifications. In the years since 1975, some have related reports of as many as eight hundred of the enemy. From what I know, that's just not historically accurate or factual. Regardless, anticipating a tough time, we made our plan.

The mission assigned to the BLT was, "Seize, occupy, and defend the island of Koh Tang, hold the island for a minimum of forty-eight hours, and rescue any crew members of the SS Mayaguez *found on the island."*

Based on that mission, on the evening of 14 May Major Hendricks and I issued our operations order to the company commanders and certain other unit leaders of the BLT. The assault wave was to consist of G Company commanded by Capt. Jim Davis, one section of eighty-one mortars commanded by 2nd Lt. Joe McMenamin, an EOD team, a helicopter support team, a couple extra medical corpsmen, a doctor, two Army language specialists, and a small core battalion command group made up of myself, Major Hendricks, Captain Cassidy, and six others, including radio operators, for a total of 175.

The second scheduled wave, using the same helicopters as the assault wave after they returned to Utapao, would carry E Company, commanded by Capt. Mykle Stahl. We recognized that it would be four-plus hours before this second wave could arrive at Koh Tang, an unfortunate reality of the time-and-distance factors and aircraft availability. Subsequent waves carrying the other two rifle companies and whatever might be needed as the situation unfolded were to be on call.

We selected LZs on the north end of the island on both sides because these were the only already cleared areas. It was in this general area that we suspected the crew might be; a landing away from there could allow whoever was on the island to escape by boat from either of the coves.

One platoon from G Company was to land on the western side and block the smaller cove with the remainder of the first wave landing in the larger eastern zone. We would then link up the two forces, check out the immediate area, and begin a sweep south to locate the crew. Air assets were to be on station and available as required but, despite my requests, there would be no prep fires or preassault strikes.

Lift off from Utapao was scheduled for 0330 on 15 May, landing on Koh Tang at 0542. The command-and-control plan starting at the BLT and going up the chain may have looked good on paper but in reality was convoluted, without adequate communications and, unfortunately, doomed to failure.

Technically, I was to report to Colonel Johnson who, with his staff, was at Utapao. They would be my link to the rest of the BLT, our supplies, etc. But I would not [be] able to communicate with them directly except through an airborne radio relay. I believe that during the planning at Utapao we coordinated face to face with a group that was to be airborne in a C-130, equipped with a diverse, long-range communications capability. We exchanged all radio frequencies and call signs with them, and they were familiar with our landing plan and tactical scheme. I don't think that aircraft ever came on station, being replaced instead by the Airborne Command and Control Center [ABCCC]. The ABCCC, I believe, came from Seventh Air Force/ USSAG in NKP [Nakhon Phanom] and had local communications and comm back to NKP, which then was relayed to Utapao.

As I understood it, the ABCCC concept was to place an on-scene commander [AMC] [sic] and staff above the battlefield. If such a per-

son and group had been in the ABCCC that day, I am almost positive that none of them had participated in the planning at Utapao, although they apparently had a message copy of what we wanted to do. To this day, I do not know who the AMC was, exactly what he knew or didn't know about the landing force, nor what his authority and orders were. I do know that the ABCCC was a continuing frustration to us on the ground throughout the day.

At 0230 on 15 May, the teams started for the helicopters on the tarmac, and everyone was on board by 0315 for the 0330 launch. At 0330 came the word, "We are holding." I'm sure everyone thought the same thing as we sat cramped and cold on the helicopter decks: "After all this, was it just a big false alarm?"

But at 0410 the helos cranked up and we were soon airborne. As the tail and door gunners test fired their miniguns in the darkness high over the Gulf of Thailand, reality hit home for any remaining nonbelievers, if there were any.

Late the night before, some last-minute photography showed what some interpretation experts thought might be an antiaircraft gun site. Based on that [finding], a further decision had been made, I believed: that attack aircraft would take a close look at first light and, if it looked like a gun site, hit it before the landings started. Both the helicopter commander and I liked that idea.

In the helicopter carrying the command group, I spent the early part of the flight sitting up front, close to the side door. Later, I moved to the rear of the helo, where Major Hendricks was. He, the tail gunner, and I were sitting on the open back ramp at just before 0600 as the helicopters came into first sight of Koh Tang. When we could first see the island out the tail of the helicopter in the beginning of daylight, there was a tall column of black smoke rising from the eastern LZ. I thought at first that there had in fact been air strikes before the landing. The tail gunner, who was talking to the pilot on his headset, came over to us and said that the first two helos into the zone had been shot down. The fight was on!

We made a quick change and directed all other helicopters into the western zone. A few moments later, as our helicopter started into *the zone and the rounds started ripping through the side of the helicopter, we realized that this zone wasn't all that friendly, either. Our pilot pulled out and circled a bit; we told him to try to get us on the ground—somewhere, anywhere. He started in again. This time he skillfully and daringly backed into a very small area that I knew wasn't either of the primary zones, but we all exited out amidst supporting fire from the tail gunner and we quickly spread out.*

Although it took a while to reconstruct it all, this was the situation at the time: The three helicopters carrying the boarding party had gone to the Holt *as scheduled. Of the eight carrying the assault force, two had gone down in the surf off the eastern zone; one was completely destroyed and burning with thirteen killed, and the other had had its tail rotor shot off, but the Marines and crew, some wounded, had made it ashore and were in a fire fight.*

On the western side things were slightly better, relatively speaking. One helo had inserted twenty Marines but had received such crippling damage that it crashed at sea about a mile off the island on the way out. Two more had inserted an additional forty. Another, the one I was on, had inserted the command group of twenty-nine along the coast some 1,200 meters south of the western LZ. One more had made several unsuccessful attempts at the western LZ, was still circling, and would eventually sneak in later in the morning. Finally, the last of the eight in the assault force had received such serious damage trying to land that it was forced to abort. It flew directly to the Thailand coast and made an emergency landing; the troops were picked up by another helo and returned to Utapao. This team unfortunately included the G Company commander. They eventually returned to the island in the second wave and played a major role later.

The fighting was the heaviest in the vicinity of the western LZ, where 1st Lt. Dick Keith, the company executive officer [XO], was in command. Despite some communication problems due to the loss of the UHF radios and forward air controllers [FACs] in the downed helos, he was running air support very close to his positions. The first platoon in on that side, led by 2nd Lt. James McDaniel, had pushed south to help secure the LZ and had hit a heavy pocket of resistance.

Soon after the command group got on the ground, I made radio contact with First Lieutenant Keith in the cove to the north of us. Knowing that we had only four rifles among our twenty-nine men (the rest were radio operators, mortar teams, and officers, all carrying pistols) and that we were extremely vulnerable from three sides while being pinned against the water line, I directed Keith to push some Marines toward us in an attempt to link up the two forces.

McDaniel's platoon got the task and started toward us. They again met heavy enemy fire. Mc Daniel was hit in the leg with grenade fragments, but led his men through the position, and personally carried a couple of the wounded from an exposed position. Lance Corporal Loney, the point man, was killed. Private First Class Bailey, also wounded, and others in the platoon distinguished themselves with their bravery. Despite their wounds, McDaniel, Bailey, and the others stayed in the fight all day, and were among the last to be extracted that evening, still under heavy fire. Second Lieutenant McDaniel deserved the Navy Cross that he later received for his actions.

Unfortunately, McDaniel's platoon was unable to continue south to effect the link-up with the command group. We knew that we had to improve our position quickly before the enemy turned on us, so we started north toward the western LZ. With Lance Corporal Branson and another brave young Marine whose name I do not recall, in the point with two of our four rifles, and Major Hendricks and Second Lieutenant McMenamin right behind them with pistols drawn, we moved along the shoreline, sometimes crawling over jagged rocks, sometimes walking on a narrow path with heavy foliage on the right. As we moved, the BLT air liaison officer, Capt. Barry Cassidy, who was with us, was working with Lieutenant Keith and running air attacks between the two converging groups of Marines.

McMenamin set up the mortars, first firing out to sea so we could observe the impact and then adjusting the rounds back onto the island (a technique, it was interesting to note, that was also used by the USS Wilson later in the day for its naval gunfire support).

As the command group moved north, a couple of enemy soldiers moved out into the surf to get a better angle to fire at us, but return fire from our point men forced them back into the cover of the foliage.

Along the way we encountered and defeated several fighting holes and small bunker positions. We picked up some enemy weapons as we went.

During our move north I had several communications, generally frustrating and unsatisfactory, with Cricket [the ABCCC] about air support, unit locations, etc. One of the most significant of these communications occurred at approximately 1100 hours. It was now about five hours from the original landing, and I was expecting the second wave momentarily. When I inquired about its status, I was informed that the second wave had been recalled to Utapao. Shocked, I vehemently demanded that the second wave be redirected to the island immediately. I made this demand, despite what might be printed in other versions of this incident, not because the Marines in this wave were needed to stabilize the situation so that all could be extracted (something we were not even thinking about at the moment), but rather because they, and probably subsequent waves, were absolutely required so that we could continue the assigned mission "to seize, occupy, and defend the island, hold the island for a minimum of forty-eight hours, and rescue any crew members of the SS Mayaguez found on the island."

At about 1230, a little more than six hours after the first landings, several things happened almost simultaneously, or so it seemed: The main force in the western LZ had pushed well out to the south. The second wave of four helicopters had landed about one hundred Marines, comprised of Captain Davis and his team from G Company returning after the morning abort along with Captain Stahl and a major part of E Company. And the command group reached the western LZ and linked up with the main force.

Three asides might fit well here. First, the second wave brought the news that the crew of the Mayaguez had been released elsewhere, and was safe. Note that this word got to me two and a half hours or so after the crew was picked up, and from our own arriving troops, not from the ABCCC or any command channel. Second, it seems to be historically accurate that the original recall of the second wave was made (by authorities unknown to me) because the crew had been recovered, but without any input from me or, seemingly, without pro-

per consideration of the situation on the ground. Interestingly, some reports indicate that the recall decision was reversed so that we could be reinforced to effect extraction, but my demands for the second wave were based on our continuing the assigned mission, as discussed earlier.

The third aside comes after years of thinking about what happened that day on the island. It has occurred to me that the landing of the command group along the coast south of the western LZ, hastily conceived out of tactical necessity, may have had the unintended but fortuitous consequence of confusing and disrupting the enemy. While we in the command group considered ourselves extremely vulnerable to being outflanked and isolated, the enemy may have thought that we were outflanking them as they pressed against McDaniel's platoon. The effective use of tactical aircraft fire between our two converging forces, the firepower of our mortars, and the rifle fire from our point men may have disguised the actual vulnerability of our group, and instead suggesting that we were a potent maneuver element.

With the second wave in and all on the west side linked up, we continued to expand and consolidate our positions. Although never explicitly stated, with the crew recovered the mission was obviously now changed. ABCCC and FACs in OV-10s, now on station for the first time, started asking questions about extraction. Meanwhile, the OV-10s marked our lines with rockets and continued to run air all along our lines. Maj. Bob Undorf, Nail-68, one of the OV-10 air controllers, was the first person all day who seemed to "see" the battlefield, and to have a grasp of which units were where and what had to be done. He definitely was a key factor in turning the tide and, in my mind, was one of the true heroes of the day.

Sometime in the afternoon came an interesting, if not tactically significant, event. In the sky appeared a parachute supporting a pallet. As it drifted toward the island, we logically thought it was water and ammunition, both badly needed. However, as it got closer it was obvious that it would land more in the center of the island, well outside our lines. Soon, there came an enormous, ground-shaking explosion. Only then did we realize it was a pallet bomb, later identified as a BLU-82—approximately fifteen thousand pounds of explosives.

What tactical effect it had I am not sure: perhaps to further demonstrate our firepower capability, perhaps to discourage them from massing to attack us, perhaps to destroy supply and ammo caches. Anyway, the ground shook and we all went back to work.

Meanwhile, starting in the early morning, quite a drama had been occurring on the eastern side. 2nd Lt. Mike Cicere and part of his platoon from G Company and the helicopter crew had run out of their downed helicopter and set up a position in the trees where they stayed all day, with no communication with us for some reason, but good communications with the ABCCC and the air controllers. Several attempts to extract them by helicopter during the day failed, despite naval gunfire and air pounding that side of the island.

Also early in the morning, the survivors of the other downed, burned helo on the east side, just twelve of them, swam out to sea, most burned and wounded in one way or the other. 1st Lt. Terry Tonkin, one of the BLT FACs, called in many air strikes with a survival radio while floating and dodging rounds from the beach. They were all picked up by the USS Wilson *after three and a half hours in the water.*

By late in the afternoon enemy activity had been reduced and the situation had been stabilized somewhat. We began to discuss extraction possibilities and options in earnest. I believe the ABCCC was no longer on station and Major Undorf as Nail-68 had assumed the primary coordinating role. Small boats from the destroyers were considered but rejected. Undorf asked me if I thought we could do it at night by helo. My answer was yes, that it wasn't going to be easy whenever we did it but I thought that the sooner we did it the less chance the enemy would have to reform, maneuver, and mass to oppose us. I was confident that we could more than handle ourselves that night if we stayed, but that during that time the enemy would move right up against us, making the next day's extraction tougher.

I stipulated only one thing, and this was nonnegotiable: once started the extraction must continue until completed. I didn't want a small force left there on their own when somebody decided, "We'll finish in the morning."

I met with captains Davis and Stahl and we concurrently made plans to stay the night and plans for an extraction. Regarding extrac-

tion, we intended to get the wounded and support personnel out first, after which Davis and Stahl would incrementally reduce the perimeter. I decided to send the support part of the command group out early; then, when the extraction flow was established, the rest of us would go. What would be needed in the later stages were infantry Marines, not BLT command groups. Davis courageously volunteered to "close" the beach, leaving on the last helo.

Just at dusk a helicopter appeared and headed toward the platoon on the other side of the island. Heavy fire broke out and I was sure he hadn't got them out. A second attempt met similar failure, but then an OV-10 made a couple firing runs and the helo came again. This time he stayed down behind the trees for fifteen seconds or so, then pulled up sharply and flew away. All hands were out on that side.

A few minutes later, now in complete darkness, three other helicopters appeared on the horizon, heading toward our western side. The first one came into our zone and was met with incredibly heavy fire. I can vouch for that because I was only about twenty-five yards from it when it landed; our troops returned the fire and quieted things down enough so that we loaded the first helo as planned with the wounded, mortar teams, some from the command group, and a few from each of the two companies.

After that it went fairly smoothly, and as each helicopter came in, the perimeter was incrementally reduced until there were just twenty-nine left under the command of Captain Davis. They waited alone on the beach for more than thirty minutes until their helo came in. At 2010 Gunnery Sergeant McNemar made a quick check of the beach, jumped on the already lifting helo and the last Marines departed Koh Tang after fourteen hours on the ground, still only forty-eight hours from the phone call at Camp Schwab.

The extraction helicopters went to Navy ships, the USS Coral Sea, and the USS Holt, with others already on board the USS Wilson, all close off shore. Immediately, we started a painstaking head count to account for everyone. At that point, we had Marines back in Okinawa who for one reason or another had not deployed with us, Marines in Utapao, those who had not come to the island, some wounded who had been returned on the helicopters that brought in the second wave, and those just extracted spread about on the three ships. After many messages among the various locations, and much checking and rechecking, we came to the agonizing but unmistakable conclusion that we were missing three Marines: Pfc. Gary Hall, Pfc. Joseph Hargrove, and Pvt. Danny Marshall, all in the same E Company machine-gun team.

Once the BLT returned to Okinawa, there was an extensive investigation concerning the three missing men. Eyewitnesses were interviewed and facts were reconstructed as best we could. Nothing was covered up. To the best of my knowledge, the investigation concluded that the three had been killed at their gun position during the heavy fire that was exchanged during the extraction. Upon review at Headquarters Marine Corps [HQMC] in Washington this conclusion was affirmed and the three were declared KIA. To this day, that conclusion remains my personal one. That is what I believed at the time and what I still believe.

In the intervening years there have been additional investigations, rumors of various intelligence reports about the men, task forces returning to Koh Tang to search for bones, gravesites, etc. I expect that even in this book there will be conflicting statements, now well after the fact, about what might have happened to them. Despite all this, to my knowledge no other realistic conclusion has ever been reached.

After the Koh Tang operation, 2/9 reassembled at Camp Schwab on Okinawa. That summer the BLT deployed as scheduled with the Seventh Fleet as part of the WESTPAC [Western Pacific] force in readiness. The deployment included training periods in Korea and Japan.

Lieutenant Colonel Austin relinquished command of 2/9 in December 1975; in January 1976 he reported for duty at HQMC in Washington, DC. He retired from the Marine Corps in 1986 with twenty-eight years of service.

PFC. ALLEN EUGENE BAILEY, 1ST PLATOON G COMPANY

Allen Eugene Bailey was born in College Park, Maryland, just fifteen miles from the White House, in late July 1955, one of five children, and was raised with a strong love of country and a belief in an obligation to serve in the military.

His grandfather had served in the Spanish-American War, and a cousin had served on Admiral Halsey's staff as an administrative officer. His father had served as a mortar man attached to the 6th Marines, seeing combat at Guadalcanal and Okinawa during World War II, and his older brother Alfred Jr. was a career Marine. Additionally, two sisters were married to military men. It seemed natural for Bailey to enlist in the Marines while still in high school.

Bailey had two passions growing up: art and baseball. Upon graduating from High Point High School in 1974, he entered active duty as a United States Marine.

After boot camp at Parris Island, he was sent to Camp Pendleton, California, graduating as a private first class on 4 April 1975. His first duty station was on Okinawa as an 0311 infantry rifleman assigned to G Company 2/9.

The Flying Tigers flew me to Alaska, Hawai`i, Guam, another small island, then onto Okinawa during the monsoon season.

In the wee hours of 13 May we were out on field maneuvers deep in the jungle; it was raining cats and dogs and I was covered in mud. We had set up our tents and I was just starting to doze off when I heard Gunny Mac giving orders to "Move out—we're on alert."

Upon arriving back on base, we were ordered to "Pack your trash in your sea bags and drop them off in a staging area; we are possibly going into combat." I scrambled to get myself squared away in clean fatigues, and in my haste, I accidentally packed away my dad's wartime Bible in my sea bag that he carried as a young teen into combat. I went back to the staging area, found my sea bag in the huge pile, dug into it, and found the Bible he gave to me when I left for boot camp just five months earlier. I almost missed the movement and caught one of the last trucks that pulled out. Most of the men were still covered in mud when we loaded up and headed to Kadena AFB fifty miles away.

The large planes were on the runway waiting for us. I remember hearing the Marine Corps and Air Force officers arguing about us be-

ing loaded onto the planes, because we were covered in mud. At this point none of us had had any sleep for well over twenty-four hours.

Before I knew it, we were in Utapao. Our staging area was in a large under-roof air wing hangar. The majority of us rested, leaning on our field gear sitting on the floor; very few had cots.

Just before sunset a high-ranking Marine Corps officer brought the battalion to formation, briefing us on the situation. This officer said, "Some of us might not be coming back. If you are not up to this mission, take one step back and fall out of formation." Some did, but most of us stood fast. During the briefing he informed us we were going to depart at 0300 hours and land just before sunrise to catch them off guard, and that there would be a small resistance force present on the island. Then a military minister came on deck and led us in the Lord's Prayer.

We moved from the hangar deck to the tarmac strip about two hours before the choppers started arriving. I was issued grenades and two boxes of ammo, and we were told to try to rest. The resting did not last long because the choppers started to arrive, making loud roaring sounds as they landed. The place bustled with activity, and with all the noise and smells, it felt like war! It really started to hit me that this was for real. In the darkness of night the choppers shut their engines completely down for a final briefing.

Twenty of us loaded in the first chopper, and I was near the right-door gunner. During our long flight in pitch darkness, the gunner test-fired his machine gun, which scared the shit out of me. Bernal and McDaniel told us to "lock and load" and point rifles to the floor. When Staff Sergeant Bernal moved to the rear I moved also, knowing to stay close to him because he was one experienced Marine. At that point I saw out the port window that the sun was coming up fast. I saw a ship below, then heavy jungle foliage.

As our chopper approached the island, rounds started going though the chopper, slow at first then at a rapid pace. The sound was like hundreds of ice picks being stabbed though cheap tin. As each bullet went through the chopper it left a vapor trail of smoke and bright beams of light. The closer we got to landing zone [LZ] the more intense it got. It seemed as though they knew we were coming.

The chopper swung the rear end around and landed on the beach. Bernal rolled out standing with his back to the enemy, feet in the sand, looking into the chopper, hollering at the top of his lungs while standing there with complete disregard for his own life. I was the first off, carrying two boxes of ammo that I dropped as soon as I hit the beach, running straight toward the tree line.

Off to my left another chopper was coming in for a landing about one hundred feet off the water and two hundred feet from the jungle line and the enemy redirected their fire from us to it. This redirection of gun fire allowed us to make it to the jungle line. I remember that chopper being diverted off and I knew from what had happened to my chopper that it was shot up just as badly since by coming in broadside it presented a larger target to the enemy gunners. I can still hear the sounds of both choppers fading away as they left us all alone and the gunfire shifted back onto us.

Two Khmer Rouge soldiers were directly in front of me. They were firing down on us as we took cover. I slung my M16 around and walked gun fire to them in a standing position. One I shot center mass, the other one I shot in the shoulder. He scurried into the jungle dragging the dead one away.

With the intensity of fire from the enemy now being directed solely on us, I did not know how long we were going to last. I remember hearing my chopper struggling for lift-off. Just beyond where it lifted off was a jetty of rocks about 1,500 feet away from my position. This is where I planned my escape route if I ended up being the last one. Beyond that jetty of rocks, within sight about a mile out, I watched my chopper make a crash landing in the ocean, roll over and disappear. Another chopper was circling just above him. I shifted my concentration back to the enemy.

We got into a half-moon perimeter about five feet apart from each other and held our defense line. The gunfire was so intense that hundreds of rounds seemed to be going by my head and body. Everything moved in slow motion. The battle seemed to last forever, and the heat was intense. The barrage of bullets would move from us to each chopper that tried to insert more troops.

From nowhere, like a gift from God, out of the heavens came a fighter jet at a 90-degree angle straight down. As it was approaching it made a hissing sound. All of a sudden the trees one hundred fifty feet in front of me started getting mowed down. Large palm leaves and jungle foliage was flying everywhere like a chain saw was at work. He was unloading his ordnance and going so fast I didn't think he was going to be able to pull out of this dive, but as fast as he came in he went out.

After that first fighter jet, another came in, then another, and then another. They kept coming in, dropping ordnance from every direction, never in the same pattern, coming in or going out, twisting and turning in sporadic timing.

The trees and foliage were being eradicated. The ground shook and vibrated from all sides with each strike. I feared they were going to miss their target on several occasions. After about the fourth run in, I knew that they knew where we were located. I was amazed at their accuracy in not hitting me or any of my brothers.

Feeling I had a wall of protection between me and the enemy and after days with no sleep and in total exhaustion, I thought, "I'm gonna roll over on my back and watch these mothers work."

After a brief rest I felt somewhat rejuvenated. The fighter jets left and then there was only sporadic firing. The pounding that the enemy took quieted them for a brief time.

I could see and hear the command center just behind me, plotting what to do next. Lieutenant McDaniel came back to us with orders and told us we were to assist in the link-up with Colonel Austin's group, which had landed farther down on the island. Our squad had just moved out single file into the jungle line when all hell broke loose. We were in their backyard, as we found out real quick. We found ourselves in a three-sided ambush of concentrated force. The enemy was at a higher elevation and had the advantage. They started lobbing grenades and locking automatic weapon fire down on us.

The Khmer Rouge were yelling and laughing at us in broken English to "Come and get some more" and, "Come and get your dinner, GI." We were only seventy-five feet from their perimeter.

A grenade fell close to my position just on the other side of a large tree and the detonation knocked me unconscious.

Our point man, Loney, was killed immediately. Henderson, our radioman, got knocked unconscious, and I witnessed another Marine taking a round in the calf, and he didn't even know he got hit. One man was crying for his momma, and I slapped him back into reality. No one was left unscathed.

Only the denseness of the trees and thickness of the foliage saved both sides from a much worse slaughter.

McDaniel was looking pretty rough: the whites of his eyes blood red and he was bleeding from both ears while giving orders for us to pull back to our defensive perimeter. Henderson was knocked out cold and bleeding from shrapnel wounds. I flung him over my shoulder and carried him to the defense perimeter then to the medic hooch.

I went back and forth and helped the injured back to our defense perimeter while engaging in close range combat, for which I later was awarded the Navy Achievement Medal with the Combat Distinguishing Device V. All I thought was that my buddies were up there and needed me.

Later, I was watching a C-130 fly overhead straight up the middle between west and east beach and deploy a large parachute, and I overheard Captain Davis say to Gunny, "Looks like we're getting resupplied, but looks like it's going to the enemy." No sooner had the words come out of Davis' mouth before it was at treetop level and we realized that rather than supplies, it was actually a bomb.

The impact of the explosion lifted me more than a foot off the ground. After the bomb dropped, the enemy drew even closer to our perimeter, but there was less fire from the enemy line and the intensity of the battle ceased for a couple hours with only occasional sniper fire.

Later, after they dropped the big bomb several of us went back and carried Loney's body. He stayed in our defense perimeter all day until we could lay him on the beach in his body bag.

I could see the officers talking with each other. The next thing Gunny came to me and said, "We're digging in, staying for the night." That was not a good thing to hear.

I was teamed up with Jeremiah "Action" Jackson and our position was on the left side of the perimeter about 11:00 o'clock, a good distance into the jungle line. We dug our foxhole six-foot deep, putting grenade sumps on both sides at the bottom. Cutting a bench seat for us to sit and stand on, we flung the dirt around the front of the foxhole and cut in our grenade shelf at eye level. Then we covered the fresh dirt with foliage. After the foxhole was finished, I spoke briefly, telling Jackson we'd have to use hand signals from here on out. The temperature dropped a bit, which was good. The sun was setting fast and it was getting dark quickly.

In our position we heard something coming toward us. It was completely dark at this point. It was Gunny Mac, telling us in a whisper, "We are leaving the island tonight. I'll come get you when it's your turn."

I heard several choppers coming in for us. At my position, the tree line started to light up with tracers flashing like a laser show. It seemed much later when Gunny finally came back, saying, "Bailey, I want you to get the f*** out of here. This next chopper is your ride." Jackson and I got out of our foxhole and made a left envelopment toward the beach through a small ravine. I saw two Khmer Rouge soldiers pop out of a hole and start shooting toward the beach. I wanted to lob a grenade, but in my rush to get out of there, I had left them in the foxhole. I aimed my rifle at them but did not shoot for fear of engaging in a long exchange and missing my ride. I did not want to be left behind. (For more than thirty years I have worried about not killing those two, and it was a great relief to learn later that there were no casualties that evening.)

At that point I had lost track of Jackson and I started running to the chopper through a dense patch of small trees. At the base of these trees were very long, thick, tapering thorns. I caught one just above my left knee; it pierced clean though my leg. But my main concern was to get the hell off Koh Tang Island alive.

The chopper was sitting in the water and was under heavy gunfire. I moved to the left of the chopper for protection, the side you're not supposed to board on. I swam around coming up very near the rear rotor blade. Someone from the chopper grabbed me and pulled me to safety just before the helicopter took off.

My chopper was only in the air for less than fifteen minutes before we jumped off from the side of the chopper as it hovered over the ship. Then, we were taken through a hatchway into the ship. I took a stainless steel mop bucket and filled it halfway up with water and drank the whole damn thing. In the beginning of the movement back on Okinawa, many of us did not resupply our water canteens and it seemed as if we'd gone days without water.

I remember someone being operated on before me, then someone gave me a shot and put me on the table for surgery. As I was drifting out I was thinking, "I made it, thank God."

The next morning I remember being moved from ship to ship in a small vessel. I was taken to the USS Wilson, and while still under the effects of anesthesia, I heard over the loudspeaker, "Now hear this: We left some men behind; we're turning back." Then hours later again over the speakers I heard, "Now hear this: All have been recovered," and the Wilson set course for Subic Bay, Philippines. The trip there took us two days.

On board the Coral Sea aircraft carrier we had a funeral for our dead. President Ford spoke to us over the loudspeaker, and the commanding general came to each one of us personally, congratulating us and shaking hands, taking his time with each one. Two marching bands and a ton of news reporters were there.

We flew back to Camp Schwab, Okinawa, and finished the last phase of our infantry training. The next four months we went on float and went to many countries.

Not a day goes by that my mind does not think of what we went through and the lives that were lost. Those men are the true heroes. Semper Fidelis—Always Faithful."

Following an honorable discharge from the Marines, Bailey went to work on the grounds of the White House, eventually becoming chief arborist, working for presidents Carter, Reagan, and Bush Sr. He later operated a successful tree and landscaping business for many years.

With his wife, Tina, he is active in the Koh Tang Beach Veterans Association, working to locate and reunite those Marines, airmen, and sailors involved with this piece of history.

LCPL. LARRY BARNETT, 3D PLATOON G COMPANY 2/9 MARINES

Larry Barnett was born in Wilmington, Ohio, on 27 September 1955, the oldest of six children. His father had served with the Marines as a tanker during the Korean War, so when Barnett was seventeen and his parents divorced, he sought independence and followed in his father's footsteps. He joined the Marine Corps on 1 June 1973.

In May 1975, as Saigon fell to Communist forces, Barnett was a nineteen-year-old lance corporal and squad leader assigned to 3d Platoon G Company 2/9 Marines at Okinawa, Japan.

In May of 1975, I was a squad leader with Golf Company. The battalion was rotating home and was short of NCOs, so I was given a squad. On the evening of 14 May 1975, we were in the field and Lieutenant Cicere called the squad leaders over to brief us on the Koh Tang operation. He told us that we would be leaving well before daybreak the following morning, 15 May.

This was when we learned that the crew of [the] Mayaguez was being held captive on a small Cambodian island called Koh Tang. We were told that the island was being guarded by a handful of Khmer Rouge irregulars and that resistance would be light, but that we could expect light sniper fire. I began to get a sick feeling in the pit of my stomach. I returned and briefed my fire team leaders, then passed out ammo and told everyone to try and get some rest.

Very early the next morning we were told to saddle up and report to the tarmac. The Air Force began to fire up the choppers and I again got a very sick feeling in my stomach. We loaded the helicopters and began our trek to Koh Tang. I believe that the trip took about three hours.

The sun was just starting to come up as we arrived at Koh Tang. The sky was blue and clear, the sun was bright, and the water below was calm. Anyone that was on that island had to know we were coming long before we arrived. As we approached the island we began taking ground fire. I remember seeing light shining through holes in the skin of the helicopter. The pilot maneuvered the aircraft around with the back end facing toward the east beach. A helicopter next to us started the same maneuver.

For some reason, our choppers got mixed up because the chopper next to us was supposed to be where we were and vice versa. All of a sudden our chopper was lit by a real bright orange glow and I felt a tremendous amount of heat on the back of my neck. I looked over my shoulder and the helicopter next to us was engulfed in a ball of flames. We were so close to the helicopter I could see Marines trying to break out the windows with the butts of their M-16s.

The gunner on my side of the chopper began to open up with his machine gun and it jammed right away. About fifty yards or so from the beach our pilot stopped the helicopter and was going to try and abort the landing, but while we were stopped in midair a rifle-propelled grenade [RPG] detonated on the tail section of the helicopter. I was looking directly out the back of the chopper when this happened, and there was a bright flash, a loud crack, and the tail section of the chopper was blown away.

The body of the helicopter began to spin out of control and the pilot crash landed the aircraft on the beach. I clearly remember getting thrown out of my seat across to the other side of the helicopter. I banged my back and knees on the row of seats on that side. I remember closing my eyes, thinking, "This is it. I am going to die." I looked up from the floor and saw Lieutenant Cicere motioning everyone off of the chopper.

I tried to get up but was stepped on. I finally made it to my feet and ran toward the beach where everyone else was headed. As I was running either something from the chopper struck me in the back or I twisted something in the crash. Either way when I fell into the tree line I had a sharp pain in my back. I asked Staff Sergeant Wyatt to look and see if I had been shot and he said no.

Everybody had pretty well piled on top of Lieutenant Cicere. The Cambodians were lobbing mortars at us and having everyone that bunched up was a real bad thing. Lieutenant Cicere told me to get the men spread out "now." I began to place them into a defensive perimeter. Once everyone was in place we set up a command post at the center of the perimeter. There were only twenty-five of us. We had no heavy weapons except for one LAW [light antitank weapon]. We only had two M-69s. Everything else was M-16s and 45s. Our radio didn't work so we had no contact with the main element on the west beach.

I looked over at the burned-out hull of the other chopper in the water and saw Marines swimming around it. They were sitting ducks and all I could do was sit and watch them die. There are no words to describe what a helpless feeling that was, especially since our chopper was supposed to have been where theirs was. We lost fourteen men on that helicopter and all I could do was watch them die.

One of the Khmer Rouge went out to the beach to look at one of the bodies that had washed up. Staff Sergeant Wyatt got mad and shot at him but missed. Everything inside of me was screaming, "Get your nasty hands off of him." Again, all I could do was watch. The demise of that chopper has stayed with me for thirty-three years. It is just as clear today as it was then. It was the first time I had seen anybody die, and I couldn't help but think that those men had died in my place.

The Cambodians continued to lob mortars at us and we were pinned down in a crossfire from several directions. One of the Air Force pilots had a survival radio and was trying to make contact with anyone who could hear us. Early on, the pilot was told to stay off the frequency because "they were trying to make contact with a downed helicopter." The pilot said, "Listen, dumbass, we are *that downed helicopter."*

Our close air support was nonexistent in the early portion of the operation. I can only assume that this was due to the chaos and how our elements were spread all over the island. Staff Sergeant Wyatt decided to take the one LAW that we had and fire it at a small gunboat next to where Knife-31 went down. He thought that the mortar position might be on that gunboat. He fired the LAW, which hit the boat, and the mortar fire quit for a while.

At one point when I got up to check on my men, a round passed just a few inches over my head. I fell to the ground and the lieutenant and Staff Sergeant Wyatt were convinced that there was still someone on the gunboat. By then we had established close air support, through the Air Force pilot with us on the beach. He called in an air strike on the gunboat and the pilots blew it to pieces. To say I was ecstatic when this happened would be an understatement.

In the early afternoon, there were two attempts to get to us. One time was an attempt to extract us from the east beach and the second time they were trying to insert Marines to reinforce our position. As soon as each chopper got close to us, the entire tree line erupted in gunfire. The second helicopter left in a trail of black smoke. It became obvious that the Khmer were closing in around us. Words are inadequate to describe how it felt to see help come so close just to be driven off again and again.

Later in the evening a small boat was stationed just to our northeast. It was decided that the boat would come in and try to evacuate about ten people off of the island. The first to go would be the Air Force people and the wounded, a total of seven. That meant that there was room for three more; Lieutenant Cicere asked for volunteers to stay behind with him.

Staff Sergeant Wyatt was the first to volunteer to stay and the Air Force pilot, John Lucas, was the second. Not another hand went up, including mine. The lieutenant looked at me and said, "Larry, you are going to have to stay here." I couldn't get any sound to come out of my mouth, but could only give the thumbs up sign. He then told me to pick ten other men to stay as well.

I looked over at my men and said, "We have been through a lot today, guys. Please don't make me pick who is to stay." On my left was a Marine named Louis Ybarra and he was the first to raise his hand. Then, one by one, every single Marine down the line raised his hand. I had to pick no one. I was so proud of them yet so ashamed of myself.

I have a write-up of the Navy Commendation Medal from the secretary of the Navy. It states that I "unhesitatingly volunteered to stay behind." I will never wear it because it reflects a lie. The write-up presents me as some kind of hero. In no way was I a hero. I was a scared kid. They should have given my Navy Commendation Medal to Louis Ybarra.

Just before dark it was decided that there would be one more attempt to get us out of there. We had already developed plans to move from our position to the north if the extraction failed. I assembled my Marines at the very edge of the tree line. Lieutenant Cicere was to cover the right side, Staff Sergeant Wyatt was to cover the left side, and I was to cover the center.

Air Force Lt. John Lucas then threw a smoke grenade to identify our position to the rescue helicopter; just like before, when the chopper got close, the entire tree line erupted in small arms fire. This time I saw two Khmers wearing black pajamas coming out of the trees. I emptied my weapon in their direction and ran like hell toward the chopper.

I was told later that it took about fifteen seconds to load the chopper. To me it seemed like an eternity. Once we were airborne and out of range, I stood up and screamed as loud as I could. I suppose I was screaming because I had cheated death again. The Marines shot down next to me weren't that lucky.

Our chopper was shot up pretty bad but we managed to make it to the USS Coral Sea *in one piece. It sure was a welcome sight! I got a count of my people, then told the platoon sergeant that mine were accounted for.*

The next morning I assembled my men on the flight deck for another count. There was a rumor going around that we still had Marines left on Koh Tang and we were going back to get them. I cannot even begin to explain the mixture of emotions I had. One side of me said, "This cannot be happening again," and another side said, "If that was me, I would hope someone would come back for me."

In the end it was decided that we wouldn't go back for them. We abandoned them. We were told that we would be subject to a court martial if we ever spoke to anyone about the operation.

Barnett left the Marines in 1978, married, and had two sons. He has worked since in construction and as a truck driver. He is a former president of the Koh Tang Beach Veterans Association.

1ST LT. BOB BLOUGH, PILOT, JOLLY-44

Bob Blough grew up in a small town near Johnstown, in western Pennsylvania, the second of three children. As a freshman in high school, he decided that he wanted to attend West Point to become an Army officer. Since his family had no political connections, Blough wrote letters to his congressional representatives and senators at the end of each semester, reminding them of his interest in an appointment to the Military Academy. Later, he changed his goal to an appointment to the Air Force Academy.

Late in his senior year, with no word from the Academy, Blough applied for a summer job at one of the local steel mills to earn money for junior college, but at the last minute the Academy appointment came through. He would later refer to his appointment as "my ticket out of the rust belt."

Blough was awarded a bachelor's degree and a commission as an Air Force second lieutenant in June 1971. He also got his first choice: assignment to the U.S. Army helicopter school. (The Air Force contracted with the Army to train Air Force helicopter pilots. With the largest helicopter school in the world, the Army could train pilots in helicopter operations more efficiently than the Air Force could.)

Excelling in flight school, Blough graduated near the top of his class, earning his wings in April 1972. After advanced training at Hill AFB, Utah, he was assigned to fly Sikorsky CH-3 helicopters at Shaw AFB, South Carolina. There he sharpened his skills, and was taught by the veteran pilots of the squadron, most of whom were combat veterans of Southeast Asia. He was upgraded to aircraft commander on the day he became eligible. He also submitted a volunteer statement to the Air Force Personnel Center requesting an air rescue assignment in Southeast Asia. A few months later, he was sent to HH-53 transition training en route to the 40th Aerospace Rescue and Recovery Squadron [40th ARRS] at Nakhon Phanom Royal Thai Air Force Base [RTAFB] in northeast Thailand. He arrived in June 1974.

NKP, as Nakhon Phanom was referred to in military acronym, was a small base next to the Mekong River, which separated Thailand and Laos. Across the narrow strip of karst mountains of eastern Laos was

1st Lt. Bob Blough,
circa 1975. U.S. Air Force

the border of North Vietnam. Earlier in the Vietnam War, the Air
Force had chosen this location for the 40th ARRS due to its proximity
to North Vietnam and to the Ho Chi Minh Trails in Laos. The 40th's
[40th ARRS's] prime "customers" had been USAF fighter pilots shot
down while attacking the highly defended targets in these areas. The
40th flew the powerful, though temperamental, HH-53 Jolly Green
Giant, the larger, modernized cousin to the H-3 which I'd previously
flown.

     Although United States involvement in Vietnam had officially
ended by the time I arrived, Southeast Asia was still a hotbed of
Communist insurgencies and unstable governments. The area around
NKP was infested with what the Thai government termed "Communist terrorists," many of whom infiltrated across the Mekong
River from Laos. The NKP base perimeter was still probed occasionally by these forces. Also, classified operations plans tasked the 40th
with responsibility for the short-notice evacuation of U.S. Embassy
personnel and their dependents from Saigon; Vientiane, Laos; and

Phnom Penh, Cambodia, should the need arise. [The Phnom Penh evacuation, code-named Eagle Pull, was prosecuted successfully in mid-April 1975. This was followed two weeks later by the Saigon evacuation.] The 40th also maintained two HH-53s with crews on alert 24/7 at Ubon, Thailand [later moved to Korat] to be closer to their potential "customers." The rescue crews and aircraft rotated twice a week from NKP.

Two other USAF flying units were also stationed at NKP during this time: The 21st Special Operations Squadron [SOS, call sign Knife] also flew HH-53 helicopters, but most of their missions were classified. During the "hot" war, they had primarily airlifted Royal Lao and other indigenous forces against the Pathet Lao Communists. Later, their "official" primary mission was to support the Joint Casualty Resolution Center [JCRC] teams tasked with MIA search and recovery. The other USAF flying unit at NKP was the 23rd Tactical Air Support Squadron, forward air controllers [FACs] flying the OV-10 Bronco, a two-seat twin-turboprop observation aircraft used to identify and mark targets for the fast-moving fighter aircraft. Their code-name was Nail.

When I reported to the 40th ARRS in June 1974 as a first lieutenant, I found myself to be one of the more experienced pilots in the unit. Most of the pilots in the unit were first or second lieutenants on their first tour of duty after flight school. Although they had more experience flying the HH-53, my experience flying the similar H-3 made me a valuable asset to the squadron. After a short stint as a co-pilot assigned to a newly upgraded aircraft commander, I was quickly upgraded to aircraft commander, then to instructor pilot, responsible for training and checking out new pilots coming into the squadron.

On 13 May 1975 I commanded one of two Jolly Green crews deployed to Korat RTAFB [Royal Thai Air Force Base] for forward operation location [FOL] rescue alert. The 40th ARRS used the "hard crew" concept wherever possible; the intent being that the same people flying frequently together improved crew coordination and effectiveness. It also facilitated the blending of individual crew members' experience levels, strengths, and weaknesses to ensure well-qualified *crews were available to man each aircraft. Being an instructor pilot, however, I had to fly with many different crew members. I rarely got to fly with my hard crew, and this deployment was typical. 1st Lt. Hank Mason, the copilot, was the only one of this six-man crew from my hard crew.*

I'd heard that Hank was due to report into the squadron at about the same time I needed a new copilot. Hank had been a year behind me at the Academy, and I had been one of those upperclassmen in charge of his training. I remembered Hank as a skinny little guy with the attitude, "Give me all you've got. I can hack it." And he could. Hank would later prove me a genius for choosing him as my copilot. The rest of the crew I knew to varying degrees.

SSgt. Robert Bounds, a flight engineer, performed aircraft pre-flight inspections, ran the rescue hoist, gave the pilot hover instructions and clearance advisories for the right side and below the aircraft, and manned the right-door minigun. I had first met Bob at Shaw AFB when he was getting transition training in the H-3. He was a tall, lean Southerner who spoke in a quiet drawl but was hard as nails, the kind of guy you just naturally want at your side in a dark alley.

SSgt. James Howell, my other flight engineer, I didn't know him well, but he was an effective and efficient flight engineer. Jimmy's duties were in the cockpit, running the checklists, managing fuel transfer, computing power available/required for hovering, and helping the pilots with other cockpit chores.

Sgt. Bruce Daly was an accomplished pararescueman [PJ], trained in medical skills designed to keep injured or wounded survivors alive for days if necessary. PJs are required to leave the helicopter if necessary to help a survivor, and to carry that survivor to safety. They're qualified in scuba, parachuting, mountain or rock climbing, and jungle, desert, and arctic survival. Their official motto, part of the PJ's creed, is "That Others May Live." Bruce's duties were to man the left gun, provide clearance advisories to the left, and be ready to go down the rescue hoist to aid a survivor.

A1C David Ash, our other PJ, was new to the squadron, and was just out of PJ school. I barely knew him. He was a big guy, but soft-

spoken. His duties on this flight were to man the minigun on the aft ramp, provide clearance advisories for the tail rotor, and assist the other PJ with medical treatment if necessary.

When we arrived at Korat, we relieved the existing alert crew, claimed bunks in the alert shack, and prepared for the usual boredom of standing rescue alert. At about 2100 I was summoned to the Tactical Unit Operations Center [TUOC]. When I arrived, an intelligence sergeant directed me to the secure telephone saying a captain from the Pentagon wanted to talk to me. The apparatus was actually a radio-telephone using high-frequency radio waves bounced off the atmosphere to reach across the Pacific. It also electronically scrambled spoken words at one end and unscrambled them at the other end. Due to the atmosphere and the two scramblers drifting in and out of synch, the captain sounded like Donald Duck.

I was asked, "Lieutenant, can you land your helicopter on a ship?" I answered that it would depend on the type of ship. The intel sergeant handed me a photo of a civilian cargo ship with what looked like semitruck trailers stacked on deck. Tall cargo-handling hoists were at the fore and aft of the deck, with the large ship's bridge at the aft of the ship. I told him that I probably could hover over the stern and pick up the injured seaman with the rescue hoist.

"No, Lieutenant" I was told. "We want you to land on the ship to offload troops." I told him I didn't know what the roofs of those trailers are made of, but I doubted if they'd support the weight of an HH-53. "Well, could you hover over the deck low enough to offload troops?" he asked. I answered, "Yes, Sir. We'd have to hover at 90 degrees to the ship between the masts, and the troops could jump down from our aft ramp. Do you expect any resistance from the crew of the ship?"

Long pause. Then, "Only light small arms, and maybe a couple RPGs [rocket-propelled grenades]." I looked at the picture again and imagined what AK-47s and, God-forbid, an RPG could do to an HH-53 and its crew hovering broadside about fifty meters away. I took a deep breath and said, "Sir, I think you should be talking to my commander at NKP."

Before he could answer, one of the PJs came running into TUOC and yelled, "We've been scrambled! An HH-53 went down near NKP." I said something like, "Gotta run, Sir," and handed the phone to the sergeant.

We ran to the helicopters, cranked up, and took off for NKP. Once airborne, we contacted Joker, the Rescue Coordination Center at NKP. He confirmed that a CH-53 with multiple PAX [passengers] had crashed forty miles southwest of NKP. No word on survivors.

We soon started receiving multiple traffic advisories of HH-53 aircraft above us, heading south. Then a call from Joker ordered us to change course for Utapao RTAFB near Bangkok. When I asked if we could stop en route to pick up gear, we were directed to proceed directly to Utapao. A quick check of our fuel state revealed that we could just make Utapao with the required reserve.

While Hank went through the mundane task of filing an airborne change in flight plan, the rest of us were all silently wondering the same thing: Who were the crew on the crashed aircraft? We knew it was a 21st SOS bird because Joker had specified it was a CH-53. Only HH-53 aircraft with specific rescue modifications were assigned to our squadron. We all had friends in the 21st SOS. The helicopter community in the Air Force is a small group. Frequently, you had either been assigned with or trained with almost everyone in Air Force helicopters. Many of them were like brothers. And who were the passengers? Probably maintenance guys, who we probably knew, too. And did my aborted conversation with Donald Duck at the Pentagon have anything to do with this? Probably! Why else would you send every Air Force helicopter in Thailand to Utapao, on the coast of the Gulf of Thailand?

When we arrived at Utapao, at about 0200, we were told to refuel and prepare the aircraft for alert. While the rest of the crew prepared the aircraft, I went into base operations to find some answers. There I found "Uncle" Vern Sheffield, our most senior captain, and I asked him what was going on. He told me that the Cambodians had hijacked a U.S.-flagged civilian cargo ship and that we were on alert to rescue the crew and get the ship back. They'd brought a bunch of Air Force security police [SP] with them, but eighteen of them had been *killed in the Knife crash. When I asked about the crew, he only knew the name of the pilot, Jim Kays. I knew him, as I'd gone through the Academy POW school with him. Jimmy Kays was the nicest guy you'd ever want to meet. Quiet and friendly, with a shy grin for everyone.*

Vern told me, "Your two birds are on strip alert tonight. Your crews will have to sleep in the aircraft because we don't have quarters for you." I walked back to the flight line to convey the good news. Hank and I tried to sleep in the pilots' seats because the rest of the crew had already claimed the troop seats in the cabin. Needless to say, none of us got much sleep.

Our two alert aircraft were scrambled early the next morning. We were told a Navy A-7 pilot had gone down in the Gulf of Thailand. It was about a one and a half–hour flight to the coordinates we were given, several miles off the coast of Cambodia, near a small island called Koh Tang. As we neared the search area, we checked in with the EC-130 acting as on-scene commander [OSC] of the search operation. He advised that we were not looking for a Navy A-7 pilot: we were searching for survivors of a Khmer Rouge gunboat that had been sunk by a Navy A-7. That changed the complexion of things. Any survivors we might find might or might not be happy to see us. But we'd cross that bridge if we got to it. Our first priority was to find any survivors.

After a couple hours, as our search pattern took us near the north end of Koh Tang, Ash on the aft ramp reported, "Somebody just fired a missile or a rocket at us, but it landed in the water behind us." A seasoned combat pilot would have taken immediate and violent evasive action in case a second missile was fired, but I just sat there digesting what David had said, and what my response should be. The fact that it had fallen short, and that David had not seen the characteristic corkscrew smoke trail of an SA-7 Grail antiaircraft missile, indicated that it had been an RPG. An RPG is fatal against a helicopter at close range, but it has short "legs." If it had been a Grail, we'd have been toast.

After cursing myself for my own lack of appropriate response to what could have been a dire threat, I reviewed with my crew the proper procedure for even a suspected antiaircraft missile launch: Fire

*a defensive infrared flare while simultaneously yelling to the pilot,
"BREAK (RIGHT [LEFT])! MISSILE!" That gets even a rookie pilot's attention.*

*We reported the missile or rocket firing to the HC-130. His re-
sponse was, "Stay clear of the island." "No shit," someone muttered
over our intercom.*

*Soon after that, the HC-130 advised us to cancel the search and
return to Utapao. We arrived late in the afternoon; while my crew
refueled and inspected the aircraft, I headed to operations for further
instructions. Vern said nothing was expected to happen that night,
and to bed down my crews in a certain barracks and report back in
the morning. The other crews from NKP were already asleep, so we
found empty bunks and gratefully fell into them, exhausted.*

*When I woke up early in the morning, the other crews had already
left. I woke my guys and told them to meet me at Base Ops. When I
got to the flight line, all the helicopters were gone, including our two
alert birds! When I found Vern, he said, "We had to launch at 0430.
You guys were out on crew rest, so we assigned your aircraft to other
crews. Your flight gear is over there in the corner. Maintenance back
at NKP is working on getting two more aircraft operational. As soon
as one becomes available, I'll let you know."*

*Vern also gave me a brief rundown on what was happening. All
available 21st SOS and 40th ARRS aircraft had launched before daylight with Marine assault troops on board with the mission of finding and recovering the Mayaguez and her crew. Damn! A war had
started, and I was left on the ground without an aircraft! I had been
in the squadron for almost a year now, and I was one of the most
senior pilots, but bad luck had left me grounded. As the rest of my
crews straggled in, I briefed them on the news while we dined on box
lunches for breakfast.*

*As the morning wore on, the mission aircraft would return to
Utapao in ones and twos to refuel, pick up some of the Marine reinforcements along with supplies of ammo and water, and head back to
Koh Tang. News trickled in slowly, and a mobile blackboard was used
to track the status of each aircraft by tail number, including the name
of the aircraft commander, the takeoff time, the ETA back at Utapao,*

and the aircraft's maintenance status. As the morning wore on, the cryptic notes in the Status column became more ominous: "Shot up," "Down on the beach," "Shot up," "Shot up," "Down in the water," "Down in the water." This was starting to look like a disaster! Then I saw my best friend's name with "Down on east beach." I asked Vern what the status was of Schramm's crew down on the east beach and I was told that they had contacted some survivors but there were few details. I recall yelling, "GODAMMIT, VERN. GET ME AN AIRCRAFT!"

After apologizing to Vern for my outburst, I returned to my crew to give them an update. We reviewed the map that showed a tiny green speck in the Gulf of Thailand about two hundred miles away, air refueling requirements, and tactical call signs for the other aircraft and ships in the operation. We also talked about some scenarios we might find ourselves in if we ever got an aircraft, and reviewed our individual duties should our status change to one of those already listed on the blackboard. After a while, we settled back again for the interminable wait.

By late morning, we got word that the Mayaguez *and her crew had all been successfully recovered. There was not much time for celebration, however, because Marines were still pinned down on the island. Reinforcements had to be landed to ensure they were not over-run before they could make an orderly withdrawal. HH-53s were making the four-hour round trip from Koh Tang to Utapao back to Koh Tang with reinforcements. As the afternoon progressed, the news on the helicopter status board in base operations continued to dete-riorate. It was beginning to look like we would run out of helicopters due to enemy gunfire before we could extract the Marines.*

Late in the afternoon, Vern finally called me over and told me Colonel McMonigle, our squadron commander, was en route from NKP with a helicopter just released from maintenance. If he was will-ing to give up the aircraft, I could take it.

My crew and I were waiting on the flight line when Colonel Mc-Monigle taxied to a stop. As soon as he shut down the engines, I ran up to the cockpit window and said, "Sir, my crew is rested, briefed, and ready to go if you're willing to turn over the aircraft." Colonel

McMonigle looked me in the eye. He and his crew had been up all night helping maintenance with engine runs and test flights to get this aircraft ready. He and his crew were exhausted, but eager to give their comrades at Koh Tang some much-needed help. I, on the other hand, had a fresh crew and more experience flying the HH-53 than he had. He could have filled out his skeleton crew with one of my flight engineers and the PJ's, or he could have taken over my entire crew for his own. But Colonel McMonigle gave me a sad smile and said, "It's all yours, Bob." I have always respected him for that decision.

We ran a quick preflight check while the helicopter was being refueled, and soon we were airborne on a "VFR [visual flight rules] local" flight plan with our tactical call sign Jolly Green-44. We headed southeast and ran through all our combat checklists, including test firing our three 7.62-mm miniguns. None of us had fired the miniguns since our training in the States. Due to our "Status of Forces Agreement" with Thailand, we had been prohibited from live-fire training in Thailand. But unlike the 21st SOS, which stored their miniguns in the armory, the 40th ARRS had insisted that they be kept on the aircraft, ready for action.

Before every flight, our flight engineers and PJs were required to preflight each minigun, which included a dry-fire test. Any glitch, such as low battery charge or other electrical malfunction, was written up to be repaired before the next flight. This ensured not only that the batteries were kept fully charged, but also that the FEs [flight engineers] and PJs stayed familiar with the gun systems, and could diagnose and fix problems in most cases. This operational philosophy was validated by the Koh Tang operation, where the 21st SOS had multiple problems with their miniguns, while the Jollys had few problems, and those were corrected by the crews on the spot. (As it turned out, Bob Bounds had to safety-wire one of the switches closed on his gun to make it work.)

As we neared Koh Tang shortly before dark, we checked in with Cricket, the Airborne Battlefield Communications, Command and Control EC-130 on VHF radio. Cricket, with a full battle staff on board, was the OSC for the operation. They hadn't known we were coming, but were glad to see us because they had just about run out of helicopters. Cricket directed us to check in with Nail-69, the OV-10 FAC, on UHF radio.

Nail-69 directed us to orbit north of the island with Knife-51 and Jolly Green-43 in preparation for the final withdrawal of the Marines from the island. The FACs were busy coordinating the final attempt to get John Schramm's crew and their few surviving Marine passengers off the east beach.

Several HH-53s had already been badly mauled in earlier attempts since morning. Finally, Don Backlund, in Jolly Green-11, was cleared in for the pickup. In an impressive display of skill and sheer guts, Backlund and his crew made a twisting approach and hovered their HH-53 over the rocky beach while the isolated Air Force and Marine survivors struggled to board and enemy gunners pounded the aircraft. One Khmer soldier ran to within a few yards of the helicopter to throw a grenade, but was cut down by M-16 fire from the helicopter. With the last survivor on board just before dark, Backlund limped his badly damaged aircraft to the Coral Sea *to end a long, arduous day. He and his crew had been flying for almost fourteen hours straight. Backlund was later awarded the Air Force Cross, and his crewmen each received the Silver Star.*

With the evacuation of the east beach finally accomplished, Nail-69 turned his attention back to the west beach. Capt. Greg Wilson was glad to see us. Of the twelve HH-53s that had started the operation, all but two had been lost to enemy action or rendered not flyable due to battle damage. Knife-51, flown by 1st Lt. Dick Brims, and Jolly Green-43, flown by Capt. Wayne "Buford" Purser, were the only other helos still on station. Both had been flying since early that morning. With darkness falling, Nail-69 moved his three remaining helos to an orbit off the west beach and turned his attention to coordinating the evacuation with the Marine ground commander.

While we waited, I checked in with Jolly Green-43 on our squadron FM frequency and Purser soberly welcomed us and briefed us that our job was to evacuate the remaining two hundred or so Marines from the west beach of the island. Ground fire had been intense all day, including 12.7-mm (50-caliber) machine guns, mortars, RPGs, and AK-47s. The beach was large enough for only one aircraft at a time, so we would cycle our HH-53s to the beach, pick up as many Marines as we could carry, and deliver them to the aircraft carrier USS Coral Sea, then return for more Marines until we got them all.

This wasn't an ideal plan, because the Coral Sea was a forty-minute round-trip flight away. If we couldn't get all the Marines in the first three loads, the few Marines remaining on the island would be hard-pressed to defend their shrinking perimeter while waiting for our helos to return. But it was the best plan anyone could come up with, considering our limited resources. Nail-69 approved the plan and briefed the Marine ground commander, who understood the risks all too well, and would plan a two-stage withdrawal. He requested we cycle back from the Coral Sea as rapidly as possible. We assured him we would do our best.

With darkness approaching rapidly, Nail-69 cleared Knife-51 into the beach LZ [landing zone]. We all silently wished him good luck, and sat back with our own thoughts to wait our turn. I'm not a very religious person, but I sent up a silent prayer from my foxhole in the sky: "God, please don't let me do something stupid to kill my crew and make everybody else's jobs even more difficult."

It was too dark by now to see Brims in the LZ, but he soon called "clear," and Nail-69 cleared Jolly-43 into the LZ. Purser responded, "I'm turning off my lights to make a blacked-out approach." It was rapidly getting darker, and any lights on the helo would only make it a better target for the Khmer gunners. But as Purser turned off his position lights, I experienced an instant of vertigo. The aircraft I had been calmly flying formation on had suddenly disappeared into the night, and I had to quickly transfer my attention to my flight instruments to assure myself that my aircraft was still upright and level.

Again, we sat back to wait our turn. We ran our before-landing checklist, and I briefed the crew to turn off our anticollision and position lights when we started our approach. I also briefed Hank to be ready to turn on our landing lights, but only if I ordered them. My plan was to descend to just above the water to avoid silhouetting the dark helicopter against the slightly lighter western sky. My plan also called for slowing our airspeed to forty knots—just enough to main-

tain translational lift and to keep salt spray from our rotor wash from coating our windshield and engine turbine blades. [Translational lift is when forward airspeed creates enough airflow over the rotor disc to reduce the high power required to maintain a hover.] It would be tricky flying on instruments at low speed just above the water, but it had the advantages of reducing our target signature while hopefully giving me enough time to see the beach or any obstacles in time to take the appropriate action.

I knew that Army and Marine helicopter pilots had made blacked-out approaches into the jungles of Vietnam, but they were practically unheard of in the Air Force at that time. My personal heroes of the Son Tay prison camp raid in North Vietnam had done it, but only after intense training and with good moonlight. During the time I flew air rescue helicopters, blacked-out approaches were strictly forbidden, so we had no experience with them. Quite frankly—and I think my Army and Marine comrades would agree—they could be downright scary. But in this case, a blacked-out approach was a necessary risk because the risk of flying into heavy ground fire with your lights on advertising "Shoot me, shoot me" was even greater. I counted on experience, a good copilot and crew, and a little luck to make it work.

At about 1854 hours, Nail-69 cleared us into the LZ. We hadn't heard Purser call "clear," but we assumed we'd simply missed it. I acknowledged, called for lights out, and began a descent toward the water. By this time it was getting really dark. No moon, no stars, and an overcast sky. We descended on instruments on a magnetic heading toward the island. Hank gave me a warning call at 150 feet, and I slowed our descent and airspeed to reach our planned forty knots at fifteen feet above the water. Absolute concentration was required, with help from Hank's occasional, "Ten feet and descending" warning. I couldn't believe Hank sounded so calm, but that's why I had picked him.

We groped our way through the dark with all hands straining to see anything looming out of the dark. Even with the instrument panel lights turned down to minimum, they still interfered with our ability to see anything in front of us in the dark. Bobby Bounds was hanging out the right door where instrument panel lights didn't glare. Just as he announced the beach up ahead, a bright light flashed right in front of us.

"Helicopter in the LZ!" Bobby yelled as I pulled in max power and turned hard away from the island. Jolly Green-43 was still in the LZ loading Marines. Her copilot, 1st Lt. Bob Gradle, had heard our call on the radio but was apparently unable to contact us. When he saw the salt spray being kicked up by our rotor wash, he flashed his landing lights as a warning. He risked exposing his own aircraft to the Khmer gunners with his light flash, but he prevented a midair catastrophe that would have wiped out two helicopters, blocked the LZ, and left only one helicopter to try to evacuate almost two hundred Marines.

By the time we had collected ourselves, Jolly-43 had cleared the LZ and we started another approach to the island using the same strategy. It was even darker now, and I was having difficulty maintaining our altitude. Hank's warning calls of "Ten feet and descending" were still calm, but more frequent. And occasionally I'd feel a slight tug as one of the landing gear contacted a wave. I was still trying to clear the vestiges of that bright landing light from my eyeballs' memory, and I was fighting vertigo.

The ground fire became more intense—red and yellow tracers. Red tracers were from U.S.-supplied weapons captured by the Khmer Rouge fighters from the Cambodian loyalist army. One trail of tracers looked like big red balls. Everything seemed to happen in slow motion. I remember thinking in a detached way, "Wow. So that's what incoming ground fire really looks like at night. That Khmer gunner is really disciplined: he's walking his tracers right up toward the cockpit!"

At that instant, Bobby Bounds yelled, "Break left!" I immediately rolled left to 45 degrees angle-of-bank and pulled in power to keep from mashing into the water. [Air Force training doctrine at the time taught helicopter pilots to never exceed 45 degrees angle-of-bank when flying in instrument or night conditions. This was to avoid vertigo.] Almost immediately, the normally stoic Bobby Bounds screamed, "Goddamn it, break left—tree!"

I was already fighting vertigo, but Bobby's tone of voice translated to "Immediate action required or die." I racked the HH-53 over to 90 degrees and pulled in max power, hoping that we had enough altitude that the rotor blades wouldn't dip into the waves and drag us into the water. Miraculously, we got clear to the west. I took several deep breaths to calm down. I can only imagine what the rest of my crew was feeling.

I briefed the FAC on what had happened, and asked him for a heading back to the LZ. He said, "I saw the 50-caliber. Follow my tracers." As we headed back toward the island, we could see the tracers coming down from the OV-10's four M-60s at what seemed to be an impossible dive angle. "Tally-ho the LZ," I called, and adjusted our heading for the tracers.

The ground fire was still intense, but not as accurate this time. The Khmer could hear us coming, but they couldn't see us. Finally Bobby called, "Beach at 12 o'clock." The beach loomed like a lighter shade of grey in the darkness. A darker line of trees and vegetation loomed to the right and front, so I eased the nose left to land parallel to the narrow strip of sand and rock. The trees were on the right, and the left landing gear was in the water. Now we had to wait for the Marines to climb onto the aft ramp. I just hoped the Marines found us before the Khmer did.

We could do nothing now but wait, feeling naked in the darkness. The entire crew strained to see human silhouettes against the lighter beach, then try to identify them as friend or foe. I reminded my crew, "Don't shoot the good guys," but in this darkness it would be almost impossible to make the distinction until they were boarding the chopper. Sitting there in the cockpit surrounded by Plexiglas, I felt vulnerable and mentally urged the Marines to hurry. It seemed like hours, but was actually only minutes until the crew reported we had a full load of Marines and no more could be seen coming. I called, "Jolly coming out" to the FAC, and he replied that he was clear of us and no other helos were in the vicinity. I took off using my instruments and gratefully climbed out over the water. Now I'd have a chance to calm down during the twenty-minute flight to the Coral Sea.

I can't remember who first suggested diverting to the USS Holt, but I think it was the OV-10 FAC, "Growth" Wilson. He thought there was only one more load of Marines left on the island, but had received no word from either Knife-51 or Jolly Green-43 on their ETA back from the Coral Sea. With only a handful of Marines left to defend an ever-shrinking perimeter, they were in jeopardy of being overrun. The Holt was less than five minutes flying time from Koh Tang instead of almost twenty minutes to the Coral Sea. If we could offload our Marines onto the Holt, it would reduce our round-trip time by a good half-hour. We had enough fuel to do this and still get to the Coral Sea if necessary.

There were good reasons none of the other aircraft had offloaded their Marines onto the Holt, a small destroyer escort. Foremost was the size of the helipad on the Holt's stern. It was designed for a heli-copter much smaller than, and half the weight of, an HH-53. Even Navy HH-53s were prohibited from landing on it. Earlier in the day, three HH-53s had offloaded the Marine force later used to board the Mayaguez from the Holt, but these helos had just hovered over the pad crosswise with their rear landing gear resting lightly on the pad and their noses hanging over the side. The Marines had then jumped off the aft ramp onto the helipad.

I understood the situation with the Marines still on the ground, so I replied, "We'll give it a shot." We changed radio frequency to the Holt and asked for their position and for permission to land. They responded with, "Jolly Green-44 cleared to the helipad, but do not land! You'll have to hover over the helipad at 90 degrees like the other helos this morning. The pad is not stressed for your weight."

This was not an option for us. To maintain a stable hover, the pilot needs to be able to see a steady reference on the ground or water so he doesn't drift around all over the place. If I attempted to hover at 90 degrees over the Holt's helipad, I'd have been unable to see any-thing but a dark void. And the HH-53 was too big to hover facing the ship without our crew door and ramp hanging out over the water.

I made a low pass over the pad to check it out. As we approached the Holt, the only thing we could see was a small square of light float-

ing in a hundred square miles of black void; we couldn't distinguish the black sky from the black ocean. I flew low and slow just to the left of the Holt so Bobby Bounds in the right door and I could both get a good look at the helipad. We could see why the Navy didn't allow its HH-53s to land on it. It was tiny! At the front of the pad, the vertical wall of the super-structure rose just inches from the helipad. I asked Bobby if he thought we'd have rotor clearance if we landed 45 degrees to the pad with each main landing gear on opposite corners of the pad. I'd have to keep it light on the wheels to avoid overstressing the helipad, and we'd have to offload the Marines through the right door. Bobby said he thought it would be tight, but possible.

I called the Holt with our proposed plan. "Stand by," was the response. I assumed he was conferring with the Holt's captain. The captain and I both understood that this was definitely a high-risk proposal. If I screwed up, it would probably total my craft and do substantial damage to his ship. More importantly, it would kill or injure my crew, my Marines, and the sailors on the flight deck. But I wouldn't have proposed it if those Marines still left on the island weren't in such jeopardy. The Holt's captain, Cdr. Robert Peterson, had been monitoring all the radio traffic, and he apparently agreed with my assessment. But if I screwed up, we'd both probably be court martialed.

The Holt radioed "Jolly Green-44 will be cleared to land on Downunder's [Holt's tactical call sign] helipad. Do not put the full weight of the helo on the pad." We completed our landing checks and I briefed my crew on my intentions. Only Bobby Bounds and I in the right door would be able to see the Holt on short final. Hank would help me out with altitude and rate-of-descent calls. Jim would monitor rotor RPM and key engine and transmission instruments. Bruce in the left window wouldn't be able to see anything until we were over the pad, at which time he'd be responsible for making sure our left wheel was indeed over the pad before we set down. David on the aft ramp wouldn't be able to see anything during approach. He was to prevent the Marines from exiting off the aft ramp, which would be hanging over the water.

We ran through the final landing checks, including locking the landing gear brakes to keep us from rolling around on the helipad, and started the approach. Depth perception and closure rate were difficult to judge without any visual references except the small, bright helipad floating in the darkness. I soon realized that our approach angle was way too steep, so I went around for another try. I also aborted the second approach because I was too steep and we began to "fall through," meaning our rate of descent was way too high. Finally, on the third try, I got the angle and rate of descent right.

On short final, Bobby switched to "hot mike" so he could give me a running commentary on approach speed, rotor clearance on the right side, and altitude above the pad. From the HH-53 cockpit, the pilot has a very restricted field of view to either side or below the helicopter. And because the rotor mast is so far behind the cockpit, the pilot is totally dependent on his crew in the back to keep him advised of how much clearance is between his rotor tips and any obstructions to the side.

As we neared the pad, I had doubts about whether we'd have enough rotor clearance to the ship and still get onto the pad. It was really tight. But Bobby kept up his commentary, confirming our clearance to the ship, and guiding me verbally to a hover over the pad. I was totally tuned to Bobby's voice and kept a light touch on the controls, trying to sense what my helicopter was going to do before it did it. We needed only a sudden wind gust to drive our rotors into something hard. Finally Bobby, and Bruce on the left side, cleared me to a soft landing with the rear wheels. I let off just enough power for the nose wheel to lightly touch the pad, figuring we were putting only about half the full weight of the HH-53 onto the helipad.

As soon as the nose wheel touched, Navy guys ran under the helicopter to chock the wheels. For a long time, I didn't see any Marines exiting the right door, and I started to get concerned. I hoped the Marines hadn't jumped off the aft ramp taking David Ash with them. In response to my, "What's going on back there?" Bobby replied that he was "getting the damned safety wire off the damned minigun safety switch as fast I can" to clear the door for the Marines to exit. David *was, indeed, doing a valiant job of keeping the eager Marines from exiting as rapidly as possible via the aft ramp.*

One of my most vivid memories of the Mayaguez operation is the sight of the LSO [landing systems officer] standing upright in the corner of the helipad with his lighted wands to guide us into a safe landing. I have to admit that my concentration and my reactions were to Bobby's guidance because I trusted him. I had no idea how much experience in guiding helicopters the LSO had. I assumed that it was an additional duty for him and that he performed his duties occasionally, unlike the LSO on an aircraft carrier. However, I was ready to react to him immediately if he had given me a wave-off signal.

The reason I remember him so vividly was that he seemed so naked and vulnerable standing there while everyone else on his crew was hiding behind something substantial. Twenty-some years later, I received an email from a man who had been a sailor on the Holt that night. His chief had ordered him to the helipad for fire guard duty, but had warned him to "find something substantial, and stay behind it; some crazy Air Force pilot is going to try to land an HH-53 on our helipad." To this day, I admire the courage of that LSO who had no idea if I had the skill to pull it off, and most likely would have sacrificed his life had I erred.

Shortly, Bobby had cleared the door, and I could see Marines running off the aircraft following the sailors' hand signals to safety. As soon as the last Marine was clear, the Navy guys ran under the helicopter to remove the wheel chocks, and Downunder gave us takeoff clearance. They also said they counted thirty-five Marines offloaded, which we confirmed. With a silent salute to the LSO, I carefully eased away from the Holt and we got airborne again.

We checked in with Nail-69 and he advised us that none of the other helos had yet returned from the Coral Sea. He thought that only one more load of Marines was still on the island for extraction. As we neared the island, Nail-69 advised us that one of the Marines had thrown out a strobe light onto the LZ to help us locate them. The strobe light was a great help in finding the LZ in the dark, but it was a mixed blessing. It not only told us where to land, it also told

the Khmer gunners where we would land. And it would spotlight the
helicopter every time it flashed.

Obviously the Marine commander was taking a calculated risk.
And the fact that he was taking that risk told us that the Marines were
in desperate circumstances. They needed to get out now! I briefed the
crew that I planned to land on top of the strobe light to hopefully kill
it, or at least to avoid having our helicopter lit up like a neon sign.

Again, we used our low-and-slow tactic on our run-in as the
strobe light guided us toward the LZ. I avoided looking directly at the
strobe to try to protect my night vision, and the beach came up faster
than I had anticipated. I had to haul the nose up high to stop in time,
and dragged our tail in the water in the process. Salt spray engulfed
the aircraft as water ran up into the open aft ramp. As Jimmy hit the
windshield wiper switch I could see trees on our left illuminated by
the strobe light. I kicked in right rudder pedal to position us over the
strobe light, while Bobby started giving me directions to a hover over
the strobe. The right side of the helo was over the water on a steep
part of the beach, so Bobby was trying to position our right landing gear on a rock projecting from the water. I was having a hard
time complying with Bobby's instructions. Every time the strobe light
flashed, it lit up the waves rolling in from the right. I kept drifting left
toward the trees and was fighting a bad case of vertigo.

Finally, Hank asked if I had a hover reference, meaning a stationary
object I could see. "Negative," I replied. "I've got it," Hank rogered,
and I immediately released the controls to him, saying, "You have the
aircraft." All my senses told me Hank was drifting to the right, and I
had to fight the urge to grab the controls. But Hank could see a solid
rock on the beach to his left, and was providing a rock-solid hover for
Bobby's directions. Hank and Bobby set the helo down with the right
wheels on the rock while my head finally stopped spinning.

Marines started boarding the aircraft, but they were having a hard
time getting onto the ramp because our tail was over the water and our
ramp was almost chest-high. It was taking a long time to get loaded
while we watched tracers fly over the helicopter. By now my "gyros"
were again stabilized, and I took over the controls from Hank. We
just had to hold while those exhausted Marines climbed on board.

Suddenly, I saw movement in front of us; a dark silhouette against the lighter gray of the beach. He was trudging slowly toward us. I hadn't seen any Marines loading because they were all coming from the left rear of the aircraft. This guy was coming from the wrong direction, and he was small. He was either a very small Marine or a normal-sized Khmer Rouge soldier.

None of the miniguns on the HH-53 pointed to the front. They were meant to be defensive, and the pilots were all taught to point the nose of the aircraft away from ground fire. I gave the controls back to Hank and grabbed my GAU-5 (a chopped-off M-16 with a collapsible stock) from beside my seat. The pilot's window was hinged at the top, so I had to push the rifle down and out through the window. I couldn't reach it with my left hand, so I had to hold it with one hand, Rifleman style. I flipped the safety to full-auto. I remembered to aim low and left because the muzzle would rise to the right as it fired, especially with only one hand holding it.

"Please don't make me do this," I thought as the silhouette slowly got closer. If I see a muzzle flash, or if he raises his arm like he was about to throw a grenade, I'll blast him, I thought. But I didn't want to have to explain to a grieving mother why I had shot her young Marine son. Not even in my nightmares. But why is he coming from the wrong direction?

Finally, he got close enough that I could see from the strobe light peeking out from under our belly that he was, indeed, a young Marine. He was lugging what looked like an olive drab laundry bag, probably filled with grenades or ammunition. As he started to pass me on the right, I put my GAU-5 back on safe and stowed it beside the seat. "Young man, I hope you never realize just how close you came to dying of friendly fire," I thought.

I was proud of that young Marine: he had refused to leave anything behind for the Khmer, and he remembered his training to put the helicopter between him and the enemy. It would have been a lot easier for him to go around the dry land side of the helicopter, but there he was, now up to his chest in the surf, still dragging that heavy bag. He was panting for air as he slogged through the water around

our right fuel tank, and my guys in the back told me they were ready to take off. I ordered "Stand by. We still have one Marine coming around the right. David, be ready to give him a boost up the ramp. He's going to need help."

Finally, Bobby said, "Last one's on board. We're gonna be heavy. Let's get outta here!" I gave Nail our "Jolly coming out" call and pulled in full power for an instrument takeoff. I planned to take off straight up initially, then lower the nose while turning right to clear any trees that may be in front of us. But something was wrong! I was pushing full forward on the cyclic stick, but the nose kept rising! That HH-53 felt like it wanted to roll over on its back! "Guys, I can't get the nose down," I reported. Bobby replied with a breathless, "All the Marines are stacked up in the tail, we're throwing them forward as fast as we can." As the Marines had clamored up the aft ramp in the dark, they had tripped over David's gun mount and were literally stacked up on the floor at the rear of the helicopter. Their combined weight was enough to exceed the center-of-gravity limits of the aircraft, so I didn't have enough flight control authority to lower the nose.

"Nail, we're coming straight up out of the LZ," I radioed. "Nail's clear," came the response. All we needed now was a midair between a blacked-out helicopter and an OV-10 rolling in behind us to protect our withdrawal.

But now the cockpit was lit up by the bright yellow glare of numerous caution lights indicating mechanical problems. The caution lights notified the crew of the malfunction so corrective action could be taken. I had inadvertently jerked the controls when the minigun went off, sending a surge through both hydraulic systems, and momentarily activating the bypass function in both hydraulic systems.

We were still climbing, and the controls were responding normally, except for the nose-high attitude. In fact, the nose was slowly starting to come down as the weight of the Marines was shifted forward. I turned my attention to the caution lights. We needed to verify that we didn't have a serious hydraulic flight control problem. First, I directed Hank to reset his SERVO BYPASS circuit breaker. He squirmed around in his seat to reach the circuit breaker located on the panel to the left of his seat. One caution light went out.

About this time, Nail-69 asked, "Do you plan to go back to the Holt?" "Stand by, Nail," I responded curtly.

"OK, Hank, you've got the aircraft," I directed. Hank grabbed the controls and rogered, "I've got the aircraft." Now it was my turn to squirm around in my seat to reach the other circuit breaker. I reset the breaker and the other caution light went out. Good. That verified that we didn't have a hydraulic problem.

I reclaimed the controls from Hank and was glad to see we were regaining flying speed. The PJs reported several of the Marines were wounded and asked for the white cabin lights to be turned on so they could better treat the wounds and start IVs. I said, "Hold off on the white lights for a minute; go ahead with the red lights for now." The white lights would destroy everyone's night vision, and I wasn't sure yet what our next step would be.

My quick assessment went something like this: (A) We were getting critically low on fuel. We could aerial refuel with the HC-130 orbiting a few miles away, or we could refuel on the Coral Sea. The Holt had no fuel for us. (B) Our turbine engines had ingested an unknown amount of salt water spray during our two landings on the beach. When the salt spray hit the hot turbine blades, it instantly evaporated, depositing salt crystals onto the turbine blades. These deposits degraded the aerodynamics of the turbine blades, decreasing the engine power, and could cause engine failure in extreme cases. (C) My crew counted thirty-seven Marines on board, which equated to more than nine thousand pounds of weight. We couldn't have lifted that much straight up out of the LZ if we hadn't already burned off most of our fuel. But their weight made us heavy, degrading our critical power margin for a landing on the Holt's small pad. (D) We had wounded on board, and an aircraft carrier had better medical facilities than a little destroyer escort. (E) Knife-51 was en route from the Coral Sea. All these factors combined to convince me that the risk of trying another landing on the Holt was no longer justified.

The decision made, I radioed, "Nail-69, Jolly 44 is headed to the Coral Sea with wounded. ETA 20 minutes."

Hank gave me a heading to the Coral Sea as I climbed to 1,500 feet. I told Jimmy to turn on the white lights in the cabin to help the

PJs with their medical treatments. As Hank dialed in the Coral Sea's *Tactical Air Navigation [TACAN] and their radio frequency, I realized that my neck and back were cramped up from all the stress. But there was no time to relax. We had to figure out how to land on an aircraft carrier.*

I called Coral Sea *with our position and altitude, advising them that we had wounded on board and that we needed a hot refueling (a rapid refueling done without shutting down our engines). I also requested radar vectors for an approach. I radioed, "This will be our first landing on a carrier, so we'd appreciate any help you can give us."*

I had been hoping for a ground-controlled approach [GCA] where the radar operator gives constant heading and glide slope corrections to guide you to a specific landing spot. Apparently, they didn't have a GCA on aircraft carriers, probably because the carrier could be pitching up and down so much that a precise glide slope could not be established.

Again, we went through our landing checklists as the radar controller lined us up on final and gave us "recommended" descent altitudes. ("Recommended," of course means that if anything goes wrong it's the pilot's fault. But I was glad for all the help I could get, and followed that youthful-sounding sailor's recommendations to the letter.)

Soon we could see the lights of the Coral Sea *at twelve o'clock, a tiny speck of light floating in the dark. It didn't look any bigger than the* Holt, *but we knew it was. Our controller brought us down to about three hundred feet. I could see the landing area outlined in lights; as we got closer, I could see the LSO with his lighted wands.*

We landed without incident, and I hoped the LSO wouldn't give me taxi instructions to move the aircraft. I knew the Navy used some hand signals that were very different from signals the Air Force used, but I had no idea what they meant. Fortunately, he let me sit where I had landed. I could see stretcher bearers running to the aircraft and some Marines running from the back of our aircraft. Bobby deplaned to supervise our refueling as Jimmy ran us through our hot refueling checklist.

Once we refueled, we headed back to Koh Tang. When we checked in, Nail-69 directed us to hold west of the island with Jolly

Green-43, who had preceded us back from the carrier. Knife-51 was picking up the last load of Marines from the island.

Dick Brims, another friend from the Academy, was having fits trying to land on the dark beach. Finally, in a desperate act of defiance and bravery, he turned on his landing lights, despite the enemy gunners, to get to the Marines on the beach. After ensuring he had all on board, he joined us in orbit. Our three remaining helicopters orbited off the west beach while Nail-69 and Cricket tried to determine if we had recovered all the surviving Marines.

This was not an easy task, because Marines that had been evacuated were spread out all over the Gulf of Siam. Some had been taken back to Utapao, with some of those in the Air Force hospital there. Many had been taken to the Coral Sea. A few had been taken to the Holt. Some survivors of one of [the] helicopters shot down had been rescued by the destroyer USS Wilson. One of the missing Marines had been found in the head on the Coral Sea. Golf Company Marines were now mixed with Echo and H&S [Headquarters and Service] Company Marines. Officers and sergeants were separated from their enlisted men.

Those of us in the helos hoped, of course, that we had managed to extract all the Marines. We didn't want to go back into that hellhole, but we were all prepared to do just that if necessary. We all knew that our worst nightmares would be realized if we left any of our guys behind. Finally, Cricket called with the good news: all Marines were accounted for. All aircraft were to return to Thailand.

In all, we lost forty-one airmen, Marines, and Navy corpsmen in the successful recovery of the SS Mayaguez and her forty-man crew. That's a horrible cost. But all those men died helping to rescue their fellow Americans. "Greater love hath no man."

For their actions in recovering seventy-two Marines from Koh Tang under heavy fire, Bob Blough was awarded the Silver Star, and each of his crew members was awarded the Distinguished Flying Cross.

Blough left the Air Force in 1978 to pursue a career in automotive engineering. He continued to fly air rescue helicopters in the Air Force Reserve until his retirement in 1993.

PFC. TERRY BROOKS, 3D PLATOON E COMPANY 2/9 MARINES

Terence Lynn Brooks, a native of Portland, Oregon, was born the second of four brothers in March 1957. He left Sam Barlow High School at age seventeen to enlist in the Marine Corps in September 1974. In May 1975 he was an eighteen-year-old private first class assigned to the 3d Platoon E Company 2/9 Marines.

I had joined the Corps to get into heavy equipment but after boot camp I found out that I was going to be an infantryman (0311). On 14 May 1975 I was in training at Camp Schwab on Okinawa, and we were all in the field when I overheard the radioman get a call from Camp Schwab ordering us all back to camp and to get all of our gear packed up and ready to go. Once we got back to camp, we were told to pack all of our belongings in our sea bags and not to take time to call home or send a letter.

Once I heard that, it scared me and even though we were told not to write or call I sent my parents a short letter stating that something was up and that if they didn't hear from me for a while not to worry. After that, we all were put on trucks and driven out to Kadena AFB.

When we arrived, C-130s were already waiting for us. Off we flew, eventually landing in Utapao. We were told to form into our platoons at the hangars and stand by. After a while, some gamma goats [trucks] came out filled with live ammunition, hand grenades, smoke canisters, and the good old face-painting stuff so that we could become invisible in the jungle. This whole time no one had mentioned to us what was going on.

Not long after the first helicopters left, one came back with a huge hole in its side and that's when I figured it out that this was no game to see how quick we could be ready for the real thing. This was the real thing and we were next in line to go.

I was in the first chopper from Echo Company that left and the first to land on the west beach. I remember flying in the chopper for about maybe an hour when all of a sudden we were told to lock and load. Not long after that, we started descending and the ocean got closer and closer. All of a sudden we heard the [helicopter] minigun start firing and we didn't even know what he was firing at until the chopper turned 180 degrees and there in front of us was an island and we were coming in to land. We later learned its name was Koh Tang.

We came in and the back end opened up and we were told to go, so we did. My good buddy Steven G. Haun was the first off and I was right behind him. Steve fell about ten feet from the back of the chopper and I thought that he had already been shot and possibly killed. I went out farther and started setting up the perimeter and the other guys did as well. Once I hit the ground I rolled a few times and opened up on the tree line. Then I started yelling at Steve until he finally answered me and then I knew he was all right.

After the chopper left we all got up and walked single file to the south part of the LZ [landing zone] and headed through the jungle to try and link up with Golf Company Marines that were on the east beach. We didn't get very far because the jungle was so thick and we didn't have any machetes to help cut our way through. I can't remember who was running the show—Staff Sergeant Hale or Lt. Walt Davis—but they decided to return to the beach and to start digging in.

As we were coming out of the jungle, I saw three men that I thought were from Golf Company taking all the gear off of a Marine that had been killed and that Marine was Loney. We headed to the tree line and started digging our foxholes. My foxhole buddy was Steve and so we started digging only to find out that once you get past the sand, it was all solid rock. Our foxhole only got to be about two feet deep; we stacked a bunch of logs that we found on top of each other to create our cover.

When we finished Steve noticed that not too far in front of us was another foxhole—only this one was the enemies' and it was at least six feet deep the way they should be. When you're young and dumb, you do stupid things. Well, the stupid thing Steve did was to go inside that foxhole to see what he could find. It could have been booby-trapped, but thank God it wasn't.

Captain Stahl came up to us and after chewing us out over our stupidity asked for volunteers to go capture a 90-mm cannon that was down the beach a little ways. Of course we volunteered, because we were Marines and that's what Marines do. Off we went. Steve, Jeff Kern, Wagner, and myself. We carried the cannon back to the LZ and put it in the water and someone went out and blew the barrel.

The whole time that all this stuff is going on, the Navy and the Air Force are dropping bombs about one hundred yards in front of our position. For an eighteen-year-old kid, it was pretty scary. As it was getting dark we were told that a big bomb was going to be dropped so be prepared to take cover. Sure enough they did and it shook the whole island. Not long after that the radioman got a call that said the enemy was coming our way so to be on alert.

Lieutenant Davis told us to take cover and to be quiet. Sure enough not long after, we could hear them crawling at us through the jungle and just before they got to within about twenty feet, the lieutenant ordered us to open fire so we did. It seemed to last an eternity. I looked back and saw that Lieutenant Davis was standing straight up, not even behind any cover, yelling "Fire, fire, fire!" So we did and I even had time to throw my hand grenade that I had received back in Thailand. We ceased fire and were told that the choppers were on the way to get us off the island so we needed to get our asses up and head toward the LZ.

Mind you we weren't just walking down the beach, we were moving and shooting at the enemy the whole way there, making sure everyone was present and accounted for, working our way back to the place where we had started in the morning. Every time a chopper came in, all you saw were these tracer rounds coming out of the jungle toward the choppers.

At the time I didn't know it, but my buddy from boot camp, Dave Fowler, had been shot three times before he even got off the chopper. He was on the east beach and laid there all day until a chopper pilot noticed him moving his hand and saved him.

When it was my time to get on a chopper, as it came in the enemy opened up from the jungle, tracer rounds going out to meet it. We opened up on the tree line to stop the enemy from firing. We stopped firing and the helicopter's miniguns started firing to help us get on. We were all running for the chopper, helping each other as we went. We finally made it off an island that I wish I had never been on.

We were told to check each other out to make sure none of us was wounded on the way out and we headed for the USS Coral Sea. When we landed on the aircraft carrier, the Navy guys were there to help. They really took care of us for about two days and gave us head-of-the-line chow privileges and fresh clothes because we were stinking pretty bad after sweating on that island all day. We were told that we were headed to the Philippines for a day of R&R and that we would be there in a couple of days.

In the meantime, we had a ceremony on the deck for the men that had died. That's when we found out we had left a machine-gun squad, that didn't get the word to move out, on the island. Of course we were all pissed off and wanted to go back to get them but I guess that wasn't an option. I don't know why we couldn't have gone back, but we didn't. A lot of the guys today have a pretty big problem with post-traumatic stress disorder [PTSD] and I think that has a lot to do with it.

Brooks was honorably discharged as a corporal in September 1977 and married his high school sweetheart, Katherine Ann, with whom he had four children. He returned to Oregon where he has worked for the past thirty-one years as a carpenter.

2ND LT. RICHARD COMER, COPILOT, JOLLY-12

Richard L. Comer was born in Gastonia, North Carolina, in July 1951. As early as junior high, he'd set the goal of attending the Air Force Academy and becoming a pilot. He applied for a congressional appointment during the Vietnam Tet Offensive in 1968; his appointment in the summer of 1969 marked the first time any member of his family had attended college.

In 1970, during his sophomore year at the Academy, he visited Norton AFB in California and flew on board an HH-53 helicopter piloted by Maj. Frederic M. Donahue, who later that year was awarded the Air Force Cross as one of the pilots involved in the effort to rescue prisoners of war from the North Vietnamese POW compound at Son Tay, outside Hanoi. Inspired, Comer decided on a career as an HH-53 rescue pilot.

*Maj. Gen. Richard Comer,
circa 2005.* U.S. Air Force

Following graduation and his commission as a second lieutenant in the U.S. Air Force on 6 June 1973, he was assigned to Fort Rucker, Alabama, where he attended the helicopter training course from September 1973 until June 1974. This was followed by a five-month HH-53 qualification course at Hill AFB in Utah.

In December 1974 Comer, a twenty-three-year-old second lieutenant, was assigned as an HH-53 pilot with the 40th ARRS at Nakhon Phanom RTAFB, Thailand.

In 1975 I was with the 40th ARRS [40th Aerospace Rescue and Recovery Squadron] and we flew rescue missions under the call sign "Jolly Green." We belonged to the Military Airlift Command and we were a tenant unit on the Pacific Air Forces [PACAF] base at Nakhon Phanom [NKP], Thailand.

The other helicopter squadron there, the 21st SOS [Special Operations Squadron], also flew the HH-53 using the call sign Knife but they didn't have air refueling probes on their CH-53s. They were part of PACAF.

Both squadrons had participated in the evacuation of Phnom Penh, the capital of Cambodia, and later in the evacuation of Saigon, the capital of South Vietnam, in April 1975.

In Cambodia the Marines did most of the evacuating from ships to the south and the Air Force had only a little play. In Saigon, the PACAF guys got first call and placed all of their aircraft on the USS Midway. The Jolly Greens got the spots left over. Only two of our ten aircraft played in that mission.

The fall of Phnom Penh was on 12 April and the fall of Saigon followed on 29 April. The two aircraft returned to NKP on 2 May. The war in Southeast Asia was officially over and we all expected to rotate home very soon and close up Thailand.

On 13 May the seizure of the SS Mayaguez made the news. We didn't take much notice as it was a regular day. My crew, with Capt. Barry Walls as the crew commander, was scheduled for a day/night training sortie, but our bird [aircraft] was broken and the maintainers were moving very slowly. Nothing seemed important. We had lost the war and were just waiting for the call to go home.

At about 1730 hours Barry, who was the chief of flight scheduling, said everything was cancelled since no aircraft were flyable and everybody should go back to their hooch [quarters]. We had just arrived there when the phone rang and we were ordered to report back to the operations building.

When we got there, the squadron commander said he had been directed to send three aircraft and crews to Utapao Air Force Base on the southern shore of Thailand to be part of a task force to recover the Mayaguez and its crew.

We were to be a search and rescue [SAR] force to back up an assault force that would be carried in by the 21st SOS. We were to launch and go to Utapao and we would be briefed further when we arrived. The three crews chosen to go were Walls' crew, Wayne Purser's crew, and Joe Gilbert's crew. We were excited to go because none of these crews had flown the earlier missions and now we had our chance. We went out to the flight line where there were now six or seven Jolly Greens ready to fly.

We took off at about 2145 hours and dodged thunderstorms most of the way. We overflew Korat [Royal Thai] Air Force Base a little over two hours out and observed two Jollys on rescue alert as they took off. I called them on the squadron common radio and Hank Mason, copilot on Bob Blough's crew, told me that one of the Knives had crashed when leaving NKP and they were heading north to help out. We discussed what was going on and reasoned that since there were plenty of other helicopters going toward the crash, we should proceed on to our mission at Utapao.

We landed just before 0200 hours on 14 May, parked, and got a quick briefing by someone from the command post who advised us that there would be a mission briefing at 0530 hours. He told us to go to billeting and get rooms and we piled into waiting crew buses, but most of us only had enough time to take a quick shower before we went to the chow hall for breakfast.

At the 0530 briefing, we found out that there were four more helicopters from the 21st SOS and their crews were also present at the briefing. We learned that the SS Mayaguez was anchored off Koh Tang Island, about 140 miles out to sea from the Thai coast.

The Knives of the 21st SOS were to carry a force of some Army guys and mostly Air Force security police [SP] out to the island. The Jollys were to carry SP to the SS Mayaguez and hover over the containers on deck low enough for the SPs to jump off onto the vessel. Little resistance was to be expected at either place. After dropping off the SPs, the Jollys would provide a SAR airborne alert, refueling off the HC-130 helicopter air refueling tankers.

The Army guys apparently could speak Cambodian and were along to negotiate the release of the Mayaguez crew, which was assumed to be on Koh Tang Island. We looked at photos and could see that only two small strips of beach could support HH-53 landings. Those of us who were to hover low over the Mayaguez worried about being sitting ducks if there were a bunch of armed guys there to defend the boat. The PJ [pararescuemen] gunners seemed to yearn for a real gunfight.

We went out to the aircraft and prepared to crank up for the launch, which was scheduled for 0730 hours. The enlisted guys had gone out to the line first while the pilots had stayed back for a brief-ing on formation procedures. When we all got together at the aircraft, about twenty or so SPs showed up and the PJs briefed them on the aircraft and passenger procedures. I compared notes with a sergeant on what our jobs would be on the upcoming mission.

At our earlier briefing, our squadron operations officer and sec-ond in command, Lt. Col. Gordon Hall, gave us our assignments. His assistant was a senior captain named Vern Sheffield, and both these men were greatly respected. They were working like mad to organize things, and Hall told us that Sheffield would come out to the flight line later to give us the final "go" order for the mission.

We waited for a while in the cockpits, ready to crank up our engines. Vern came out a little later than we expected and gave us the cut sign across the throat meaning to shut down, instead of the windup hand circle signal that would have meant to spin the rotors. The mission was on hold and we would have to wait, standing by at our aircraft for further word.

We waited for the next seven hours. We were tired, and by 0800 the aircraft ramp was already scorching hot. After sitting in the cock-pit for a while, we got out to avoid the sun coming in through the cockpit windows. I remember lying down on the concrete ramp using the aircraft for shade. The auxiliary fuel tank on the right side of our helicopter became my shade. Lying right under the tank, which was full of fuel, was cooler because the fuel seemed to be good insulation and stayed cooler than the air. I took short naps using my helmet bag as a pillow. I think it was about noon when I noticed that C-141s had come in and parked near the helicopters and that there were Marines disembarking.

A group of them were led to our aircraft and told that we were their ride. The SPs who had been there all morning were being re-lieved from the mission. The mission would now be done by Marines. I talked with one of the Marine lieutenants, and told him what we had been told to do in taking them to the SS Mayaguez. He didn't say what he had heard about their mission, but said he needed to go over to one of the other helicopters to talk with his captain. I went back to sleep.

During the early afternoon more and more HH-53s from both squadrons arrived. Bob Blough's flight arrived, refueled, and then flew out toward the Mayaguez on a rescue mission of some sort. I didn't know much except we were told to remain in place with our Marines, waiting for orders.

It was about 1500 hours when Don Backlund and his crew came up to our aircraft with their flight gear. They informed us that, due to the need for a fresh crew on the aircraft, we were being displaced on the mission and the aircraft was now theirs to fly. Colonel Hall was with them and confirmed the order. We were told to go to the BOQ [bachelor officers' quarters] and get some rest. Thirty minutes later all the crews showed up at billeting with orders to rest and be ready to brief for the mission at 0400 the next morning. I remember I told Barry that since everyone was now getting rest, we should get our aircraft back and be returned to the mission. He said, "Go to sleep."

When the phone in our room rang, I answered it. Captain Sheffield told me to bring the crew. We got to the flight line in less than twenty minutes.

Sheffield told us that the Mayaguez recovery had turned into a small war and that several of the helicopters that went to the island had been shot down. There were people in the water and on shore needing rescue and medical evacuation. The helicopters that had dropped their Marines on the destroyer were trying to help.

He said we should remain close and stand by, but that the PJs assigned to our crew had been assigned to a 21st SOS helicopter that was here and on alert when everything started happening. He had placed our PJs with that aircraft and they had already launched out to help.

Vern [Sheffield] told Barry that our crew should stay available and keep informed. He promised that when he could put us together with other PJs and an aircraft we would go out as well. He hoped to get us an aircraft from a crew when they returned from the battle. Or we might get one from NKP, because the rest of the aircraft in both squadrons were being fixed and flown to Utapao as quickly as maintenance could get them ready. He said that a few extra crews were around, because they had been flown in on C-130s yesterday *evening, and he would find us some PJs from those crews as quick as he could.*

I loitered in the operations building, listening to what was being said and began to learn more of what was going on. The mission had remained essentially the same as we had been briefed the day before.

Helicopters had been assigned to carry the Marines to two places: the larger group went to Koh Tang Island while a smaller group was offloaded onto a Navy destroyer [USS Holt], which then came along-side the SS Mayaguez. Marines then boarded and took back the ship.

The destroyer had not been part of our plan the day before because it was too far away. The extra day had given it time enough to become part of the plan. A carrier [USS Coral Sea] was also on the way and would soon be close enough to provide support.

The 21st SOS squadron commander, Lt. Col. John Denham, had flown the first helicopter to the island and had been shot down. So had his second in command, the squadron operations officer, in an-other of their helicopters. The last 21st SOS aircraft that had been sitting on the parking ramp at Utapao was still there because it had been grounded for excessive vibrations. The pilot, 1st Lt. Dick Brims, had cleared it for a flight and had asked the Jolly Green squadron for a couple of PJs. That was how the PJs on my original crew had gone out to the action. They were on Knife-51 with Brims flying.

The first Jollys out were the ones that took the Marines to the destroyer; those Marines now had control of the SS Mayaguez. The Marines on the beaches were under fire and calling for more Marines.

At operations, there was a Marine colonel named Andersen who was getting reports about the situation on the island and on the Maya-guez. He seemed in control as he gave orders and listened to reports.

Colonel Hall, our squadron operations officer, was also there, tracking where each of the Jolly Green helicopters were. I wanted to ask when he thought my crew would get into the action. I desperately wanted to find a way to the action, but without PJs we didn't yet have a full crew.

Lieutenant Colonel Denham came walking into the building a couple of hours after I got there. We'd been students together in an HH-53 transition course. He was a truly nice guy, polite in every way, *and a strong born-again Christian. His predecessor at the 21st had been a part owner in one of the Thai massage parlors and had held squadron parties in the local bar and massage parlor. Needless to say, Denham had been a big change over at the 21st.*

He had been shot down just off Koh Tang Island three hours earlier. I learned later that day that his flight mechanic, Woody Rumbaugh, had gone down at sea with the helicopter. Denham and the other two crew members had been hoisted out of the water by another 21st SOS aircraft and had just arrived back at the base. We spoke briefly. I said I was glad to see him alive. I had heard he had been shot down and until that moment I had not heard that he had been picked up. He put his hand on my shoulder and squeezed, then went over to the desk that was assigned to his squadron and started tracking where all his people were. He had several dead, including all of the crew that had crashed on the first night.

Aircraft from the 21st were also cycling in and were loading more troops, refueling, and leaving again. I needed a flyable Jolly Green helicopter. Vern said the Marine colonel was moving more troops toward the island because he thought it would be the best way to keep those Marines on the beaches safe. He did not regard the recapture of the SS Mayaguez ship as the end of the mission.

We heard sometime around 1000 hours that the Mayaguez crew was back in American hands. I remember thinking that, no matter what, the mission had succeeded.

Our crew was assigned three PJs at about 1100 hours and we were told to get ready to go. One of the Jollys was returning and, if it was flyable, we would relieve the crew, who had been on the bird since 0300.

The aircraft coming in was Jolly-42 with Lt. Phil Pacini's crew. I grabbed my flight gear and went out to the parking ramp to meet it as it taxied in. It looked good to me as it parked. The maintenance guys who were talking to the crew after plugging into the intercom began to point at the sides of the aircraft and at the auxiliary fuel tank on the left side.

I saw one of them put his finger into a couple of bullet holes. Lt. Bob Dube, the copilot, talked with me after they shut down the engines and rotors. They had taken a good bit of fire from the island, which had punctured both auxiliary tanks. They also had some flight control problems that they thought needed to be fixed. Their judgment was that the aircraft was not flyable. The maintenance guys didn't have any spare aux tanks to hang on the aircraft either. It hurt, but we'd be staying in place.

An hour later, another Jolly came in and the pilot said his bird was in good shape. We got together and got a quick brief that we were to take some maintenance guys and Joe Gilbert's crew with us. We were first to fly out to the carrier USS Coral Sea and place the maintenance guys and Gilbert's crew there. Then we were to join in on the extraction of people on the island.

Orders had come from somewhere that the troops on the way out had to return. No more Marines were to be placed on the island and those on shore had to be extracted. Aircraft carrying troops toward the island were turning around to come back.

Capt. Paul Jacobs and his crew in Jolly-12 landed and parked a perfectly flyable HH-53 at about 1300. It got refueled by the maintenance guys who were going with us. Jesse [Sergeant DeJesus], our flight mechanic, did a quick walkaround and preflight check, then we took off with a pretty large load of people.

It must have been after 1400 when we tracked outbound from the Utapao Tactical Air Navigation [TACAN] on a radial that pointed us toward Koh Tang Island. Barry briefed the crew through the combat ingress checklist but expressed his belief that everyone was competent in their jobs and knew their procedures. Sticking to procedures and concentrating on getting the right things done was how we'd best be able to help out.

I got all the radio frequencies up and, about fifty miles out from Utapao, I switched to the TACAN frequency of the aircraft carrier. We heard a good bit of chatter on the radios and listened intently to get up to speed on the situation. At about one hundred miles out to sea from Utapao we had good radio reception and locked onto the ship's TACAN, which showed it was about thirty-five miles farther out. We made contact with them and told them we had some helicopter maintenance and extra crew members to drop off on their deck. They told us that they would hot pump [refuel] us when we landed.

Barry made the landing and it was the first time on a Navy deck for any of us so we made the best we could as to what their hand signals meant. Undoubtedly, the Navy guys had a number of things to say about the AF guys they saw that day. There were two other HH-53s on the deck, but they were shut down. Refueled, we took off and headed toward the island, fifteen to twenty miles away.

We got up on all the right radio frequencies and heard Lt. Don Backlund, aircraft commander of Jolly-11, talking to the airborne FAC [forward air controller].

The airborne FAC had not been part of the original plan but had been called up from the base at Korat, Thailand, when the first wave of helicopters had encountered strong resistance. Three of the first four helicopters to land on the island, all of them in the 21st SOS, had been shot down. Backlund was telling the FAC that the Marines and surviving crew members on the beaches were under fire and needed to get off the island.

Several attempts to pick up wounded during the day had resulted in battle damage that had put other helicopters out of commission, and the two or three helicopters still out there flying wouldn't last long if previous mistakes were repeated. Backlund was really laying things out and advised the FAC that it would be dark soon and the chances of successfully getting everybody off the island would be greatly reduced.

Barry knew the FAC by name and mentioned that he was a major named Bob Undorf. Backlund challenged him to make things happen, and quickly, or he would become the newly arrived OSC [on-scene commander] of a miserable failure.

During that conversation we had arrived on Jolly-11's wing and we were now joined in a formation of two Jollys. There was also Knife-51, Dick Brims and his crew, with my crew's original PJs on board, who were orbiting nearby and ready to work with us. This was complicated by the fact that squadrons from different AF major commands didn't fly formation using the same exact procedures.

The FAC went to work, talking with the people on the beach, identifying their exact positions, and lining up the strike assets he had available. He called in an F-4 to drop a couple of bombs. The bombs went badly, with one falling short of the island and the second landing long off the island. Both were closer to the Marines on the beaches than to any of the enemy.

Undorf sent the F-4s home and asked who could hit a target. He then called in the AC-130, who hit some of the spots near the Marines on the east beach. After that, he cleared in a flight of C-130s that were carrying daisy cutters. One of the C-130s dropped its load at the far end of the island. The daisy cutter was designed to blow holes in the jungle, with the concussion of the bomb designed to cut the trees off at ground level and open space to create a landing area for helicopters.

The guys back at Utapao had sent them out to create an alternative LZ if the beaches became unusable. I couldn't think of a good reason for that as the Marines seemed to be trapped on the beaches and wouldn't be able to move to the far end of the jungle island. But I was a helicopter copilot and what did I know about whether the Marines could push through. I needed to concentrate on my own job.

Finally, it was time to go to work. The shock wave from the explosion made our helicopter rock and roll like a ship on a rough sea; our SERVO caution lights came on, indicating our hydraulic flight controls had experienced low pressure and might be failing. Since the lights were caused by the turbulence and nothing else was wrong on the instruments, I reset the lights and completed the checklist items.

Undorf called in Backlund's helicopter to land and pick up all the Marines remaining on the east beach. We went in with them and Brims followed. As Backlund slowed and turned his helicopter to place its tail facing the trees just off the beach, we set up a slow circle over and around his helicopter.

Backlund's two side guns were both blazing away as they set down. I saw Brims' helicopter on the other side of the circle we were making over Jolly-11, and his guns were also blazing. Our guns shot out a couple of short bursts. Technical Sergeant Patterson was the lead PJ on board and he had the gun on the left side. Airman First

Class Rhinehart was on the tail, and Sergeant Styer was on the right. Jesse had stayed in the seat. We took a few rounds, a good number up the belly of the cabin, but neither Jesse nor I observed any damage on the flight instruments.

Backlund's helicopter came up out of the LZ; he called that he had wounded on board and that the east beach was clear of friendlies. He headed for the Coral Sea and we returned to our holding pattern about four to five miles off the island.

Undorf told us to prepare for a hoist pick-up. There was one person left on the east beach and he was in one of the shot-down helicopters. We had seen the hulks on the first run in and had a good look at them. One was sitting upright with the tail broken off and the other was farther out in the water lying on its side. We were told an American was in the one lying on its side. Undorf called the AC-130 back in and cleared them to shoot everything on the beach. The AC seemed to cover it well with sparkling rounds hitting all along the beach.

Barry had given me the flight controls in the holding pattern. I had the primary radio and told the FAC, "Request you expedite." Since it was now getting to be almost dark, I imagined it was going to be a tough hover in the dark out over the water. I figured we had better get all the fuel we could into the main tanks from the auxiliaries, since if they were punctured we wouldn't be able to get any of that fuel, and I began a fuel transfer to the main tank.

Jesse had gotten out of his seat to run the hoist on the right side, which meant the right-side gun had to be swung out of the way and not used during a hoist. Styer put on swim gear in case he needed to get into the water to help the survivor.

The AC-130 finished its work and Undorf called us to go in for our hoist. We were now getting close and I began the approach with nose up. Barry took the controls at just that moment and did a steep turn while slowing to put the tail toward the places where we thought the enemy positions were and Rhinehart began to open fire with the tail gun. It jammed. He said the gun was shot. This was a literal statement as we learned later that a round hit the gun in the feeder and made our tail minigun useless.

We took a couple of rounds through the cockpit and I could hear impacts into the fuselage. Undorf was on the radio calling out fire. I felt some more rounds hit us and looked toward Barry. He was hovering and moving the helicopter to the left as called for by Patterson. The shot-down helicopter was off to our left as we came to a hover. We needed to move about a hundred feet. All those former Marine foxholes on the beach were now full of angry Cambodians shooting at us.

I saw Knife-51 come into the lagoon and hover just about two hundred yards away, level with us. Their crew had knocked out all the cabin windows on one side and crew members, to include our former PJs, were shooting at the shore with their personal weapons. They were putting out a lot of bullets all over that beach.

Jesse took over direction of the aircraft as he directed Barry in placing the craft over the hulk below us. He advised when the hoist was out the door and on the way down. After a bit, the hoist was in the water and it was by the hulk. I heard Jesse grunt loudly in the middle of his calls for "right two, down five" etc. Barry asked Jesse if he was OK. Jesse just kept giving directions for about twenty more seconds, then softly said, almost in surprise, "I been shot, I been shot, my leg, my leg."

Styer was on the floor by him, looking for the reported survivor. There wasn't one that anyone could see. He pulled Jesse from the door and unplugged Jesse's intercom cord. Barry began the takeoff from a hover and somebody got the hoist coming back up and brought it back inside. I made the radio call that we had one crew member wounded and were coming out from the beach. Barry asked what heading to fly and I said we could go to the USS Holt, which had been near our former holding pattern.

The Holt lit up and said they were ready to receive us. From the back, Rhinehart and Patterson advised us that the aircraft was badly damaged and they thought we were losing fuel. I looked at the gauges and it looked to me like the aux tanks were losing fuel. Barry said that the Holt's helipad was too small for us to land on so we needed to go to the Coral Sea where we could park and shut down. I made the radio call to the Holt that we were aborting the approach due to battle damage and were en route to the carrier.

Barry asked the PJs how badly Jesse was hurt, while I gave him the heading to the carrier, based on my memory of where it had been in relation to the island. I checked the TACAN and saw that the needle that should have pointed to the carrier was spinning around, indicating that we had no lock on the carrier's transmitter. I used my flashlight to look at the TACAN control and it was on the correct frequency channel, but it wasn't working. I assumed it was damaged.

Barry had me take over flying the helicopter so he could check things out. He took his flashlight and shined it on the TACAN control panel. He said it was the right channel. I called the Coral Sea for landing directions and advised them that we were damaged and had one wounded on board. The ocean lit up with the ship about five miles directly in front of us.

Barry told me to make the landing and I made the approach to hover beside the ship, then followed their directions to move sideways to park between two HH-53s already shut down on the deck. It was challenging from the left seat, but I felt good to be the one making the landing. We tipped some to the right as we settled on the gear, learning then that the gear strut on the right was collapsed and the tires on that side were flat.

As we shut down, sailors carried Jesse off the helicopter to take him to the ship hospital. After we got out of the seat, I looked at some of the bullet holes in the cabin. Rhinehart said that he had laid behind the tail gun and used his personal weapon to fire back after his minigun had failed. Both of the aux tanks had holes in them and there was some damage up around the rotor head.

After about ten minutes, our maintenance guys were all over the helicopter, saying they had to get it configured to go down the elevator or the Navy would push it over the side. They wanted to take off the rotor blades, and Barry gave them the go ahead, while the rest of us went to the hospital to see Jesse.

We had a short visit, and the doctor said the leg had taken the punishment fairly well and the bone hadn't been damaged. Jesse was *groggy but awake. As we went back to the flight deck we met Joe Gilbert.*

Gilbert told us to take Backlund's aircraft and fly back to Utapao. Barry said we had no flight mechanic and Joe told us to take Backlund's crew with us and to put his flight mechanic, Harry Cash, in the seat. We did that and took off about fifteen minutes later, flying the helicopter that we had originally taken to Utapao two days earlier.

Right after we took off, we heard Knife-51 saying he was going in to the west beach to extract the last of the Marines. This confused us and we asked one another why we were going to Utapao when it wasn't over yet. I told Barry that we should return to the Coral Sea and drop off everyone but a crew and head back to the island.

Lt. Gary Weikel, Backlund's copilot, asked over the intercom what we should do. If Knife-51 was getting the last Marines, what was there left to do? I called Knife-51 and asked what was left. Brims said that the copilot of the helicopter down on the east beach, Lt. Johnny Lucas, was still there and someone had to get him.

Weikel told us that Johnny Lucas was one of his best friends and that he was already on board the USS Coral Sea. Lucas had boarded Jolly-11 when they extracted the Marines from the east beach.

We then heard Jolly-44 radio that they were airborne from the Holt, where they had disembarked the Marines they had picked up from the west beach. Jolly-44 was Bob Blough and crew who had gotten on a helicopter that had arrived from NKP that afternoon.

They had arrived to join Knife-51 just as we had headed for the Coral Sea after getting shot up on the island. Knife-51 reported that they were airborne from the west beach with the last of the Marines and that Jolly-11 and -44 could head for Utapao. So we did.

What I remember most of that day was an intense desire to get in the fight, a desire that was frustrated by circumstances.

Comer returned to Nakhon Phanom, where he remained until December 1974 when he was assigned as an instructor pilot with the 601st Tactical Airlift Support Squadron at Sembach AFB, West Germany.

Following assignments with the Marine War College and at the Air Force Academy, Comer commanded a squadron of HH-53s during operations Desert Shield and Desert Storm, and retired from the Air Force in May 2005 with the rank of major general after thirty-two years of service.

CAPT. JAMES W. DAVIS, COMPANY COMMANDER, G COMPANY 2/9 MARINES

Davis enlisted as a private in the United States Marine Corps in September 1967 and was sent to boot camp at Parris Island, South Carolina. After completing infantry training at Camp Lejeune, North Carolina, he attended officer training at The Basic School [TBS] at Quantico, Virginia, in February 1968 before shipping out to Vietnam as a newly minted second lieutenant.

Assigned to "The Walking Dead" (1st Battalion 9th Marines, part of the 9th MAB [Marine Amphibious Brigade], which was operating in the area of the Quang Tri Province), Davis saw combat as an infantry platoon leader and company commander.

Following his tour, Davis returned to Camp Lejeune to assume command of K Company 3/6 Marines. He attended the Aerial Observers School at New River, North Carolina, before taking command of the Marine Detachment on board the USS *Holland* (AS-32) in Rota, Spain.

Following completion of jump school and after he had attended the Infantry Officers Advanced Course at Fort Benning, Georgia, Davis was deployed to Okinawa and given command of G Company 2/9 Marines.

I arrived on Okinawa during November 1974. I was immediately assigned to 2nd Battalion 9th Marines as the commander of Golf Company. I smiled when they showed me my company office since it was the very same one I had departed from in January 1969, after my company returned from Vietnam. I honestly smiled to myself, and thought, this may be an omen? The company personnel had already finished their deployment so the men I initially commanded were old "salts." They had completed most of their tour and were doing routine training and inspections until their final days were over. As the months passed, the old guys returned home and new Marines arrived to start the evolution all over: join the unit, train, deploy, return to Okinawa, and await orders back to the States.

Prior to the seizure of the Mayaguez, *Golf Company was in the "forming" and early training stage, which means we were building up the battalion with new Marines to get them trained and then depart on routine deployment to places like the Philippines, Korea, Japan, etc. Training incrementally starts with individual skills, fire team, squad, platoon, and finally company tactics and patrolling. Subjects like offense, defense, fire support, leadership, and logistics are all part of this training.*

When we were notified to prepare for departure on the evening of 13 May 1975, the company was training in the central training area on Okinawa. We had been listening to the Mayaguez *seizure on the company portable radio, but earlier events like the fall of Saigon and Phnom Penh overshadowed our interest. I had approximately forty-two Marines that had detached from my company to deploy and participate in Operation Eagle Pull [Cambodia] and Operation Frequent Wind [Vietnam]. These Marines had just recently returned to my company and we were just learning their names and putting them back into platoons. This meant that one-fourth of the company hardly knew their counterparts.*

On the evening of 13 May I received a call on the radio that truck transportation was coming ASAP to pick up my company and return us to Camp Schwab, our base. I was not given a reason. We had just been resupplied, and I was told to bring home all blank ammunition, but just leave the C rations for the locals. This was a little unusual, and I knew that something was going on, but I had yet to associate any of this with the Mayaguez.

Upon returning to the barracks, the troops showered, packed an extra set of utility uniforms, and were ready for inspection within less than two hours. It rained that night on the way back to the barracks so the Marines, having ridden in open trucks, were wet, tired, and generally not in a real good mood. Being Marines, they did their job. We trucked to Kadena AFB, got a quick meal, rested, and awaited the flight to places unknown.

We departed Okinawa on board USAF C-141s. No one slept during the flight for more than a few moments at a time. The pilot came over the intercom and said, "There is Vietnam off to your right." At least I knew the general geographic area we were heading in. We were somewhere between Vietnam, Cambodia, and Thailand. I had not made a firm connection, but I became suspicious that this would somehow involve the Mayaguez *since Vietnam and Cambodia were now out of the U.S. strategic picture for the "big" war, but Cambodia was back in the picture for the* Mayaguez *seizure.*

When the aircraft landed at Utapao, the battalion S-3, Maj. John Hendricks, walked up to me on the landing strip as I was leaving the aircraft, and asked, "Jim, how would you like to conduct a raid?" He then smiled. What was I to say but yes! My head was racing for the lack of information and what I knew raids involved: rehearse, rehearse, rehearse, like the Israelis had done at Entebbe. I had recently graduated from the Infantry Officers Advanced Course at Fort Benning and was fairly savvy with the military planning process.

As we walked over to the command center at Utapao, I remember seeing a U-2 Black [Blackbird] reconnaissance aircraft parked well within view. I remember that I was briefed with a group of Marine and Air Force officers and we were told that, as well as could be determined at that point, the civilian crew of the USS Mayaguez *were being detained on the island of Koh Tang.*

One of the 3rd Marine Expeditionary Force [III MEF] colonels interviewed a Cambodian navy lieutenant commander in the hall of the command center and asked him who normally occupied the island and in what strength. The man replied that we could expect around forty irregulars or possibly pirates on the island. I was standing with the colonel when this comment was made. The lieutenant commander would not make eye contact with either the colonel or me when he made this comment, and I was suspicious—not that he was purposely lying, but that he made up this intelligence assessment. The colonel joined a few more MEF officers and made the remark, "Those Khmers won't fight!" That was an obvious assumption.

When we returned to the main briefing room in the Command Operations Center [COC], a lot of speculation, piecemeal planning, and talk was going on. Capt. Gene Smith, who had attended the advanced course with me at Benning, shared smiles with me since some of the ideas were not really practical. Since we were the junior officers in the briefings, we sat on the floor with our backs against the wall.

Within an hour or so I raised an obvious question. "Has anyone seen this island or taken any aerial photos?" To my surprise, the answer was no, despite the U-2 I had seen. I had attended the Aerial Observers Course at New River, North Carolina, when I was a junior captain, so I asked if we could have an airplane made available for a reconnaissance. A few ideas were discussed and the answer was yes. There was an Air Force staff sergeant in the room so I asked him if he could go to the PX and purchase some high-speed black and white film for my 35mm Minolta camera. He complied. By then it was mid- to late afternoon on 14 May.

We took off in what I remember was a twin-engine olive-drab civilian aircraft, probably a Cessna twin. On board were two pilots, Lieutenant Colonel Austin and the air liaison officer from the MEF. The flight to the island took more than an hour and was uneventful. As we approached Koh Tang, a fighter aircraft was on station. Because of possible ground fire, I took the pictures at around four thousand– to five thousand–feet altitude. Since it was getting late in the afternoon, the details were very poor. We returned to Utapao, arriving at dusk and I sent the film to be developed on base.

After the overhead photos were developed, I met with the gunny [gunnery sergeant] and my XO [executive officer], 1st Lt. Dick Keith. The details within the 8 x 10s were nonexistent because of the altitude they were shot at and the haze of late afternoon. I did, however, see what looked like a "sliver" of beach on the eastern and western sides of the island. I did not see what was found later to be a partial clearing and buildings between the beaches. The 1:50,000 map had only one contour line and a hill described as fifty feet high. That was all the details I had to plan the operation.

I went off by myself to write a five-paragraph order (situation, mission, execution, admin and logistics, command and communications) with the only guidance that we were not to use preparatory fires against the island that might hit the crew of the Mayaguez, *which was assumed to be on the island. We were initially to go into the two beaches "cold" with the helicopters and try to negotiate the freedom of the crew with whomever held them captive.*

The second paragraph of the order (mission statement) went something like this: "At 0630 on 15 May (when) portions of BLT [Battalion Landing Team] 2/9 (who) lands (what) on Koh Tang Island, Cambodia, (where) to rescue the crew of the USS Mayaguez (why)." Notice I did not use the words attack, assault, seize, etc., in the order. That was not the mission guidance given to me prior to writing the order. We were never really told to take and hold the island, but I did brief my platoons that in the event we had to spend the night, we would together seize and hold a portion of the island.

The other important paragraph in the order was paragraph three (execution). Seeing that I only had two possible LZs [landing zones] that were on opposite sides of the island, I had to plan a simultaneous double envelopment via helicopters that is risky to coordinate even with seasoned troops and officers that have done this type of training. Double envelopments are not a recommended form of maneuver because of coordination of fires between units, complexity of link-up, communications, etc., but I had no other choice. I had to get as many troops ashore as soon as possible to gain strength and fire superiority should the case arise—as it later did.

The battalion and company staffs agreed to my plan since there weren't a lot of other options. We were down to less than twelve hours before departure to Koh Tang. We had supplies and ammo to distribute and had to organize the helicopter teams. The company command element returned to their platoons to brief the staff and troops. After the briefings we passed out the chow, water, grenades, and ammunition. There was no time for sleep, and we were into the third night with little or no sleep and fairly untrained Marines. I knew that this was going to be a little tricky to pull off if we had a lot of resistance, but I had a lot of faith in my new officers and the staff NCOs who for the most part were Vietnam vets.

I can't remember at what point in time the Air Force CH-53 helicopters arrived that evening, but after we finished briefing the company staff on the operations plan, GySgt. Lester McNemar and I sat in the tail end of one of the CH-53s awaiting a go/no go to depart from whomever would make that final decision.

We were not there long when a staff sergeant walked up to me and handed me several aerial photos from the U-2s who I guess finally did their aerial reconnaissance over the island. Unfortunately, what I was looking at was worse than I would have expected. There were buildings and defensive positions everywhere, and several areas that looked like antiaircraft positions. My intuition had been correct. We were going to fly into someone else's fight!

I knew that I had little time left to brief the company staff, so I told the gunny, "Gunny, we don't have time to brief the troops. We are going in anyway, and I'm not going to show this to the troops, but I think we are in for a world of shit!" Within what seemed less than a minute the pilot said to us, "Saddle up, we are going in!" We boarded the choppers and took off for Koh Tang.

Needless to say, I was full of anxiety on the flight in, which lasted less than two hours. At one point we were fired at by tracers, but our altitude was beyond tracer range. We could see the guns light up the sky below us.

As we approached the island, we had lost any chance of surprise. The sun was out and the sky was cloudless, a beautiful day for a fight! As my helicopter made a feint on the island's west beach and crossed over the trees, no shots were fired. As we passed back over the beach, I could see smoke starting to rise from the east beach. I initially had no idea what was causing that billowing smoke.

We started back in to land the troops, and all hell broke loose from the ground. I was hit in the left side of the face, in the cheek bone, with shrapnel or something. The hole was the size of a pencil and it penetrated the bone. I almost turned a complete back flip and my vision was temporarily covered by a white flash as I fell to the floor of the chopper.

I looked to the front of me as I was trying to get back on my feet and the gunner of the helicopter grabbed his stomach and fell back among the life jackets piled behind him. "Oh my God," I thought. "He's been hit in the stomach!" The gunner then felt his stomach and looked at the buckle of his flight safety belt. The buckle had taken the

*round and was creased by the bullet. He had had the wind knocked
out of him, but that was the extent of his injuries. He then jumped
up, mounted behind the gun, and continued to fire into the direction
of the incoming fire. "What a brave airman!" I thought.*

*I got to my feet and again took my position near the window of
the helicopter, trying to understand the situation. The chopper took
quite a beating so the pilot waved off and headed back to sea. As we
were out over the water, another chopper hit the water and rolled
over. We hovered, trying to see if there would be any survivors, but
unfortunately none appeared. It was the pilot's decision to head back
to Utapao since we were leaking large amounts of fuel and hydraulic
fluid.*

*We were unsure of our location when the pilot stated, "I've got
to set this bird down! We are out of fuel!" The helicopter actually
dropped the last several feet onto the ground. I jumped out and set
the troops in a hasty perimeter around the chopper. Talking with the
pilot, we were unsure if we were in Cambodia or Thailand. The pilot
got on the radio and asked for a pickup by another chopper. In the
meantime the gunny disabled the helicopter with his M-16. The situation remained uneventful until we were picked up several hours later
and returned to Utapao.*

*When we returned, I went to the temporary S-3/operations shop
and briefed Capt. Gene Smith, who was the S-3A. He was my old
friend from Vietnam and Fort Benning's advanced course. "I'm going
back in with you," he said. I replied, "No, Gene, you have a wife and
two young kids. We will be OK!" With that, I took my troops, loaded
up, and we took off again for Koh Tang.*

*As we flew back to Koh Tang, the crew chief advised me that the
crew of the* Mayaguez *had been rescued, but that we were going in
anyway. He wrote on a C-rations sleeve with a red pencil, "LZ very
hot!" We were as prepared as we could be.*

*The helicopter landed without taking any serious hits, and the
troops disembarked in an orderly fashion into knee-deep water. The
first thing the gunny did when we saw the troops was to order them to
put on their helmets. I got with Capt. Mike Stahl and started organizing the perimeter and digging in. Lieutenant McDaniel had returned*

CH-53 helicopter that crash-landed on a Thai/Cambodian beach after taking heavy fire over Koh Tang is disabled by GySgt. Lester McNemar, USMC, to prevent enemy capture of aircraft. Department of Defense

from his patrol where they took one KIA, Lance Corporal Loney, and several wounded, to include himself. At this point, fire was sporadic and inaccurate.

The company calmed down and settled into the perimeter, and occasionally returned fire to keep the Khmer Rouge too far away for them to throw hand grenades, although a few grenades were exchanged between the opposing lines.

Lieutenant Colonel Austin and the command group stayed on the beach with the mortar section. Austin was coordinating the extraction of 2nd Lt. Mike Cicere from the eastern side of the island. Several of the troops wanted to move forward, but I stopped them, since nothing would be gained at that point except more casualties.

As the afternoon passed, my gunny became restless and approached me with the question, "Captain, can we take this damn island?" He was ready, although by this time we were running low on water and ammunition. When the gunny came to where I was sitting to get my answer, I replied, "Gunny, we are not going to take this

island. There is no reason to, and I am not willing to risk the lives
of more Marines. We may have stepped out of the pages of history,
but this is my decision." Saying nothing, the gunny walked off and
rejoined the troops.

It was less than an hour later when I looked out to sea and saw
helicopters returning over the horizon to begin the extraction. Lieutenant Colonel Austin ran over to my position from the beach and
asked, "Jim, how do you want to pull this off?" I replied, "Sir, you
had the morning shift, I will take the night shift and get the Marines
off the island." We still had the entire west beach and Captain Stahl's
Echo Company to extract.

I reduced the perimeter incrementally, getting Captain Stahl's
company on the right side [south end] of the perimeter out first. My
troops remained in place and covered Stahl's company withdrawal
as they moved onto the beach and boarded the helicopters. I clearly
recall asking Captain Stahl before he got on the helicopter, "Mike, do
you have all of your troops?" He replied yes, and I told him to get on
the chopper.

The gunny and I continued to reduce the perimeter down to one
heli team. We moved back to the beach and our boots were literally
almost in the water as we took advantage of the defilade rendered by
a small dune to our front. It probably saved lives as the fire from the
Khmer Rouge went over our heads. With their rifles pointing into the
jungle to our front, I passed the word down the line to my Marines to
load two full magazines, put one in their rifles and have the other next
to them. When I gave the word to fire as the helicopter came in, they
were to provide protective fire, emptying both magazines, and then
get on the chopper.

At this point we had only two alternatives if no helicopter came
in: swim or fight to the death. The gunny and I discussed this, and
since we had nonswimmers we had vowed to fight to the death if necessary, but we were not going to leave troops behind.

I had a small strobe light which I had traded something for from
a recon Marine back in Okinawa. I knew it would draw fire so I
tossed it to our front as I turned it on. It was something for the helicopter to guide on because by then it was dark.

Around 2000 hours the helicopter finally arrived and the Marines fired into the jungle on my order and backed into the helicopter. The gunny and I were the last ones to load on board. The crew chief did not have time to raise the ramp, and as the helicopter began to gain altitude, he started sliding back. I reached out and grabbed him, and started sliding myself. We had a very dangerous human chain leading to the back of the ramp that wasn't working very well. Several of the Marines saw what was happening and came to our rescue, pulling me and the crew chief to safety. After several minutes of flight time, we were on board the USS Coral Sea.

When I departed the helicopter on the flight deck of the Coral Sea, a Navy doctor ran up to me because of the blood on my face from a wound earlier in the day. He wanted me to go to sick bay and get treated, but I declined and headed for the officer's mess [wardroom]. I wanted to check on Lieutenant Cicere and his platoon and talk to Lieutenant Colonel Austin. When I walked in, Mike Cicere came up to me and we gave each other a hug, glad to be still among the living, not knowing if we were dead or alive. Mike assured me that he had extracted all of his people, and I assured Lieutenant Colonel Austin that everyone was off the island. Captain Stahl had yet to discover that he had three missing Marines. After that, we indulged in conversation about the events of the day while we drank coffee and reflected. It all happened so fast!

Later that night a naval flight officer came into the wardroom and offered me a place to spend the night in officer's country. He was one of the pilots that had run air strikes against the patrol boats and runs on the island. He led me to a stateroom and gave me clean pajamas in exchange for my filthy, sandy, and still wet utility uniform. After the exchange I entered the stateroom and was surprised to see writing gear, a stamp, a large bottle of rose wine, and a pack of cigarettes, my brand. The U.S. Navy was looking out for me. I drank the wine and just stared at the top of the desk reflecting until after 0100. Sleep came hard, but the wine helped. Depression hit me hard that night. I was beginning to realize the tragic events and the losses I had suffered.

Early the next morning the ship's communications officer woke me and told me that CINCPAC [commander in chief-Pacific] wanted to talk to me. I went to the ship's communications center and assured the admiral by teletype that all the troops were successfully extracted from Koh Tang. After breakfast the BLT command group was gathering information from Utapao, the USS Coral Sea, *the USS* Wilson, *and the USS* Holt, *attempting to locate Marines who had been deposited at these locations during the rapid extraction from the island.*

At that point the muster looked OK. That ended early in the afternoon when we held a muster of my company and Captain Stahl's Echo Company. After a headcount of Echo, Captain Stahl walked up to me in front of both companies and reported that he was missing three Marines. There was a very heated exchange between Stahl and myself that I won't detail. We then went to Lieutenant Colonel Austin and reported the missing Marines.

After talking to Lieutenant Colonel Austin, the gunny and I came up with a proposal. We wanted to return to the island with one of the small boats from the ship, carrying a hidden M-60 machine gun in the forward compartment, and if necessary fight our way out if the Khmer Rouge did not accept a white flag of truce. All we needed was a boat and boat driver from the Coral Sea. *We proposed to launch fighter aircraft, drop leaflets on the island in French and Cambodian explaining our intent, and if necessary use the aircraft to run air strikes if needed. Lieutenant Colonel Austin had no problem with my plan. I wanted to get those troops out, dead or alive!*

The commander of Task Force 73, Rear Admiral Coogan, was told of the missing men, and he had a fourteen man SEAL [U.S. Navy Sea, Air, and Land] team flown in from Subic Bay. We held a meeting with the SEAL team commander, Lieutenant Colonel Austin, Gunnery Sergeant McNemar, and myself in attendance. The admiral wanted the SEALs to go to the island during daylight under a flag of truce and attempt to recover the Marines. The lieutenant junior grade refused to go in during the day, but did volunteer to do a reconnaissance at night. At that point I pushed the issue with the admiral, and the exchange became heated as I insisted that he let the gunny and me go in as planned.

Finally the admiral had had enough and said, "Captain, you do not talk to me like that. Understand?" I had pushed the issue as far as I could. At that point, he had not said no. The admiral never directly told me no, but I knew the answer when we departed the area for Subic later that day. I was terribly disappointed because I realized that I would have to live with this for the rest of my life. Regardless of whose company they were in, they were Marines!

Obviously, the Mayaguez *affair was an intelligence disaster. I feel that the president was let down by the intelligence community. With Cambodia and Vietnam falling, President Ford was out of options, and did the right thing. To us, the operation was tactical, but to the nation it was strategic. We had to demonstrate to the world that we could still act decisively in Southeast Asia.*

For his actions in the *Mayaguez* operation, Davis was awarded the Bronze Star with Combat V and the Purple Heart. Following his tour in Okinawa, Davis returned Stateside to serve as commanding officer of A Company, Headquarters Battalion, Headquarters Marine Corps [HQMC] Washington, DC, followed by command of the Weapons Training Battalion at Quantico.

He attended the Command and Staff College and served with the 1/24 Marines before retiring in command of the Marine barracks at Charleston, South Carolina, with the rank of lieutenant colonel on 26 September 1988. After a period working in law enforcement, Davis took a position working in the government.

SGT. JESSE DeJESUS, FLIGHT ENGINEER, JOLLY-12

Jesus ("Jesse") Perez DeJesus was born in San Lorenzo, Puerto Rico, on Christmas Eve, 24 December 1949. He hoped to become an aircraft mechanic, and after graduating from high school in 1968 he enlisted in the U.S. Air Force, since there were few aviation schools. He saw military service as a way to get training and experience as well as to travel the world.

After basic training at Lackland AFB in Texas, he was sent to Chanute AFB, Illinois, where he trained as an aircraft mechanic. He was posted to McClellan AFB in California, then to Robins AFB in Georgia to work on C-141s.

In 1970 word came down that the Air Force needed helicopter mechanics; he volunteered and was sent to Sheppard AFB in Texas for helicopter school. He volunteered to go to Vietnam or Thailand; after about
four months he received an assignment to go to Udorn RTAFB in Thailand as a helicopter mechanic to work on HH-53 helicopters. He was
reassigned to Tyndall AFB, Florida, in August 1972, but volunteered to go
back to Thailand; in less than a year he was back in Thailand at Nakhon
Phanom.

*During that time we pulled alert duty at Ubon RTAFB [Royal Thai
Air Force Base] with two HH-53 helicopters. We would rotate every
three days; one chopper was a high bird and the other a low bird. The
low bird would make the rescue and the high bird would provide cover. The Vietnam War was slowing down so we didn't have too many
missions. In 1975 things changed. South Vietnam was being overrun
by the North Vietnamese and we were involved in getting people from
Saigon to the Navy carriers. The next mission was the evacuation of
our embassy personnel from Phnom Penh. We had about eight Jolly
Greens [HH-53s] involved in that mission.*

Our next mission was the SS Mayaguez *incident: 13 May started
as a regular day for our air crew (Capt. Barry Walls, 2nd Lt. Richard
Comer, and me). We were scheduled for a three-hour night training
mission. We had just started the number two engine when we received
a radio call to shut down and come in for a briefing. After we shut
down, three PJs [pararescuemen], Technical Sergeant Patterson, Sgt.
Randy Styer, and Airman First Class Reinhardt showed up, then a
munitions maintenance crew arrived at our helicopter (#793—code-
named Jolly-12).*

*Needless to say, I never made it to the briefing. I stayed with the
helicopter to get it ready for flight. Three miniguns were installed and
ammunition was loaded on board. About an hour later the pilots
arrived and told me that we were heading to Utapao RTAFB.*

*About thirty minutes after we were airborne, I saw two other
Jollys heading north on alert duty. Major Walls told the crew that
a helicopter went down and the Jollys were scrambling to look for*

survivors. I found out later that it was a helicopter from the 21st SOS [Special Operations Squadron]. On board were four crew members (two pilots and two flight engineers) and about twenty SP [security police]. One of the main rotor blades [MRB] separated from the main rotor head [MRH], causing the aircraft to crash and consequently fireball. Later, I found out that the blade had been defective.

We arrived at Utapao and waited. Another Jolly arrived not too long afterward. It was a long night and the following day dragged. I believe it was 0200 on 14 May, and I was passing through a lounge when I saw a Knife crew hanging around. I saw their flight engineer, SSgt. Woody Rumbaugh, with a strange look on his face. I remember because it was such a weird look. I never told anyone because I was busy doing something else and I completely forgot about it until after my return from the Philippines. Later, his helicopter, piloted by Lt. Col. John Denham (who was my commander later at Eglin AFB in Florida), was shot down and landed in the water. Staff Sergeant Rumbaugh drowned. I heard two stories: one was that he was trapped in the helicopter and the other that he was weighted down with an armor vest and didn't know how to swim. Both pilots survived.

The mission to rescue the SS Mayaguez started first thing in the morning on 15 May, but our crew waited almost the whole day without taking part. I don't know all the details on why we weren't involved in the morning mission, but later on, as the mission was coming to a close, we were tasked with the extraction of the Marines.

We got airborne and flew to the USS Coral Sea. We had some maintenance personnel, as well as a munitions person on board. En route, we checked our miniguns and mine malfunctioned. The munitions person helped me correct the malfunction. After an hour or two, we landed on the USS Coral Sea, dropped off the maintenance personnel, and refueled. That was our first landing and refueling on an aircraft carrier. We got airborne again and headed toward Koh Tang Island. On the way there, the PJs and I set up our miniguns and received permission from the pilot to go hot. I put the armor vest on which was very heavy and I wondered if I'd have enough time to remove my vest if we went down. I figured my LPU [life vest] wouldn't help me stay afloat if I kept my [armor] vest on.

As we approached the island, we were ordered into a holding pattern, circling for only a short time about five to ten miles from the island. I could feel the vibration when a Navy F-4 dropped a five hundred–pound bomb, or so I thought. There were a lot of things going through my mind.

Pretty soon we received a radio call ordering us to pick up a survivor who was supposed to be in a downed helicopter about twenty-five to fifty feet out from the island in a cove, radioing positions and information on the enemy. The helicopter had been shot down earlier in the day. I disarmed the minigun at the personnel door by the hoist and stowed it away. I didn't know the status of the other helicopters that were nearby, but since we were a fresh crew, I guess they wanted us to pick up the survivor.

Anyway, we were called in for the pickup. The pilot went in fast and when he got there he turned the helicopter toward the sea. The tail was not far from the beach. He got into a hover over the downed helicopter. At the same time I opened the bottom personnel door and lowered the penetrator with the flotation collar. Sergeant Styer was ready to get on the penetrator and I signaled him to wait. We had earlier decided that we would put him into the water in case the survivor was unable to help himself. Also, I was thinking that if we got fired on, it would only be the penetrator and not him.

I looked down at the helicopter and noticed that the whole aircraft was under water and the only thing that was above water was the MRH. I asked myself, where was this guy hiding? Maybe he was hiding by the MRH or just underneath. So I put the penetrator down near the MRH, figuring the survivor would be able to see and grab it.

After we went into a hover, we took heavy gunfire from both sides of the helicopter. I was so focused on what I was doing that I didn't hear all the damage inside. We were an easy target, hovering about fifty to seventy-five feet above the water in a cove, not far from the beach. When the penetrator had been in the water for only a few seconds or a minute, I felt a sharp pain on my left thigh. I looked down and noticed blood on the floor. I had my AR-15 just aft of the door but now it was lying on the floor.

For a second, I thought I had shot myself, but actually AK-47 rounds had passed through the right auxiliary fuel tank, the helicopter skin, and then me. I continued to look for the survivor, moving the penetrator around the downed helicopter. I didn't mention to the pilot or crew that I was shot, but when I looked down again at the floor, there was a puddle of blood. Right away I notified the pilot that I was shot. When he heard that, he was going to abort and get us out of there.

The penetrator was still outside, and as he was pitching nose down for forward flight, I noticed the penetrator swinging toward the MRH. I thought that was all we needed, for the penetrator to get stuck underneath the MRH. So I pushed out on the cable, got it away from the MRH, and put the handle up, causing the cable to retract at about two hundred feet per minute. The aircraft was still going forward as the hoist was coming up. Finally, I got the penetrator inside the helicopter as Captain Walls headed toward the Coral Sea.

Technical Sergeant Patterson came over to look at my wound. We arrived at the Coral Sea *and the ship's medics carried me off and took me to their emergency room to work on my wounds. Apparently, I had taken two AK-47 rounds in my left thigh. (Years later, I had an x-ray done on my thigh, and it showed numerous pieces of shrapnel.) A doctor checked me out and put an IV in my left arm and I was taken to the medical ward.*

After the mission the USS Coral Sea *headed toward Subic Bay Naval Base in the Philippines. I was on the ship for a few days until we arrived at Subic Bay. The next day I was put on a CH-47 and taken to Clark. A couple of days later, Maj. Gen. Leroy J. Manor, Pacific Commander of PACAF [Pacific Air Forces], presented me with a Purple Heart. I think it was a couple of months before I was put back on flying status.*

DeJesus remained in the Air Force and, as a member of the 67th ARRS at RAF Woodbridge in England, was among the air crews designated to take part in a mission to rescue Americans during the hostage crisis in Iran in 1980, a mission that was later canceled.

A helicopter accident during a night refueling mission in 1982 resulted in the death of the pilot, Maj. Barry Walls, and the flight engineer, SSgt.
Buddy Fortner, who was stationed with DeJesus at Woodbridge.

He retired from the Air Force as a master sergeant in September 1992
after earning a bachelor's degree in occupational education from Southern
Illinois University.

1SGT. LAWRENCE L. FUNK, G COMPANY 2/9 MARINES

Lawrence "Larry" Funk was born in a small town in Pennsylvania on 31
August 1938. He enlisted in the U.S. Marine Corps at the age of seventeen
on 17 January 1956.

After recruit training at Parris Island and infantry training at Camp
Lejeune, North Carolina, Funk had many assignments before shipping
out for Vietnam in February 1965, serving a tour with the combat engineers at Danang.

Funk was promoted to first sergeant in 1973 and reported to G Company 2/9 Marines at Okinawa early in 1975.

*I returned from evening chow about 1700 on 13 May to find the com-
pany XO [executive officer], Lieutenant Keith, in a frenzy. The 2d
Battalion had been put on alert and we were to be prepared to move
out that same night.*

*We went on board Air Force C-141s and flew to Thailand. After
several meetings throughout the day, we boarded Air Force CH-53s
early the next morning and flew out toward Koh Tang Island.*

*On our approach, I could see helicopters down in the water,
burning. Our pilot tried to fly in, but there was no LZ [landing zone]
available. We had to back onto the beach, only to receive heavy enemy
fire. In less than thirty minutes, I estimate we had at least thirty-four
wounded in Golf Company.*

*After making my way to the center of the beach, I ran into Lieu-
tenant Keith. He informed me that the CO [commanding officer] and
the company gunny were also shot down, whereabouts unknown.
After much confusion we reorganized and set up a defensive perimeter.*

*About noon that day, Captain Davis and Gunnery Sergeant Mc-
Nemar flew into the beach area. They had made it back to the Thai*

*mainland before crashing. They were picked up by an Air Force heli-
copter and returned to the island.*

*Our next concern was how we were going to extract from the
island, since by then we had learned that the Mayaguez crew was safe
and in American hands.*

*We started the extraction about dusk, and once again the helicop-
ters had to back in and hover over the landing site on the beach itself.
We received heavy fire each time a helicopter came in for an extraction. The helicopter I was on landed on board the USS Coral Sea.*

*As we steamed toward Subic Bay, we had a lot of counting of
personnel and a lot of radio traffic to Washington, DC. After a few
days on board ship and a couple of days in Subic Bay, we flew back
to Okinawa.*

*For me, Koh Tang was just a bump in the road of a very long
career in the Marines.*

For his part in the *Mayaguez* operation, Funk was awarded a Bronze
Star and a second Combat Action Ribbon. He retired from the Marines
on 1 March 1986 as sergeant major after thirty years of service.

SSGT. JON D. HARSTON, FLIGHT MECHANIC, KNIFE-31

Jon D. Harston was born 29 July 1948 in Newport News, Virginia, the
son of a retired Air Force chief warrant officer (CWO) with twenty-five
years of experience working in aircraft maintenance. After graduating
from high school, Harston followed his father and enlisted in the U.S. Air
Force in July 1966. He was trained in aircraft maintenance.

Initially assigned to work on a variety of fixed-wing aircraft at Travis
AFB, California, he requested retraining for rotary aircraft (helicopters)
to qualify for assignment to Vietnam, and he served his first tour (1969–
1970) at Phan Rang, Republic of Vietnam, as a flight mechanic on board
HH-43B rescue helicopters.

He returned to Vietnam (1971–1972) assigned as a door gunner on
board UH-1Ns of the 20th SOS [Special Operations Squadron], the Green
Hornets. As part of the 56th SOW, he was involved in covertly inserting
Studies and Observations Group (SOG) special forces teams into Cambodia and Laos.

SSgt. Jon D. Harston, flight
mechanic on Knife-31, recipient of
the Air Force Cross. U.S. Air Force

His third tour in Southeast Asia (1974–1975) was as a flight mechanic–
gunner on board CH-53s; he was assigned to the 21st SOS at Nakhon
Phanom RTAFB, Thailand, where he participated in the evacuations of
Phnom Penh [Operation Eagle Pull] and Saigon [Operation Frequent Wind].

One evening just a few weeks after returning from the aircraft carrier
USS Midway, *the chopper crews of the 21st SOS [Special Operations*
Squadron] and the 40th ARRS [40th Aerospace Rescue and Recov-
ery Squadron] were celebrating the completion of the evacuation of
Saigon at the NCO [noncommissioned officers] club on NKP [Nak-
hon Phanom]. It seemed at that time the final events of the Vietnam
War era had finally come to an end and now all we had to do was sit
back, relax, and await the completion of our tours of duty at NKP.
The jovial spirit of the crews was suddenly broken, however, when
a PA announcement at the club instructed the crews to immediately
proceed to their respective squadrons. We soon found out that we
had one last, unanticipated, mission—the rescue of the SS Mayaguez
and her crew.

Although we were all excited to have one last combat mission to participate in, the flight from NKP to Utapao was not one of anticipated excitement we thought it would be. Tragically, we had to witness the gut-wrenching fiery crash of one of our own choppers that threw a blade shortly after takeoff from NKP. All on board, the crew and eighteen security police [SP], were killed. All other choppers were ordered to continue to Utapao while one Jolly stayed back to investigate the crash and recover the bodies. It was a very quiet flight to Utapao.

Initially, we were going to insert Air Force SP on Koh Tang, but someone of higher authority came to their senses and decided to delay the mission until Marines from Okinawa could be flown into Utapao. After a delay of about twenty-four hours, we gathered up our Marine landing force that had arrived on C-141s and headed out to Koh Tang Island. I was on board Knife-31, piloted by Maj. Howard "Al" Corson.

We approached Koh Tang Island at daybreak. It was eerily quiet on the low-level approach toward the east beach. Randy [Hoffmaster] and I readied our miniguns for the approach and landing. As Corson turned the chopper southward and began his approach, all hell broke loose. Out the right door I saw Knife-23's tail get blown off and watched it crash onto the beach. An instant after opening up with my minigun into the tree line, one of the rounds coming through the floor caught me in the left leg and knocked me to the floor. As I struggled to get back up I saw the outside of our chopper was engulfed in flames and relayed [yelled] over interphone to the pilots that we were on fire.

Within the next instant, I remember an explosion and we impacted into the shallow water. Again, I was knocked back to the floor. At that moment, and in a daze, I was unaware of what was happening to Randy, the pilots, or the Marine landing party. All I could see were flames all around the chopper and I felt a relieving coolness as ocean water entered the right door.

I instinctively swam out under the right door gun far enough to clear the fire that was burning on top. Upon surfacing, I realized I was in the middle of a fierce fire fight and only had my .38 sidearm with me. I guess the cool water helped bring me to my senses so I swam back under the water to the burning chopper to retrieve my AR-15 that was hanging by the doorway. Upon reentering the chopper, I saw many of the Marines trying to bust out the clear Plexiglass windows to escape the burning wreck. I yelled at them to come out under the doorway where the water would protect them from the fire. As the Marines started to head in my direction, I grabbed my AR-15 and headed back out into the surf myself.

When I surfaced the second time, I came up next to Randy, who was facing the beach with his .38 in his hand. I remember Randy making some sort of disparaging comment about the situation we were in (don't remember exact words); with rounds kicking up the water all around us, I leveled my AR-15 and returned fire into the tree line until I was out of ammo. A few of the Marines that had got out of the chopper tried making it for the beach and tree line but never got any farther than a few feet onto the beach, if they even got that far. They were killed immediately. The rest headed out to sea.

Turning my attention back to the chopper, I saw Major Corson was still in his seat in a daze and still trying to fly the damn thing. I made my way to the front of the chopper and attempted to open the pilot's side window using the emergency escape latch but quickly realized that was not necessary as the whole front of the chopper was missing. I reached in and unlatched Major Corson's lap belt and yelled at him to get out. He seemed to come to his senses and stepped right out over his rudder pedals into the water.

I then made my way around to Lieutenant Vandegeer's side of the chopper but was driven back by fire. I could see Vandy was dead and slumped into his shoulder harness. He was pretty well shot up. One of the exiting Marines, I think it was Trebil, had also made an attempt to save Vandy, but had been also unable to do so.

As I saw the survivors heading out to sea, I thought that was a pretty good idea and started heading out myself. At some point, while backing out into the water, I stepped off a ledge and went straight down under the water. With all my flight gear, including my helmet, still on, I sank like a rock. Startled, I pulled the lanyards on my LPU [life vest] and when they instantly inflated, I shot up and out of the water like a rocket. Those big bright orange bladders were probably the best targets the bad guys ever had. Almost immediately, one of the bladders was shot away and I was frantically letting the air out of the good bladder so it had just enough air to keep only my head above water.

I probably had made it about twenty-five yards off shore when I saw an injured Marine moving in the water near the chopper. I yelled at him to swim out to me but he seemed to be having a difficult time of it. I swam back in toward the chopper and met him about halfway. He hung on to my back and I used the LPU oral inflation tube to add a little air to the bladder so it could hold both of us up. I realized he was pretty badly burned and that's why he needed a little help. Thinking he was the last of the survivors, we headed back out to sea.

After getting back out another twenty-five yards or so from shore, I was shocked to see yet another Marine moving around the chopper. I figured he must be in the same shape as the one I now had with me. I kept low in the water and dogpaddled back toward him. We joined up, added a little more air to the LPU bladder, and the three of us headed back out to sea. It turned out that he would be the last survivor off Knife-31.

The entire time we were swimming out to sea, the Cambodians never stopped trying to kill us. Rounds were constantly zinging past our heads and grenades were blowing up here and there in the water around us. One round found its target and struck me in the helmet about two inches above my nose and right between my eyes. My helmet split right in two and the impact drove me back into the water. While the impact did make me see stars for a few seconds, the helmet did its job and prevented the round from splitting my head open. That was, no doubt, the closest I've ever come to meeting the grim reaper. I'm pretty sure my newfound Marine friends thought I was a goner.

After swimming for several hours, during which time we never saw any other survivors, we saw a ship moving our way from out in the distance. At first the Marines were a bit worried that it might be a Cambodian gunboat, but I assured them that with all the fire power we had in the air at the time, it was not likely to be a bad guy. As the ship got closer we could tell it was much too large to be a gunboat. The ship turned out to be the USS Wilson.

Eventually, *we saw a rescue boat dispatched from the* Wilson *and it began picking up survivors. That was the first time we could tell where the other survivors were located, but they were still quite a distance off. After picking up the first batch of survivors, the rescue boat headed back to the* Wilson, *and that action really made our hearts sink. We figured that they thought they had picked up everyone and therefore would not continue looking for us.*

As I was told later, that was the case, except Major Corson and Randy Hoffmaster told the crew of the rescue boat that we were last seen alive and to go back out and look for us. It took about half an hour, but the rescue boat headed out a second time. After watching it do a zigzag search pattern, it finally spotted us and came to our rescue. I cannot begin to tell you how good it felt when we realized we were finally spotted. On a humorous side note, the rescue boat had an M-60 machine gun manned on her bow and evidently wanted a little piece of the action. After we were picked up, the boat headed in toward shore to shoot up the shore line a bit. I mentioned to the boat captain that we had been through quite a lot, we were wounded and had no weapons, and would therefore like to be dropped off at the Wilson *before they engaged the enemy. Fortunately he saw my point of view and agreed. We all had somewhat of a chuckle.*

We were taken to the USS Wilson *where we were provided medical treatment and were well taken care of. The Navy personnel gave me a dry pair of khakis to wear and a pair of flip-flops. Somewhere along the way I had lost my flight suit and boots.*

After a few hours on the Wilson, *I was flown over to the USS* Holt *where there were better medical facilities. The next day, at my request, I was choppered over to the USS Coral Sea where the rest of my squadron buddies were located. I was asked to fill out a locator card and was eventually placed in a room with a Navy ensign. It was not normal for an enlisted man to be placed with a Navy officer and it didn't take long before the error was discovered. A Navy petty officer came to relocate me to enlisted quarters, but the ensign told him that*

I was staying right where I was. That seemed to be OK with the Navy and they let me stay.

I asked about taking a shower and the ensign showed me to the head. When he discovered that I didn't have any skivvies (they gave me khakis on the Wilson, but no shorts) he pulled out a brand new pack of skivvies that he was saving for shore leave and gave them to me. I can't say enough good things about that ensign.

I soon discovered that the Coral Sea was headed back to the Philippines and I really didn't want to go there. I wanted to head back to Thailand to find out what had become of the rest of my squadron buddies. I asked the Navy if there were any ships in the area that might be heading to Thailand and discovered that the USS Kiska [a Navy supply ship] was nearby and heading there. The Navy was kind enough to chopper me over to the Kiska and they put me in their medical ward and took good care of me for the two-day trip back to Thailand. Randy Hoffmaster discovered what I had done and got choppered over to the Kiska himself. We both made it back to Thailand together.

Upon arriving just off the shores of Utapao, an Air Force HH-43B flew out to the Kiska and picked both Randy and me up and gave us a ride to the base. We were both happy to join up with our buddies and we began grieving for those close friends and fellow crew members that were lost.

For his actions during the mission, Harston was awarded the Air Force Cross and Purple Heart. He retired from the Air Force in 1992 with the rank of chief master sergeant (E-9) after twenty-six years of service. His other awards include the Defense Meritorious Service Medal, two Meritorious Service Medals, and ten Air Medals.

MAJ. JOHN B. HENDRICKS, S-3, 2/9 MARINES

John Beverly Hendricks was born on the family farm neat Douglassville, Texas, on 11 August 1939. The house, built by the great-grandfather for whom he is named, rests on land granted to the family by the Spanish when the family migrated to Texas before the Texas War of Independence.

All four great-grandfathers fought for the Confederacy during the Civil War, and all came home afterwards.

Inspired by his Uncle Bodie's accounts of war in the Pacific, he enlisted in the Marine Corps Reserve at seventeen while still attending Kirwin High School in Galveston.

Accepted by St. Mary's University in San Antonio, he was bound for the San Diego Marine Depot, but recruiters detoured him to the platoon leaders class. After two years, Hendricks transferred to Texas A&M University, where he graduated in January 1961 with a bachelor's degree in English and a commission as a second lieutenant in the Marine Corps Reserve.

Hendricks married and then attended The Basic School [TBS], followed by four years at Camp Lejuene with 2/6 Marines; he then deployed afloat to the Caribbean and Mediterranean. A year assigned to Headquarters Battalion 2d Marine Division was followed by two years on board the USS *Duluth* (LPD-6), an Austin-class amphibious transport, including operations along the coast of Vietnam.

He returned to San Diego with the *Duluth*, and transferred into the 4th Reconnaissance Battalion as S-4. Shortly after taking command of a reconnaissance company, Hendricks was back in Vietnam, working with the Army's 1/9 Cavalry Squadron of *Apocalypse Now* fame. After a stint as operations officer of the 1st Reconnaissance Battalion, Hendricks returned to Washington, DC, to learn Vietnamese at the Defense Language Institute. The assignment he was training for was aborted after the North Vietnamese discovered and terminated the unit to which he was to be assigned.

After Amphibious Warfare School at Quantico, Virginia, and four years in the Counterinsurgency Branch of G-3, Headquarters Marine Corps [HQMC], Hendricks was sent to Okinawa in 1974 to command A Company Headquarters Battalion, Marine Corps Base, Camp Butler. Now a major, Hendricks volunteered for the S-3 spot with 2/9 when it became available in April 1975.

I joined the battalion just after it had formed and begun its cycle of training and preparation for deployment. I was assigned as the

S-3, operations officer. Lt. Col. Randy Austin was the commanding officer and Maj. Larry Moran was the executive officer [XO]. The battalion was at nearly full strength with no major shortages in number or in technical skills. The battalion was already well into individual and weapons training when I arrived.

We had completed the weapons familiarization for small arms and the crew-served weapons and were beginning the squad and platoon-level training exercises. We had experienced and competent company commanders. Captains Jones, Davis, Stahl, and McCarty were putting their units through their paces and the training was coming along according to schedule. Our weapons training told us that we had old but serviceable rifles, functioning machine guns, light [short a few] 60-mm mortars, and better-than-average 81-mm mortars. We were equipped to fight and the crews were formed and had live fire practice.

We were out training in the northern training area in the rain and mud of Okinawa in May when, while working with the company commanders, I received a call to report to the regimental command post at Camp Schwab.

The regimental operations officer, Maj. David Quinlan, quizzed me at length on the readiness of the battalion to deploy and to conduct small unit operations. I gave him as clear a picture as possible on short notice. I had no idea what was in the wind nor did he give me any hint. As soon as possible I let Lieutenant Colonel Austin know. He was in contact with the regimental commander who had been at division headquarters. It did not take us long to figure out that this was no routine checking up on our training efforts. Later, Lieutenant Colonel Austin returned to tell us to saddle up and prepare for airlift. To where, he did not know.

Within hours the battalion assembled on the service apron at Kadena Air Force Base just as Air Force C-141 Starlifters began arriving. After a short wait we were instructed to fall into our plane teams and prepare for boarding. We still had no idea of where we were going; the flight leader—I recall him being a brigadier general—had no better idea. The order came to enplane and we started to board the aircraft.

While we were in flight the flight leader, who was piloting the aircraft that Lieutenant Colonel Austin and part of his staff were on, met with Lieutenant Colonel Austin and informed him that his sealed orders were to deliver us to Utapao Air Force Base in Thailand. A little later someone produced a copy of the Far East edition of Stars and Stripes. *Right on the front page was the story of the seizure of the SS* Mayaguez, *an American-flag merchant ship en route to Thailand. Finally we knew where we were going.*

As we landed plane after plane at Utapao we were met by Air Force arrival personnel who asked us to stay near our aircraft while they decided what to do with us. After a while, Lieutenant Colonel Austin hitched a ride to Air Force headquarters to see what was going on. In the meantime, two air force captains—one USAF and the other Thai Air Force—drove up in a blue jeep. They were curious as to who the dirty, heavily armed people were who were standing around in the Thai sun as their aircraft rolled over to refuel and take off again. It turned out that both officers were graduates of Texas A&M University, my alma mater. We all examined each other's rings, shook hands, and introduced ourselves as is customary in Aggie land. The two officers learned of our plight standing in the sun and sped away. Perhaps it was coincidence or Lieutenant Colonel Austin's efforts, but within half an hour guides appeared to take us to a nearby hangar; port-a-potties were staged near the hangar and trailer loads of cots and folding chairs appeared. Most welcome were the containers of ice water. The two captains hovered around us through the afternoon and evening. Anything that we asked them for appeared shortly thereafter. Busses arrived to take us to a mess hall for meals and then the Marines settled down to get some rest.

The Marines were in place and the Marine Expeditionary [MEF] staff from Okinawa arrived; a number of Air Force planning and operational unit commanders and staff also began to arrive. We were about to get serious and figure out what we had to do and how to do it.

The first order of business was to take an airplane ride in an Army U-21 aircraft and see the island for ourselves. Members of the battal-

ion and task force headquarters plus company commanders boarded the Army two-engine aircraft for a first-hand overflight of the island. I remember Lieutenant Colonel Austin and Capt. Jim Davis with me on the flight. There were at least three others, but I do not recall who they were. We already knew that no topographical maps were available. Jim had his little 35-mm camera and he took pictures out the window of the aircraft as we circled the island at a very high altitude. We could see the SS Mayaguez at her anchorage, the general shape of the island, and the oil slicks from the sunken gunboats in the little harbor on the east side of the island. Aside from that we were able to obtain almost no detail but did get a perspective of the lie of the land, where the ship was, and where the harbor lay. This turned out to be very helpful.

After our return to Utapao we met with members of the Air Force at Utapao, coordinators for fixed wing, a brigadier general from General Burns' staff at Nakhon Phanom, air intelligence, and the crew of a C-130 air rescue aircraft. The task force colonel and Lieutenant Colonel Austin took the lead in questions designed to elicit the most information about the circumstances of the seizure of the SS Mayaguez and the situation on the island. No maps and only a few localized photos taken by aircraft were available. Initial estimates were that about sixty to seventy former Royal Khmer Navy personnel from the sunken gunboats and a very few soldiers, believed to be Khmer Rouge, were on the island. All in all, less than a hundred effectives were present on the island. This was based on information given by a Royal Khmer officer who had fled to Thailand. Aerial observation seemed to confirm this.

After we had almost finished with this coordination process, the major operations officer from the task force stopped me in a passageway and let me know that he had received more information about the Khmer on the island. He said that, rather than the "less than one hundred" originally briefed, there appeared to be at least 150. He had no further information about the makeup of the force. I relayed this information to Lieutenant Colonel Austin and our intelligence officer. After the exchange of information about the opposing forces and the assets available to rescue the crew, we returned to our hangar. Once there we set up a briefing board and got down to drafting options and beginning to develop an assault plan.

According to the limited photos and information available to us, and with an overview by Captain Davis' 35-mm photo, we saw that we had four possible LZs [landing zones] on the island. Two were over halfway down the island to the south. One was to the east on the southern side of a small peninsula, another was on the western side (very small, and, it would turn out, the one the command group later went into), a third was on the western side of the northernmost neck of the island, and a fourth was right on top of what appeared to be a small fishing village on the east side of this neck. The two zones to the south were deemed to be too far from the probable location of the captured crew and it would take us too long to land there and then fight our way north. The two zones on the northern neck of the island presented the best opportunity to get on the opposing Khmer quickly and rescue the Mayaguez *crew members while the Khmer were still under pressure.*

Lieutenant Colonel Austin approved the detailed plan and the company commanders began their process of briefing their troops and arranging the logistics of the assault. We had met with the helicopter commanders and with the commander of the C-130. Radio frequencies, call signs, authentication codes, etc. were exchanged. A jump staff of the task force was to be on board the C-130 to coordinate between the battalion assault force, the Air Force assets, and the Navy.

The plan was to time the flight to the island to arrive just before first light. The first aircraft were to land in the zones with the first glimmer of dawn and the troops were to use the first light to secure the immediate landing areas. The battalion headquarters was then to land and set up supporting arms. The plan was for a quick link-up between the forces in the western and eastern zones and to then to quickly begin the search for the crew.

The operation was planned as a raid. We not only planned the assault, but the withdrawal as well. (Later, when things went awry, the company commanders in the western zone executed this almost to the letter.) Sometime late that evening the two assault company commanders reported their preparations complete and troops ready to go in the early morning hours. We all caught a quick nap and got as much rest as possible.

At the appointed time, we moved out to the helicopters and formed up our sticks [groups], ready to board. At about this time the intelligence officer showed up with copies of aerial photos and distributed them to the commanding officer, the company commanders, and me. We were ready to go. We lifted off into the early morning darkness of 15 May, a few minutes late from our planned departure time.

We later learned the C-130 was taken off our mission and instead a C-130 ABCCC [Airborne Command and Control Center] from Nakhon Phanom had been given the mission of coordinating the air and ground assets. Our communications codes, the coordinating staff, and our plans thus never made it to the battle area.

Our departure was selected to have us arrive over Koh Tang Island at first light. The flight was some two hundred forty-six miles. Some of the CH-53s were the air rescue models and had refueling capability; others were cargo support aircraft and had to land to refuel. These latter could not loiter or make more than two passes before having to abort and return to the nearest friendly base for refueling.

During the flight the sea below was invisible in the darkness. After what seemed a long, long time, the crewman gunner who was also near the rear ramp gave me a shake and commenced pointing around the side of the aircraft. As we began turning, he shouted that the first birds were making their approach and that we would be going in behind them. As the aircraft turned, its tail swung from pointing west through south and finally a little east of south. At that moment there was a faint glow of light on the eastern horizon. Within minutes the sun appeared to leap into the sky and it was full light of day.

In this brilliant and clear light the first columns of smoke rose from the eastern side of the island. The first aircraft had closed the island and had been promptly shot down. The crewman told me that another aircraft in the western zone had been hit and was going down. It was 0701.

We caught glimpses of burning aircraft on the eastern side of the island and two other aircraft flying away from the island on the west, and Lieutenant Colonel Austin was faced with a dilemma. Relayed messages from forward in the cargo compartment made it clear that we could not land in either primary zone, east or west. During planning, when we had no maps or charts and only a few copies of a high-altitude photo with which to work, we had identified three other possible LZs on the island: two on the little peninsula on the southeastern side and a small one about 1,200 to 1,500 meters to the south of the western zone.

As soon as he learned that there were troops on the ground and engaged in the western zone, Lieutenant Colonel Austin selected the little zone south of the western primary zone. He was not going to leave his troops on the ground without him.

The pilot approached the zone at a high speed, flared the aircraft, turned it, and commenced to back into the small LZ. The pilot backed the aircraft right into the zone and was chopping branches with his tail rotor. Just as we got ready to jump off the rear ramp and clear to each side of the aircraft, the crewman gunner commenced to chop down trees with his minigun. Before he had finished his long burst, every Marine was off the aircraft and forming a perimeter. The jungle was right up against us and we could not see more than a few feet in front of us. The Gulf of Thailand was to our backs.

As we were taking stock of our situation we could see that a trail led along the waterfront through our little clearing. A quick count determined that only my two S-3 clerks, Branson and Healy, were armed with M-16 rifles. Otherwise, we had an 81-mm mortar section, and an awful lot of .45 caliber pistols.

Lieutenant Colonel Austin made a quick estimate of the situation and we began to move north along the trail. Branson and Healy were point, with me following close behind, and Lieutenant Colonel Austin was just behind me. Behind him came a collection of air liaison officer and party, interpreters, mortar men, and radio operators. A couple of senior NCOs formed the rear guard with their .45s at the ready.

About a hundred meters up the trail the scout/clerks encountered a small, heavily overgrown ravine that the trail went through. On the other side was a typical Southeast Asia field encampment. There was a raised platform with a palapa [thatched] roof and eating and drinking utensils hanging from the poles and rafters. Several fighting holes were positioned around the shelter and oriented toward the sea. Branson moved across and right to cover the area and Healy covered from the other side. When I went into the clearing, no one was visible and so both clerks moved through and to the other side.

On the raised platform were clothing, some U.S. military web gear, a brand new M-16 rifle with bandoliers of ammunition and extra magazines, and the keys, logbook, and some personal letters of the chief engineer of the SS Mayaguez. *The crew was on the island.*

Lieutenant Colonel Austin gained radio contact with the Marines in the western zone. Nothing was heard from the Marines who were supposed to be in the eastern zone. We started to move slowly north. As he spoke with the western group, he directed them to move a party south and link up with us. Shortly thereafter, word was received that the link-up party had encountered an ambush, suffered at least one killed, and was withdrawing to the western LZ perimeter.

The command group became the maneuver group. We were the only ones that could move, and move we did. Within another couple of hundred meters we encountered a larger ravine with the brush cleared around it and a sizeable covered bunker built to cover the trail to the south and the seaward approach. A stream ran through the ravine from the jungle side of the island. Several individual fighting holes were set at the edge of the jungle.

There followed a frustrating period of trying to get the A-7s that were flying support to bomb the bunker and fighting positions. We were too close for their rules of engagement and nothing could budge them. We even moved back thirty or forty meters but we were still too close. Finally one aircraft did drop ordnance into the jungle to our east but air support was now not an option.

Shortly after that we decided that the bunker had to go. Lieutenant Colonel Austin requisitioned my measly two hand grenades and used his baseball expertise to try for the apertures. The Khmer Rouge who had built the bunker knew what they were doing and the bunker stood fast. Finally, with Branson and Healy covering me (I now had the third recaptured M-16), I went down into the water as nearly masked from the bunker as possible and tried to flank the bunker. My reward was to slip on the seaweed of a submerged rock and achieve a double dislocation of my right shoulder. Pressing on and climbing the escarpment to the side and back of the bunker, I saw a black-clad Khmer several feet back in the foliage firing his weapon. As I stuck my head up over the edge of the escarpment, he vanished into a trail that angled off toward the major terrain feature on the island.

That was our only excitement. The bunker proved recently vacated. What turned out to be our only major obstacle was now out of our way but a scout was now on the way to the Khmer forces to announce our presence. We headed north. Lieutenant Colonel Austin was on the radio talking to the western group and they were under probing attacks from the east and southeast.

As the gunfire grew in strength and the western group announced that the Khmer appeared to be massing for a major push, Little Mac, our mortar platoon commander, expended his entire inventory of 81-mm mortar rounds into the trees surrounding the western perimeter. The results, as we found out later, were devastating. Many of our Marines took splinters and some small shrapnel, but the helmeted and armor-vested Marines were unfazed. The lightly clad Khmers, on the other hand, immediately broke contact and pulled back.

At this point, another flight of CH-53s descended on the island with captains Davis and Stahl. They had some of Captain Stahl's company and the remainder of Captain Davis' troops that had turned away because of damage to their helicopter. They had landed in Thailand, were picked up and returned to Utapao, and boarded the second-wave aircraft to join the fight. During this lull, Lieutenant Colonel Austin took the opportunity to push us along at a rapid pace and the link-up was quickly accomplished.

Austin held a quick meeting with the officers in the zone and made some adjustments to their perimeter. Along the way we had also recovered some 60-mm mortars and their munitions. These turned out to be brand new and much better than the battalion's mortars, which had been with the turned-away aircraft and were sorely missed.

As we walked the perimeter and made sketches of who was where and took stock of their armament, we were notified that Staff Sergeant Tuitele was missing on the northern side of the perimeter. Shortly thereafter, the "missing" sergeant appeared from the undergrowth loaded like a mule with ammunition of every sort. He had conducted a little reconnaissance mission and scouted several abandoned positions. He, being a good Marine, was not going to leave anything useful behind. His "resupply" proved very useful as the day wore on and night approached.

During the afternoon I could hear Lieutenant Colonel Austin talking to the ABCCC staff, on a different aircraft than that to which we had entrusted our radio frequencies, codes, names, and organization for combat. This group was from Nakhon Phanom and was now "in charge." I tried to make a standard Marine sitrep [situation report] with which the airman on the other end was totally unfamiliar. After that, I tried a unified service version of the situation report with which he appeared to be more familiar, but which was not suitable to let higher headquarters know of our situation.

Finally Lieutenant Colonel Austin found an air controller who appeared used to working with ground forces and proceeded to request air support and relay what we needed. It was about this time that he was informed that the Mayaguez crew had been returned and that we could withdraw.

I don't remember much for the next few hours. The corpsman had given me a shot to relax me while he and another person reset my shoulder. I stayed pretty much out of focus for the rest of the afternoon and drifted in and out of consciousness.

The next item on our agenda, now that the crew was reported safe, was just how to leave the island. We knew that we had lost more than half the aircraft that had landed us and the second wave, but did not know how many were left flyable or if there were any reinforcements.

As the day of 15 May waned, Lieutenant Colonel Austin gave up on the ABCCC and found an airborne FAC [forward air controller] who spoke the same language. As I recall, he used this FAC (A) to coordinate air support and relay information. At one time I can recall Lieutenant Colonel Austin becoming very adamant that the Marines needed either reinforcements and resupply or "off the island" before nightfall. With nightfall rapidly approaching, we received the word that we would be withdrawn. There was still plenty of light when we saw a huge parachute deploying in the sky above the highest part of the island to our southeast. We all thought that resupply was being dropped and that it was going to land in the Khmer-controlled part of the island.

Our "resupply" turned out to be a behemoth of a bomb, deployed from a C-130 and slowed by parachutes. The resultant blast was crushing in its over-pressure. We all stood around about half-dazed wondering what was going on. After a few minutes of the most profound silence everywhere on the island, the Khmer opened up with everything they had. The first aircraft taking us off the island showed up at about the same time and was being targeted by the Khmer gunners.

The headquarters group, with all the supporting technicians, mortar men, etc., was gathered on the beach behind a ridge of sand and rocks at the high-water mark. The helicopter came in on his approach and commenced his now-familiar turning around movement to back onto the beach.

We loaded the wounded, interpreters, and a few other non-riflemen personnel into the first aircraft. Tracers were zipping through the LZ and bouncing all over the place. Our infantry companies were returning fire and the din was enormous. I checked out with Lieutenant Colonel Austin who was going to stay with captains Davis and Stahl for the final withdrawal and boarded the second aircraft with the last of the non-riflemen. We next met up on board the carrier, USS Coral Sea.

I was taken to sick bay for medical treatment and later Lieutenant Colonel Austin and the other officers went to meet with Admiral

Coogan. I believe Lieutenant McDaniel was in the sick bay with me as well as about two dozen of our Marines.

Another shot from the medical people and more pulling and pushing with my shoulder and I went to sleep. The next thing I knew someone was shaking me and telling me that Lieutenant Colonel Austin had left for Subic Bay and I was in charge. For the next couple of days my working uniform was a set of blue hospital pajamas, a pitcher of water (we were all very dehydrated), and report forms, casualty reports, and muster lists. We were still sorting out where people were and exactly who was missing.

During our repeated formations, weapons inventories, and head counts on the hangar deck of the carrier, I had the opportunity to check many of the Marines' weapons to see if they had been fired. In Vietnam I was often told by other Marine and Army officers that many of their men never fired their weapons, even in close contact. It had also been my personal observation that in reconnaissance units as small as eight men an intense firefight left two or three men who did not discharge their weapons at all. When we were checking the weapons of the Koh Tang raiders we found almost every one had been fired. Only a few of the captured M-16s did not bear evidence of having been fired.

We held a memorial service for our dead and missing on the carrier deck after things settled down. I can still remember the wreath that a chaplain had produced rapidly being left behind as it floated down the side of the carrier and into its long, long wake.

The XO of the ship told me that Admiral Coogan had about worn out the flag bridge deck in his eagerness to reach the vicinity of Koh Tang. The carrier aircraft removed any threat of the Khmer reinforcing the island or otherwise interfering with our withdrawal.

It was interesting to read the accounts of the seizure of the Mayaguez and the U.S. operations to recover her and the crew. In the Stateside papers everything was a failure, we were lucky to be alive, there were repeated references to the "rescue of the Marines." [The comic strip] Doonesbury even had the Marines landing on the "wrong island" in landing craft.

At the end of the day, the Mayaguez *incident was just a footnote to U.S. involvement in Indochina. The footnote, however, was appended to this long chapter in our history with a bang rather than with a whimper. It was only proper that Marines would play a central role and typical that it would be bloody.*

Hendricks retired from the Marines as a lieutenant colonel in December 1984.

PFC. MIKE HENNEN, 3D PLATOON G COMPANY 2/9 MARINES

Michael Hennen was born in Butte, Montana, on 15 February 1956. His father had served with "Chesty" Puller in the 1st Marines at Palalu; when he was eighteen he followed in his father's steps and joined the Marines.

After boot camp at the MCRD in San Diego and advanced infantry training, Hennen was assigned to G Company 2/9, 3d Marine Division, at Okinawa, but found himself detached to C Company 1/9 Marines.

As soon as we arrived at Okinawa, we wound up as a special detachment assigned to Charlie Company 1/9 which was in the middle of rotating back to the States.

About two weeks following the evacuation of our embassy in Vietnam, in late April 1975, I was with my company in the field on a training exercise when we were put on alert. We'd had little sleep in the three days prior and we numbly packed our gear and boarded aircraft, destination unknown.

We landed in Utapao, where we loaded up on grenades and ammunition and waited. Eventually, we loaded up on choppers. I loaded on board Knife-23. It was early morning, still dark, and a very quick intelligence briefing informed us that we were en route to an island called Koh Tang, and that the only opposition would be a small number of Cambodian militia. I remember Staff Sergeant Barschow, an Air Force photographer who accompanied us, tossing me an orange and saying, "This is going to be like taking candy from a baby."

A short time later, the sun began to rise behind us, silhouetting us in the morning sky as we flew over the Mayaguez. *I looked at it as we passed over, headed toward the east beach.*

Pfc. Mike Hennen.
Mike Hennen collection

Our timing was off, as the plan had been to arrive before the sun came up. In the rear, one of the crew test-fired the minigun, the first shots I heard that day.

Suddenly, there was a loud explosion, and I looked out to see Knife-31 on fire and going down. About fifteen seconds later, an RPG hit Knife-23, the chopper I was on, and fuel began spilling from the tail like a waterfall. The tail had been blown completely off the aircraft.

Our chopper went into a wild spin as it fell, and bullets were fly-ing around in all directions as we landed hard on the beach facing the tree line. It was a terrifying, wild ride. Lieutenant Cicere regained his composure and shouted, "Let's go, you Devil Dogs," and, like in the movies, we followed him and charged up the beach.

I was a fire team leader, in charge of three other men. I yelled to Bob Dochniak, one of the guys I was in charge of, "Keep your damn head down. Those bullets are skimming off your helmet!" We advanced about twenty-five yards. The squad leader, LCpl. Larry Bar-nett, yelled, "All right people, they know we're here. Let's do our job!"

We moved ahead another twenty-five yards and set up a perim-eter. I noticed a Cambodian on my right waving toward my platoon, and I thought he was crazy until I realized he was waving at other Cambodians to pinpoint our position.

I put myself and my three men—Dochniak, James Pearson, and a guy we called "Skinner"—into position. Staff Sergeant Barschow had been shot three times, but we couldn't get to him, so we told him to just lay low. He was finally able to crawl into our perimeter, and was treated for his wounds. Dochniak felt a cramp in his ankle, but upon removing his boot discovered that he'd been shot through the ankle.

Meanwhile, that Cambodian on our right continued to pour fire into our position. A staff sergeant (I don't recall his name) had a Marine take a couple shots at the Cambodian, without effect. The staff sergeant then emptied two 30-round magazines, and the other Marine took a couple of more shots, but the Cambodian remained unharmed. Finally, a 2.3 rocket launcher took him out.

Later that day I noticed someone on the wreck of a Cambodian boat offshore, and I called Pearson over to take a couple of shots. Lieutenant Cicere came over to ask what we were firing at. We told him about the Cambodian on the boat, and he called in naval gunfire and we had no more problems from that quarter.

We remained pinned down under fire for most of the day, and we were worn out and exhausted from lack of sleep and adrenaline rush overload. We had no water; even though we each had a C-ration, nobody felt like eating. At one point, Pearson got up to stand behind a tree to take a leak, which drew an enormous amount of enemy fire. After that, the rest of us dug a hole and relieved ourselves while lying on our side. .

In his book, The Last Battle, *author Ralph Wetterhahn stated that we were in dug in positions, but he was in error. There was too much sand and coral for us to dig in. All day long, explosions from bombs, naval guns, jets, and mortars erupted near our positions. Trees fell, and smoke was everywhere.*

At one point, a jet on an air strike run dropped a cluster bomb about ten feet in front of our downed chopper, almost taking out some of us. Fed up with just sitting like a target, and in danger of being overrun, I told Barnett that I was going into the jungle and take out everyone I could or I'd lose my mind. He told me to remain in position, assured me that I was doing a good job, and reminded me that I couldn't lose my mind without his permission.

No *helicopters seemed able to make it into the east beach to extract us, and it looked like we were destined to become POWs. All the other helicopters dropped their Marines on the west beach. The Cambodians had better fortifications on the eastern side and the loss of two helicopters made further insertions inadvisable.*

The lieutenant told us that the Navy was sending something like a captain's boat in to remove us, but that it could only carry ten to twelve of us out. This meant that half of us would have to remain on the beach while the other half was removed. No one wanted to stay behind, but no one wanted to leave other Marines behind, so every man down the line raised his hand to volunteer to stay. If one died, we all would die.

Finally, after about ten hours under fire, a helicopter made its way into position to remove us. As we made our way toward the chopper I told Pearson to pick up Barschow and make his way to the helicopter. I laid back and fired several magazines of M-16 rounds into the tree line because I could hear Cambodians nearing our position.

Daylight was fading and Dochniak, high on morphine, went in the wrong direction and had to be redirected toward the chopper. Concerned about being left behind, I made my way toward the helicopter only to find Pearson lying in the water under Barschow's dead weight. We assisted Barschow into the helicopter that was hovering over the beach by lifting him and literally tossing him inside.

The helicopter was moving up and down anywhere from five to eight feet in the air, and Marines had to time their jump to get on board. Enemy fire seemed to be coming at us from all directions. I recall it was like a slow-motion movie, and I could actually see the rounds hitting the sand.

When it was my turn to board the helicopter, I made my way to the left side, timed my jump, and was pulled on board. Only then did I realize it had taken us only about forty-five seconds to load. I was the last man off the beach, and the helicopter lifted off.

I thought about my last Disneyland ride on board a helicopter and was afraid we'd be shot down again. I didn't relax until we landed on the Coral Sea.

They did a head count and discovered three Marines from Echo Company were missing. There was talk that we were going to go back to the island to get them, but it never happened. This ran counter to a Marine tradition that Marines don't leave Marines behind, but we were told to keep our mouths shut.

Afterwards, it was mostly the officers that received medals, while we just did our job and tried to rescue the crew, then were ordered to keep quiet about the missing Marines, and threatened with courts-martial. There is still a lot of resentment over that among those of us that were there.

Mike Hennen left the Marines in 1976.

LCPL. GABRIEL HERRERA, WEAPONS PLATOON G COMPANY 2/9 MARINES

Gabriel Herrera was born in San Francisco on 19 October 1956. He graduated from Questa High School in May 1974 and enlisted in the USMC in March 1974 under the delay program. He joined the Marines for two reasons: first, his parents were not able to help pay for college, and second, he was influenced by his uncle, a former Marine.

His uncle, Sgt. Maj. Robert Mossman, was a highly decorated Marine who was one of the few enlisted pilots in the Corps who flew under Col. Pappy Boyington in World War II. His medals and the stories of what he accomplished hooked Herrera. Mossman was in the credits of the John Wayne movie *The Flying Leathernecks*. Once, when he landed at Kirtland AFB, he got off the plane and was nearly arrested because he was an enlisted man.

When Herrera joined the Corps, a few of his classmates also joined different branches of the service; two were Leo Archuleta (USMC) and Norman Sanchez (USN). He arrived at boot camp at Camp Pendleton, California, on 2 September 1974.

I enlisted for two years. I was going to be a grunt [infantry] but was classified a 0351 antitank assault-man. After basic and infantry training I went home on leave before my deployment to Okinawa. Upon arrival in California, while standing in line depressed and sad, I met my classmate Leo, who also was on the flight to Okinawa. This was the middle of March 1975.

Also on that flight was Lance Corporal Lutz who was making his second enlistment in the Corps. He was a Vietnam veteran who said he couldn't make it in the real world so he rejoined. His advice then, even though we were supposed to be over all hostile situations, was "listen to your NCOs [noncommissioned officers]." After arriving in Okinawa, Leo went on to Nam and Lance Corporal Lutz and I were on our way to Camp Hansen. As soon as we got there we were told we were on Red Alert. My thought was what the "f" is going on? I didn't sign up for this. We were handed M-16s and live ammunition. We were assigned to "A" Company for Operation Frequent Wind on 12 April which was a pretty uneventful operation, since we remained on board this command ship, mainly on standby off the coast of Cambodia.

Operation Eagle Pull on 15 April was an operation to get the U.S. ambassador to Vietnam, Graham Martin, safely out of the country. We were on board the USS Blue Ridge [LCC-19], which was a command and control ship with enough room for a couple of Hueys at best. During this mission our job was to strip any chopper that landed of all contraband—weapons, liquor, etc. We then pushed them over the side of the ship to ensure that when the ambassador landed there would be sufficient room for his chopper. This operation took thirty days. We watched the fall of Saigon from off the coast. Every night the bombing would be closer and closer. We watched pilots that could not land due to lack of fuel ditch their choppers in the sea, after which Navy boats would rescue them from the water. One chopper hit the side of the ship, which was scary.

In late April, while on leave in Subic Bay, I found out my old classmate, Norman Sanchez, was on board the USS Coral Sea which was docked next to ours. After a ship-to-ship phone call, we went on one of our all-nighters till the Shore Patrol brought us back. Upon arrival back in Okinawa, I was reassigned back to G Company.

We were just a green crew when we went out on a training exercise around 10 May. I recall it was raining that day and we were getting ready to set up two-man tents. It was dark and soaking wet. A clear memory was of Lance Corporal Lutz looking up at the sky and telling us "something's going on." He just had a sort of sixth sense about him. Shortly after that, we were ordered to report back to camp and off we went, dragging all we had through mud and rain to the deuces [trucks] that would take us back.

At daybreak we were again issued weapons, and this time I was handed my bazooka and rounds and off we went on trucks to an airfield from which we flew to Utapo AFB, Thailand. There we slept in the hangar bay not knowing what we were there for or what our mission was. Come daybreak, we were told to muster up. We were told that our mission was to go to a small island and rescue a crew of men from a ship. That's all I heard. Then I was in line to board the chopper.

The sun had not yet risen when we were on our way. There was an eerie feeling with no talk and serious looks from all. All I can remember when descending down toward the island was talk of a chopper that was hit and the fear set in. I remember thinking, "Oh my God, what are we doing?"

I was with Lieutenant McDaniel's group in the first chopper into the west beach. We made a sweep with the rear gunner opening up with all he had, then we turned and dropped down hard onto the beach, and I had impressions of blue water, wind on grass, and bush. We started to exit out of the chopper when the lieutenant told me to fire the three rounds with my bazooka; there, there, and there. Afterwards, I charged off onto the island and ran for cover. I'm not ashamed to tell you I was scared.

I recall F-4 aircraft strafing rounds that I thought was way too close to our positions. There were shells from naval ship support and a big explosion that I now know was the largest conventional bomb in the U.S. arsenal. That explosion shook the whole island.

Afterwards, a calm quiet settled in, and by late afternoon, with darkness setting in, choppers started to extract us out. As it got darker and darker, I started to wonder if and when we would get off this hellhole of an island. It would be quiet, with nothing happening, until a chopper tried to land and then the tracer rounds would start up and we'd return fire. I remember being in the water when that last chop-

per arrived and we were all in line, pushing each other, until we were on board.

The aircraft was vibrating like it was going to fall apart and we were afraid it would be unable to get up into the air. But it did. We landed on the USS Coral Sea, although at that time I did not know or care where I was. All I knew was that it was an aircraft carrier. After all the roll calls we were taken to the chow line where I asked one of the servers what ship this was and he told me it was the Coral Sea. I pulled out my soaking wet wallet and showed him the name and address of my classmate Norman. The server said he'd help find him, then placed a call and not two minutes passed before Norman showed up.

What an emotional reunion. He took me to his quarters, gave me skivvies, and let me sleep in his bunk. Norman was able to call his parents back home and tell them that I was OK. They in turn called my parents. I did not know of this until a few weeks later during mail call. When we were awarded the Combat Action Campaign Ribbon, I remember Lieutenant Colonel Austin making the comment of how young I was. That has stuck with me, as I believe I am still the youngest Vietnam Combat Service Ribbon recipient. Records show the average DOB at the end of Vietnam was 1954, and I was born in 1956.

Herrera was honorably discharged from the Marine Corps in September 1976.

2ND LT. DAN HOFFMAN, WEAPONS PLATOON COMMANDER
G COMPANY 2/9 MARINES

Born and raised in Gary, Indiana, Dan Hoffman enlisted in the Marine Corps after graduating from Purdue in the summer of 1973. He reported for duty on 4 January 1974 for Officer's Candidate School at Quantico, Virginia. Commissioned a second lieutenant on 29 March 1974, he then attended The Basic School [TBS] at Quantico, and was assigned as an infantry officer in October 1974. He requested and was assigned to the 3d Marine Division at Okinawa, and reported for duty on 10 December 1974, assigned to the 2/9 at Camp Schwab.

2nd Lt. Dan Hoffman receiving the Bronze Star. Dan Hoffman collection

After the Mayaguez *was taken, our battalion was hurriedly called up and ordered to report to Kadena Air Force Base for transport by C-141 aircraft to Utapao Air Force Base in Thailand. Not all of the battalion was to leave our home base of Camp Schwab. There were about seven or eight Marines who were only seventeen years old and could not legally be sent into combat. They were told they had to stay back and provide security for our various buildings and equipment. I was originally also scheduled to stay behind but I spoke with the battalion executive officer [XO] and at the last minute was assigned to Golf Company as Weapons Platoon commander. Golf Company was to be the lead company in the operation.*

After a six-hour flight to Thailand, we arrived at Utapao and were shuttled out onto the tarmac. I remember that we were located not far from an SR-71 Blackbird, a super-secret spy plane. We were walking all around it when Air Base Security decided we weren't really supposed to know it was there and shuffled us away.

Early that evening, we were issued live hand grenades and as much ammunition as we could carry. The mood changed to somber and everyone started paying attention.

As an officer, I sat in on the briefings. There were no published orders and intelligence was lacking. The plan was to make two simultaneous amphibious assaults on opposite sides of the north tip of the island. We could not prep the island with fire before we landed because, we were told, the Mayaguez crew was being held there.

We thought we were going up against a few pirates and local fishermen and we had nothing to worry about. Koh Tang Island actually was being defended by a Khmer Rouge battalion of combat-experienced troops that had been fighting in Cambodia for years. Unknown at the time, possession of the island was disputed between Cambodia and Vietnam, and the Khmer Rouge had fortified the island to prevent it being seized by Vietnam.

Golf Company was designated the lead company. We were to go in first with the battalion command element, and Echo Company would come in to reinforce us a couple of hours later. Our forces would be inserted by nine helicopters, which were all of the air assets available. Another three helicopters would carry Marines from Delta Company 1/4 from the Philippines to retake the Mayaguez .

We had no maps, only hand-drawn outlines of the shape of the island. The island had very dense jungle, and the only place helicopters could land was on two narrow strips of rocky beach on opposite sides of the north end of the island. We were to land simultaneously on both the east and west beaches, then sweep into the middle of the island where there were a number of buildings where the Mayaguez crew was supposedly being held, then sweep south through the entire island.

I loaded on Jolly-42, which was supposed to be the third helicopter in on the east beach. It was a long flight, and I remember seeing the other helicopters in flight and watching the sun come up.

I was on an Air Force HH-53 Jolly Green helicopter, which was used for search and rescue [SAR], and I was not trained in assault tactics. Lucky for me I was on a Jolly Green. Several of the other choppers used on the assault were CH-53s [Knives], the difference being the HH-53s had more armor, miniguns instead of M-60 machine guns, and most importantly, self-sealing fuel tanks. The majority of

the casualties in the initial assault were on CH-53s. We were sup-
posed to arrive at dawn but something went wrong; we were late, and
by the time we arrived, the sun was already up. There was no element
of surprise. The enemy knew we were coming. They could see us and
hear us, and they were ready for us. It was an immediate disaster.

On the east beach where my chopper was supposed to go, two
helicopters were immediately shot down. This is where the majority
of our fatalities occurred. Another helo crashed into the ocean off west
beach after they dropped off their Marines. The pilot was attempting
to make a landing but the defensive fire was too intense.

At about 0700 the chopper went in again to attempt another
landing. We were taking a lot of fire. There were holes being shot in
the side of the chopper with the light shining through. The ramp went
down and I charged off. The minigun in the rear of the chopper was
blasting away. There was green and trees in front of me as I came off
the ramp. The water was behind us.

Almost immediately the Marine next to me went down from rifle
fire. His name was David Fowler. As the helicopter lifted off, I had no
idea where the rest of my company was. I was supposed to have land-
ed on the east beach with the majority of our company and six other
helicopters with very little resistance. Instead, I had landed at the
northern end of the west beach and we were coming under heavy fire.
There were, however, other Marines already there giving us defen-
sive fire. I set up a little perimeter, after which I searched around and
found Lieutenant McDaniel and moved over to join forces with him.

His chopper had been the first one in about thirty minutes be-
fore us; his chopper had landed with only twenty Marines on board.
They had been alone and under heavy fire for some time, including
an intense hand grenade battle. McDaniel had a very bloody shrapnel
wound on his right leg when I found him, but he was walking around
and we were glad to see each other. I spread my Marines around and
we were now in a pretty good horseshoe-shaped defensive position
with the beach and water at the base of the horseshoe. McDaniel
had his troops on the south end and I was spread out to the north. It
seems humorous now, but for the first hour on the beach, I had my
directions all screwed up because I thought we had landed on the east

beach. No one told me different, so for the first hour I had my directions reversed, thinking north was south and vice versa.

Landing on the same chopper with me was the company XO, 1st Lt. Dick Keith. He took command of the situation and set up with his radios in the center of our perimeter. In the center of our position was an abandoned grass hut with a roof and trenches dug around it. There was a large quantity of weapons and lots of ammunition. We put several wounded Marines around and in the hooch [hut] with the corpsmen, and I checked the lines. I also distributed some of the captured ammo to our guys. We were taking fire so we just sort of held our position. Choppers were flying in and out, but with the heavy ground fire they were unable to land. But they kept trying.

Keith, in command, was being held down talking on two to three radios pretty much at the same time. Our communications were really messed up: the command and control structure had everyone talking on the same net and it was difficult to get a word in. Dick was trying to call in air support and get additional choppers in. He did a magnificent job that day but he spent way too much of his time giving situation reports telling higher headquarters what was going on rather than doing what needed to be done. This was one of the many mistakes in this operation that would be reviewed and corrected for future operations.

I set up a machine-gun team on the edge of a clearing to face to the south and had two Marines with M-79 grenade launchers. We had lots of captured 20-mm grenade ammo so I had them pepper the jungle in front of them, returning a large amount of fire.

About this time I learned that several of the choppers on the other side of the island had been shot down or crashed, and the knowledge that many of our company were probably dead did not help morale. A close friend who I had been through TBS with, 2nd Lt. Mike Cicere, was pinned down on the east beach with about eighteen guys. Several of them, including some of the crew from the downed helicopter, were wounded, and couldn't maneuver. Getting them safely off the east beach would be a major problem for most of the day. The enemy had them pinned down and was using them for bait. They sat quiet until a helicopter came in to get them out and only then fired on the chopper.

This kind of fire discipline showed how well trained and experienced they were.

Throughout the day, several helicopters attempted to extract the guys on east beach but they were badly shot up, resulting in fewer available choppers to be used in our extraction later. It wasn't until almost dark that the Marines stranded on the east beach were rescued.

Despite the continuous fire, somehow about 0930 a third chopper made it into our LZ [landing zone] on the west beach. It offloaded Marines from 3d Platoon, then rapidly lifted off. They set up in the high grass pretty much in the center of the LZ. The platoon commander was 2nd Lt. Rich Zales, who I went through Officer Candidate School and TBS with. They had been unable to land during the initial assault. The pilot had made several unsuccessful attempts and, low on fuel, flew off to refuel in midair. He finally got it in around 0930.

I had Zales fill in the lines and we strengthened our positions. With Zales' reinforcements, we had about eighty Marines, including some wounded. This was the largest force on the island until the second wave with two platoons from Echo Company came in around 1230 hours. Enemy fire was pretty much continuous.

I kept walking the southern sector of the lines talking to the Marines and resupplying ammo. We had captured large amounts of mostly U.S. ordnance, which of course we could use. Ammo and weapons were never a problem that day but it was very hot and everyone was running out of water. By this time I had armed myself with an M-16. I'd picked it up from one of the wounded. All of the wounded were moved to the hooch in the center of our position but no helicopters could get in to extract them.

Unable to land because of the heavy volume of fire, the battalion command element had been offloaded on the beach about 1,500 yards south of our position. The helicopter had on it the battalion commander, Lt. Col. Randall Austin, the S-3, the FAC [forward air controller], all their radio operators, the battalion doctor and his team, and two tubes of 81-mm mortars and their crews. Additionally, they were hampered by having only three M-16 riflemen with them. It is very hard to fire and maneuver twenty or so Marines with only three riflemen and .45 caliber pistols. Initially they could only hold a defensive position. They eventually started moving north up the beach utilizing what arms they had and effectively using air cover provided by the Navy fighters off the USS Coral Sea.

The fighters were having a difficult time: they couldn't register their targets well because they had little time on station. The Navy fighters were trying to drop their ordnance between our position and the command element that was separated south of us. The command element had been slowly advancing toward our main position. They were directing some of the aircraft and also firing their mortars ahead of them. The problem was the area between our two positions was getting smaller and their advancing fire and the directed aircraft strikes were coming very close to our position. Air support was starting to work better about this time and I somehow got hold of a radioman with a working radio and kept him with me for the rest of the action.

There were heavy bunkers between our position and where the command element was moving up the beach. We took some mortar fire at this time and got a few more wounded. I kept walking the lines bringing up more ammo, mostly machine-gun and M-79 ammo. Somewhere around 1100, I got a call from Lieutenant Colonel Austin. He wanted the LZ cleared. We had pretty much already done that. The command element was slowly moving north toward our position. They had captured a few AK-47s and the 81-mm mortars were firing. The problem was the distance between us was getting smaller and their mortars were getting very close to our position. I remember being under fire, lying down between some large rocks and calling Lieutenant McMenamin on the radio and strongly letting him know that his fire was coming way too close to our lines, and suggesting he cease fire. I wasn't polite and used words my mother would not have appreciated. The mortar fire stopped.

I went to Keith saying we needed to do something. He was bogged down on the radios. I started to grab whoever I could find. I took LCpl. Gilbert Lutz, the radioman I had earlier commandeered. I also grabbed the company first sergeant, Larry Funk. I told him he was now a rifleman and was coming with me. I also grabbed a staff sergeant, Seferino Bernal, who was Lieutenant McDaniel's platoon sergeant, the machine-gun team I had used before as well as one of the M-79 grenadiers and a couple of stray riflemen. I took this composite assault squad of ten Marines to our frontline position and took off south in a wedge formation. The jungle was extremely thick and it was very difficult to advance. We were making a lot of noise but for some reason at that time were not taking fire. I decided we just couldn't effectively move through the thick foliage and signaled for everyone to move west to the beach.

We formed in a single file and proceeded slowly south toward the enemy positions between us and the command element. We were hugging the tree line; it was rocky and uneven terrain with several outcroppings, but at least we were able to maneuver. The water was to our right, but the beach was very narrow and rocky. We slowly headed south with the dense jungle to our left and the water to our right, all the while Navy fighters were trying to drop their ordnance on the enemy positions directly to our front, between us and the command element.

About this time we also came under heavy mortar fire, which I determined was coming from our own mortars; I had them stop firing. I moved my Marines a little farther south and we came upon a point in the island. There was a heavy log bunker with overhead cover and we were taking some fire from it. I advanced closer by crawling along a tree that was lying down along the beach. I signaled to my Marines that I was going to throw a grenade at the bunker, and that after it went off we would all charge through.

Everybody spread out, still lying flat in the sand or behind the one downed palm tree. I stood up, threw the grenade, got back down, and the grenade went off. I stood up and we just got on line and charged through. When we got through the bunker, we found three dead Cambodian KIAs, an M-109 90-mm recoilless rifle, an antitank weapon that could have wreacked havoc on any amphibious landing, and a large quantity of various types of ammunition.

There was also a lot of gear in this bunker. There were at least three AK-47s and two M-16s (the old ones with the three-pronged flash suppressor) stacked up in the bunker. We also captured a U.S.

radio exactly like the kind we were using. Amazingly, it was tuned to the same frequency we were using. They had been listening to our communications. I also kept this radio and carried it back up the beach later.

At about 1230 three things happened almost simultaneously. A second wave of helicopters with reinforcements from Echo Company came in. I know this was right after I captured the bunker because I was using the radio I had just captured. I was talking to the lead helicopter pilot who wanted to know if the LZ was secure. I radioed back that it was secure and to bring them in. At that time there were several officers on the net who were senior to me but I distinctly remember that I was the one who gave the go-ahead to come in.

As that was happening, the command element came up the beach to my position in the bunker. Austin spoke to me and told me I had done a great job and to hold my position until I was relieved. They started to pass through my position. Shortly thereafter Marines from Echo Company came up to my position. At that time I delegated some of my men to help the guys from the command element who were lugging all the heavy ammo and parts for the two 81-mm mortars we had.

Some of my guys asked me if they could go and recover Loney's body. He was the Marine from Trinidad who I had ridden next to when we departed Okinawa. Loney had landed on the first chopper with McDaniel and had been killed early in the morning. Since they said they knew exactly where he was, it was close-by, and the Cambodians seemed to have cleared out, I let six guys go out and bring him back. We tried to take as much of the ammo back with us as we could, especially the M-16 ammo and hand grenades. There was also a lot of M-79 ammo. Before we withdrew north, we destroyed all the ammunition we couldn't carry, throwing it into the water. We also destroyed several AK-47s and numerous three hundred–pound sacks of U.S. #5 milled Louisiana rice.

We then gathered all of our equipment and started back up the beach. I will never forget the little "parade" I led: I was followed by four Marines carrying Loney's body in a poncho, then four Marines lugging the heavy barrel of the 90-mm antitank gun, and then guys

*carrying the tripod for it. We passed through the lines and I met up
with my company commander, Captain Davis.*

He had been supposed to land on the first wave but his helicopter
was badly shot up and couldn't land. It limped away and was forced
to land in Thailand. The Marines and crew were picked up and returned to Utapao. Captain Davis came back in with the second wave
containing Echo Company. Incidentally, even though that chopper
was shot up to prevent enemy use where they left it in Thailand, it
was eventually retrieved and put back in service. That particular helicopter saw combat again in Iraq and Afghanistan, was eventually
retired, and is now a museum piece at Hulbert Field in Florida.

I was very happy to see Captain Davis but that changed quickly
when the first thing I did was give him Loney's dog tag. I had his body
taken to the beach where I was told it would go out on the next chopper. In the confusion in the darkness hours later, his body was never
retrieved. If I had been instructed to ensure his body got on a chopper
I would have carried it on myself.

I walked the perimeter with Austin and Captain Davis and they
had me adjust the positions of some of the machine-gun teams from
Golf Company. The plan at that time was that we were to dig in for
the night. The men were exhausted but I remember them aggressively
digging their fighting holes. The temperature had to be close to 100
degrees with no breeze inland and a very high humidity. Everyone
was soaked in sweat and out of water. We came in with two canteens
apiece and most had been low or out of water for hours.

With the two helicopter loads of reinforcements from Echo Company, we now had about 160 Marines on the west beach. At about
that time I learned that the entire crew of the Mayaguez had been
rescued. They weren't on the island after all. Again, lousy intelligence.
Now the problem was how were we going to get off the island?

Late in the afternoon the air control was greatly improved because of the arrival of OV-10 Bronco aircraft. They were able to stay
on station and made a big difference utilizing the Navy fighters and
the Air Force Spectre planes. After several tries and several helicopters
being shot up, the Marines stranded on the east beach were finally
rescued. That left only our group.

The plan was changed, again, and the word was passed that we would be extracted after dark. The only aircraft available were the remnants of those that had brought us in. They had not trained in making assaults with troops on board. We had started the day with twelve available aircraft but by now most had been shot down or were unable to fly. Those that could still fly were being used judiciously.

I went to the water's edge where members of the 81-mm mortar platoon were throwing rounds out into the water to lighten their load and to prevent them from being captured. As dusk came on, things got real tense. The enemy was well trained and very disciplined. They worked their way up very close to our lines. Echo Company was to be taken out first and they worked their way back to the beach.

As that first helicopter came in to get them, the jungle just roared out with an extremely heavy volume of fire, including heavy machine guns. I remember seeing their tracer rounds, which are green as opposed to the red tracers of the U.S. machine guns. We of course returned fire and it seemed that everyone was shooting all at once. We also had close air support from planes overhead and a small boat that had a couple of machine guns; I learned later it was from the USS Wilson.

The tide was coming in and the little strip of beach, the only place the helicopters could land, was getting pretty narrow. A second chopper came right behind the first and quickly left, leaving our force that much smaller.

We began reducing the size of our position. We were basically in a defensive perimeter shaped like a horseshoe. The enemy jungle was to our front and the water was behind us. We had no place else to go. We could only wait for the next available helicopter and hope that it wouldn't be shot down like so many before it.

We pulled back into a tighter position, leaving our somewhat well-built defensive positions and foxholes as we pulled back toward the beach. It didn't take long for the enemy to move up into our old positions. It was a very dark night. No moon or starlight. It was overcast and visibility was poor. We did not have any night vision devices. The biggest problem now became the number of helicopters able to remain flying. The majority of those that had brought us in were shot down or were damaged so badly they couldn't be repaired fast enough to be flight-worthy. The ones coming in now were also sustaining damage.

The other problem was time. The aircraft carrier USS Coral Sea was by now about a twenty-minute flight away, a minimum forty-five–minute turnaround time. After the two helicopters left with most of Echo Company, we knew we had to sit still for about an hour. By now the enemy, realizing our situation, was continuously firing at us. We sustained a few more wounded and our numbers were getting smaller.

After the second helicopter came in and then left, Captain Davis told me to get out on the next one. I moved closer to the beach, taking my radioman with me. It was about 1900 hours. I had been on the island for exactly twelve hours. You couldn't see the chopper but you could hear it. The helicopter of course did not have any of his lights on, and needless to say there was not a guy with lights or flags standing up trying to direct him in. As the chopper got closer, the enemy started firing at it. There was so much fire I don't know how it stayed up. There was a rapid-fire machine gun on the chopper and it was really putting out some fire. The pilot of the aircraft was Lt. Robert Blough, USAF. His call sign was Jolly-44 Alpha. He brought his helicopter in parallel to the beach and I ran to get on the rear ramp. The problem was that after the tide came in, the beach was so narrow he would have had to set his chopper down almost in the water. He didn't really put it down but hovered and the ramp was going up and down as the helicopter moved with the wind and the waves.

I went out into the surf about waist deep. As I tried to pull myself up on the ramp, I was so weak from the whole day that I didn't have the strength to pull myself up the first try. I managed to crawl up the ramp still carrying my M-16, and the helicopter lifted off. I was in the rear of the chopper with a good view as we pulled out. I couldn't believe the amount of fire coming at us and didn't think we would make it, and was very worried for those still down there. He did manage to pull it out and up. I later learned that there were thirty-five Marines taken out on that load. Normal maximum load for weight and safety reasons is twenty-five Marines, so the chopper was really loaded.

As we pulled away and started to get out of range of the enemy fire a cheer went up as we realized we had made it out of there. Guys were slapping each other on the back and hugging each other, and some were crying for joy. We had made it.

There was a mount-out box on board the chopper and the crew chief was passing around some ice cubes. With the roar of the two engines it was hard to hear, but he was apologizing as he passed out the ice. They had brought cans of coke but the previous load had drank them all. I dug in with my filthy hands. We all sucked and chewed on those ice cubes. I hadn't had anything to drink for hours and was very dry. To this day it was the very best ice I have ever had.

We had just settled down, exhausted, knowing the Coral Sea *was about a twenty-minute flight away. I was sitting near the rear of the aircraft and could see out over the rear ramp. I could see an occasional white wave in the water below. I would guess we were flying at about five hundred feet above the water. It was very dark and I couldn't see much. Once we left the vicinity of Koh Tang there were no other planes or ships. We were alone in the sky.*

Suddenly the chopper started to shake and vibrate violently as the aircraft shifted left and right. I knew we had not been airborne long enough to be near the USS Coral Sea, *the aircraft carrier that all the flights were being taken to. The aircraft kept maneuvering and I was convinced we were going down into the ocean.*

I started to warn those sitting near me to take off their helmets and flak jackets so we wouldn't drown. As I was getting ready to dive out the rear ramp I was grabbed and turned around by the helicopter crew chief and literally pushed to the front of the chopper.

There is a small door on the right side of the aircraft behind the copilot. I got to the door and braced myself as I jumped out expecting to land in the water. Instead I landed hard onto the deck of a ship. It was pitch black but I could see a few red lights and a sailor with a flight-ops plastic helmet on. He directed me to follow the rest to a nearby hatch. By now I had figured out we were on a ship and learned it was the USS Harold E. Holt, *a destroyer escort also called a fast frigate. It is an ocean-going vessel but one of the smaller warships in the Navy.*

The Holt *was not configured to have any troops on board and we had to be a scary sight, all wet and dirty, with all our weapons, live ammo, grenades, and machine guns. There were several wounded Marines, some with fresh wounds received during our extraction, and some who had been treated on the island. I saw that they got to the sick bay on the ship.*

It wasn't until later that I learned the details of our miraculous landing on this ship. The HH-53 is a very large helicopter and the Holt *had a very small landing pad. The pilot had inched his aircraft onto the landing pad, carefully avoiding the various masts and towers of the ship. If the rotor blades had touched anything it would have been disastrous. He had to put the helo down with his front wheels in one corner of the small landing pad and his two main wheels in opposite corners, basically sitting down on a 45-degree angle on the deck. The helicopter was so much larger than the landing pad that the rear ramp actually hung out over the ocean. It was the most amazing feat of flying I have ever seen or heard of.*

The pilot had been told his aircraft was too heavy and the ship couldn't take the weight of the loaded helicopter even if he could fit it on the ship. What he did was to maintain 50 percent power on his engines after he set it down so as to not put too much weight down on the deck. We Marines were offloaded while he was keeping his aircraft centered on a small landing pad, flying forward at a 45-degree angle. All this was done in complete darkness with no lights, while the wind was blowing, the waves were moving the ship up and down, while the ship was under way in a combat zone.

This unbelievable pilot held his aircraft stationary long enough for thirty-five Marines to offload, several of whom were wounded. Then, after all that, he flew back to the island under intense fire to land in the surf and pick up thirty-seven more Marines. When asked if he would attempt to offload again on the Holt, *he said he couldn't be that crazy again. He had in fact received several more hits to the aircraft from enemy fire and had taken on salt water into his engines and was concerned about engine power. They did make it to the Coral Sea.*

Blough's heroic actions that day saved the lives of more than seventy Marines. If not for his amazing feats of flying, which enabled a quick turnaround to go back for a second load of Marines, I am convinced there would be many more names on the Vietnam Memorial Wall from that day. Afterwards he was severely chastised by senior officers for his reckless actions. Later, back on Okinawa, we Marines heard he was awarded the Air Force Cross for his actions and we were upset because we believed he deserved the Congressional Medal of Honor. In fact, to penalize him for his "reckless" behavior, he was shortchanged by his superiors and only recommended for the Silver Star.

Despite terrible intelligence, a hastily thrown-together operation utilizing inexperienced troops, and initially poor air support with unbelievable communication and command-and-control problems, the mission was accomplished. The Mayaguez *and her entire crew of forty-one were rescued.*

It was extremely harrowing for the last helicopter out. Somehow in the confusion a three-man machine-gun team from Echo Company did not make it out. Marines ended up on three ships, and some returned to Thailand. So once we were all off the island we had several head counts until it was determined these three Marines were missing, and that Lance Corporal Loney's body had been left on the beach. We Marines believe very strongly that we leave no man behind, so we were very concerned about this.

I was one of the few Marine officers with those taken to the Holt *and I remember being on the bridge with the ship's captain through all of this. At one point there was a discussion of sending in a Navy SEAL [U.S. Navy Sea, Air, and Land] team of scuba divers the next morning. I was not a trained military diver but had done quite a lot of recreational diving and volunteered to go in with them. I know that my going back in the next day was seriously considered because I knew the layout of the beach positions. The SEALs did not go in because superiors were concerned with the possibility of the loss of more lives.*

After much discussion, the opinion was passed that the missing machine-gun team from Echo Company had to have been killed dur-

ing the extraction or else they would have tried to get out. Their sta-
tus has never officially been determined.

When we returned back to Okinawa there was an investigation
looking for answers. We were told then that they probably all had
been killed by a grenade during the early part of the extraction. It
wasn't until after the publication of a book by Paul Wetterhan that
I learned that the three may have been captured and killed by the
Khmer Rouge.

Hoffman was awarded a Bronze Star for his actions on Koh Tang and
was honorably discharged from the Marine Corps in November 1978.

1ST LT. DICK KEITH, EXECUTIVE OFFICER, G COMPANY 2/9 MARINES

Dick Keith was born in Monroe, Louisiana, on 25 November 1948. He
attended Northeast Louisiana University on a baseball scholarship, where
he completed the Marine Officer Candidate School through the Platoon
Leaders Class (PLC) program. After graduating in January 1971, Keith
was commissioned a second lieutenant in the Marines. Originally enrolled
in the aviation program, Keith decided to change to ground officer; he was
ordered to Quantico, Virginia, to attend The Basic School [TBS].

In December 1974 Lieutenant Keith was assigned to the 3d Marine
Division in Okinawa for a thirteen-month tour. Following a temporary
duty assignment at division headquarters he was assigned to the 2/9.

I reported on board the 2/9 in early May 1975. At that time, op-
erational units of the 3d Marine Division were stretched very thin
in dealing with the aftermath of the fall of Saigon and Phnom Penh.
Upon my arrival I was assigned as the XO [executive officer] of Golf
Company commanded by Capt. Jim Davis.

2/9 was in the process of being reformed and was beginning
lock-on training prior to its scheduled period of deployment. Golf
Company, like the other rifle companies of 2/9, was very young and
inexperienced, with some squads having corporals and lance corpo-
rals as squad leaders.

Around 11 or 12 May the company went out to the Northern
Training Area in Okinawa to begin its first week of squad tactics

training. The ninety-day training syllabus prior to deployment would progress from squad tactics to company tactics. This week began the initial phase of the training. While the company went out to the field I remained at the company area with 1st Sgt. Lawrence Funk and company office staff to take care of administrative matters.

On 13 May in Captain Davis' absence I attended the weekly battalion commanders' conference and was briefed that the battalion had been placed on standby due to some activity that was occurring. The capture of a U.S. merchant ship by the Cambodian Khmer Rouge was mentioned, but there were very few details. I was left with the impression that, due to our battalion not being operationally ready, we might deploy to relieve an operationally ready unit of some security duty. This would free that unit to respond to the Cambodian threat. Based on that information we began the administrative work of preparing deployment rosters.

After dinner that evening, I went out for a run, planning to return to the company office afterward and continue working with the first sergeant and the company office staff. As I ran by the battalion headquarters, a Marine ran out and told me to report to Major Hendricks, the battalion operations officer, right away. I went directly in and saw Major Hendricks, who told me that the companies were being brought in from the field and the battalion was being deployed to Thailand immediately to await further orders. Still in my workout gear, I went directly to the company office where we frantically began preparing for deployment.

Late that evening the company returned from the field. By the time the company arrived, First Sergeant Funk and I had prepared a tentative deployment roster identifying those Marines who for some reason or another would be left behind and those who would make the deployment. This task was somewhat difficult for me because I had only been with the command for a little over a week; I knew the officers but very few of the enlisted Marines. Shortly after midnight I was able to return to my room to change into uniform and grab my gear.

At approximately 0200 the company began loading into trucks for transport to Kadena Air Force Base. During the trip I was sitting

*next to a young Marine named LCpl. Gregory Copenhaver. He was
a tall lanky southern kid who you just had to like. He was telling me
that he had just returned from a TDY [temporary duty] assignment
on board a merchant ship that had picked up Vietnamese refugees
escaping from the Communist takeover of Vietnam. He was very excited as he talked of his experience. I told him that having already
done that, if we deployed into action he would be wearing all kinds
of medals when he went home. He got this huge grin on his face as he
thought of that possibility and we laughed.*

*We arrived at Kadena in the early morning hours and began load-
ing onto KC-130s and KC-141s [transport aircraft] for transport to
Utapao. It took some time for the loading of the full battalion. Captain Davis departed with part of the company in one of the early
flights and I left with the remainder of the company on a flight later
that morning. Although I had not had any sleep for more than twenty-
four hours, I was unable to sleep on the flight to Utapao.*

*At approximately 1500 hours we landed at Utapao. I was amazed
at how hot it was as we walked across the airstrip. Captain Davis
greeted me when we got to the hangar area. He told me that the
Cambodian Khmer Rouge had captured a U.S. merchant ship and
U.S. intelligence believed the crew was being held on an island off the
coast of Cambodia. He told me that Golf Company had been selected
to make a heliborne assault of the island to locate and recover the
crew. He said he was going on a reconnaissance flight over the island
and directed me to begin preparing the company for the operation.*

*I quickly found the area where Golf Company was being staged.
I briefed the platoon commanders—three second lieutenants, Jim
McDaniel, Mike Cicere, and Rich Zales—as well as the senior staff
NCOs of the company. We assigned elements of the Weapons Pla-
toon to the Rifle Platoon and they began conducting gun drills on the
tarmac of the airstrip.*

*Several hours later, Captain Davis returned and briefed us on his
reconnaissance flight over Koh Tang Island, the island on which they
believed the crew was being held. He told us there were no aerial
photos available so he took photos of the island with his personal
35-mm camera and the film was being developed. He again told us*

Golf Company had been selected to make the assault and the assault would be made on board U.S. Air Force helicopters because there were no Marine helicopters available.

Later that evening the officers of 2/9 attended an operational briefing. It was held in a large briefing room that was packed with both Marine and Air Force officers. The senior Air Force officer conducting the briefing started off by saying that the briefing was classified Top Secret and anyone not holding that clearance would have to leave the room. That was pretty comical because at the Marine company level the officers hold only a Secret clearance. So there we were, the officers that would actually be conducting the assault, being asked to leave the briefing. I can't remember if the briefing classification was downgraded and we were allowed to stay or whether we were briefed later on a need-to-know basis. I really didn't care about the big picture stuff. I only cared about our battalion briefing that was to come later that evening. It was at this briefing that we received the operations plan for the assault.

In essence, we were briefed that the SS Mayaguez had been seized by the Cambodian Khmer Rouge and the vessel was now moored one mile from Koh Tang Island. A company from the 4th Marines had been assigned to make an "over the rail" assault of the ship and seize the vessel. Simultaneously, 2/9 had been assigned to make a helicopter assault of the island to search for and recover the crew. The number of Air Force helicopters was limited, so the initial assault would be restricted to Golf Company and an element of 2/9 headquarters led by Lt. Col. Randy Austin, 2/9 battalion commander.

The assault was to begin at first light to give some element of surprise and have the rising sun to the back of the assaulting element. Captain Davis would insert with the 1st Platoon under the command of Second Lieutenant McDaniel on the west side of the island. I was to go into the eastern side of the island with the second platoon under the command of Second Lieutenant Zales; the third platoon was under the command of Second Lieutenant Cicere. Lieutenant Colonel Austin and the battalion command group would also be inserted into the eastern LZ [landing zone].

Upon securing the LZ, the two groups would then link up in the center of the island. Lieutenant Colonel Austin would move with the second and third platoons and sweep the southern part of the island. Captain Davis would move with the first platoon and sweep the northern part of the island. I was to remain with a small force to maintain security of the main LZ on the eastern side and to direct reinforcements as they arrived. Once Golf Company was inserted, the helicopters were to return to Utapao to pick up and return with Echo Company as reinforcements. Turnaround time would be approximately five hours.

The intelligence part of the briefing was later proven to be totally off the mark and almost disastrous to the mission. We were briefed that the island was defended by approximately thirty elderly irregular enemy troops who would probably lay down their weapons when we arrived. We had Army interpreters assigned to the assault force to interrogate them upon their surrender. One senior officer made the statement that it should be a "cakewalk." If so, he must have been referring to devil's food cake, because all hell was going to break loose.

I was given the task of forming teams and assigning them to helicopters for the initial wave. We had two types of helicopters— the Jolly Green HH-53s and Knife CH-53s; these had different load capacities. I worked with our battalion air liaison officers throughout the evening on this task.

At midnight the company gathered to pass out the ammunition. This is when it really hit home, when live ammo was being passed out and we were being asked how many grenades we wanted. We knew then that this was no training exercise.

We continued our preparations and moved to the airstrip at around 0200 for what was to be an 0400 launch. The 0400 launch would get us to the island right at daylight. Sometime during this staging period I was advised that either a helicopter had been scratched or one had been added and I had to make last-minute adjustments to the helicopter teams.

I finally made it to where my team was staged and laid down on my pack for a few moments of rest. It had been about two days *since I had last slept. I remember someone walking up and asking if everything was okay. From my prone position I reached out, grabbed the interloper's boot and told him I had everything under control so go away. That interloper turned out to be Lieutenant Colonel Austin. He laughed, tapped me on the helmet, and told me just to stand by.*

We waited and waited. I knew that it was a two and a half–hour flight to the island and every minute we stayed on the airstrip would be a minute of darkness wasted. Finally, the word came down that Henry Kissinger had approved the launch. No disrespect to President Ford, but I distinctly remember that the word to go had been passed down by Secretary Kissinger. Go figure: here we were in Thailand with an operation order issued and we were waiting for go-ahead from the secretary of state. Every moment wasted placed us in greater danger.

Finally we were in flight, headed for our objective. With all the thoughts that were running through my mind I knew that the two and a half–hour flight would go very quickly. It did, especially since we were refueled in flight by a C-130. I went up to the cockpit and watched the refueling operation as the C-130 dropped a fuel line and the helicopter connected with it.

Later, I was summoned to the cockpit area and given a headset to talk with the pilots. The door gunner on the chopper let loose with a few rounds from his minigun as he prepared for the assault. That blast awoke all our sleeping Marines or those who had been trying to sleep. Everyone knew then that the time to commence the assault was upon us.

Unfortunately, by the time of our arrival it was daylight and we had missed the opportunity for a surprise assault. We could see the island as we flew toward it. There were several helicopters in front of our chopper as we closed in. Suddenly I saw a helicopter about two hundred meters in front of us burst into a red ball of flame. I saw another chopper go into the water. A missile or RPG shot below us. The pilot pulled out and told me that the LZ was too hot to get into. I told him to take us into the western LZ. We pulled out and headed over the island to the western LZ.

As we came into the western LZ, we began taking lots of small arms fire. The back ramp of the chopper opened. Rounds were impacting into the chopper and I knew we had to get out quickly. I yelled for everyone to go. We ran off into a dense field of grass and brush with rounds from automatic weapons whistling by. The Marine in front of me went down with a gunshot wound. I pulled him to cover and grabbed the next Marine close by to take care of him.

I continued forward dispersing my Marines toward the threat. The helicopter pulled out and the fire died down. I then linked up with Second Lieutenant McDaniel. He advised me that his helicopter was the first to get in. He said that Captain Davis' chopper had tried to get in but was shot up too bad and had crashed at sea. He feared Captain Davis was dead.

Very soon thereafter another chopper attempted to come into the LZ. This helicopter contained Lieutenant Colonel Austin and the battalion command group. When the chopper attempted to land, a machine gun positioned to the north of the LZ opened fire, driving it out. The chopper then proceeded south, setting down approximately two thousand meters from our position, and inserted the command group.

I immediately sent staff sergeants Tuitele and Bernal to establish the northern part of our defensive perimeter of the LZ and neutralize the enemy machine-gun position.

I then raised Lieutenant Colonel Austin on the radio and confirmed that he had successfully been inserted. He advised me that his group would be working its way to our position. At that time we were receiving very light fire from the southern part of our perimeter. I directed Lieutenant McDaniel to take a squad and move south to link up with Lieutenant Colonel Austin's group and lead them back into our perimeter.

A very short time later, I heard automatic weapon fire and grenades in the area that Lieutenant McDaniel had moved out into. I moved down toward that area and located Lieutenant McDaniel and found that his patrol had run into a machine-gun position and had to fall back. He advised me that Lance Corporal Loney had been killed and several others had been wounded. Lieutenant McDaniel had himself been wounded by grenade shrapnel.

Marines disembark from CH-53 helicopter during assault on Koh Tang Island.
U.S. Air Force

*We began to quickly organize the defense of our southern pe-
rimeter because we knew we were exposed to a sizeable threat from
the south. As expected, we received an assault from the south as the
Khmers tried to exploit our weakness. We were able to beat back
this assault, but the Khmers had moved to positions within fifteen
to twenty meters of us, separated only by thick vegetation. We were
trading small-arms fire and grenades but could see very little. Another
chopper, which contained Lieutenant Zales and his 2d Platoon, tried
to insert but was driven off by the intense fire as the enemy machine-
gun position to our south opened fire.*

*I moved back toward the center of our perimeter to assess our
position: We had set up a 180-degree defensive perimeter with our
backs to the ocean. We had a machine-gun position bearing down on
us from the north and a machine-gun position bearing down on us
from the south. We had only about fifty Marines and were obviously
outnumbered. Lieutenant Colonel Austin's group, about two thousand meters to the south, was trying to work its way to us. We had*

Lieutenant Zales' platoon trying to get in but unable to do so. We had no radio contact with anyone on the eastern side and presumed the worst, having seen the choppers go down. Our company commander was presumed to be down at sea. It would be at least five hours before we could expect reinforcements, and even that would be limited because of the number of helicopter losses. We were badly outnumbered by an enemy fighting out of fortified positions. I thought of those training films we saw at TBS where they develop a really bad scenario and then ask, "What now, lieutenant?"

Quite frankly it was at this point that training took over. My mind began running at about one hundred miles an hour and would do so for about the next five or six hours.

I first made radio contact with Lieutenant Colonel Austin and reassessed their position. I then contacted the Airborne Command and Control Center [ABCCC], flying overhead in a C-130 aircraft, to provide them an assessment of our position. The ABCCC was our higher headquarters and would be our lifeline.

Radio security was a concern because I didn't want the Cambodians to know how fragmented we were and what a dire situation we were in. I still had to get that point across to the ABCCC. In order to impress upon them that things were not going particularly well, I used my individual call sign, "Bingo Shoes Golf Five," which should have indicated to them that the 2/9 Golf Company XO was in command of the main LZ rather than the battalion commander or company commander. It also struck me that "Bingo Shoes" was a really goofy call sign to have in such a situation.

At the time I did not know that the chopper I had seen engulfed in flames had crashed into the surf line. Some survivors swam to sea. LCpl. Gregory Copenhaver, badly burned, had advanced toward the beach and been cut down by enemy fire.

The other chopper I saw go down contained Lieutenant Cicere and his platoon. They were able to escape the wreckage and establish a defensive position on the eastern side. Their radios were lost in the crash and we had no contact with them to know they had survived and were there.

I established that we had flights of Air Force jets, call sign Spectre, available to provide close air support. I grabbed a third radio, dialed in the air frequency, and began working with the flight leader. We had to establish the location of our perimeter so they could provide us with support. This was very difficult because I could not mark our lines but only talk them through dry runs until I felt secure enough to have them drop ordnance in front of our lines. The only ordnance the aircraft had was 40-mm rockets and five hundred–pound bombs. It was really dicey calling for five hundred pounders so close to our position without it being well marked. They could only make a couple of runs and then had to be replaced on station with another flight. We would then have to go through the entire process again with the next flight. This process continued throughout the morning.

The chopper containing Lieutenant Zales and his platoon continued to try to insert. The Khmers were exercising extremely good fire discipline: they would hold their fire until the helicopter got into the zone and then open up, driving it out of the zone. Lieutenant Zales and his platoon finally got in about 0930 on his fourth attempt.

I immediately directed Lieutenant Zales and his platoon to the southern half of the perimeter, which was where we were at our weakest. It gave me some hope that we would be able to buy enough time to be reinforced. However, as the morning progressed we began to run dangerously low on ammunition.

Our intelligence had been terrible, we were fighting for our lives against a force that outnumbered us, and on their turf. Amazingly enough, we never gave this any thought as we did whatever we could to even the sides.

Around noon I saw a beautiful sight as I spotted a flight of helicopters coming in from the horizon. They made radio contact with me and asked if the LZ was secure. I knew they were able to hear automatic weapons fire and grenades going off in the background, so about the only reply I could make to them was "Not really." The flight leader told me that they could not try an insertion without the zone being secure. I knew that they had already suffered heavy losses and battle damage so they couldn't take much more damage. However, I couldn't see the situation in the LZ getting any better.

My heart sank as I saw the choppers flying back toward the horizon and was told that they had to break off. I did not realize at the time that the White House had directed that all offensive action cease. Someone, somewhere, had given them the order to return to base. Here I was thinking it must have been something I said.

At about the same time, Lieutenant Colonel Austin and his command group had worked its way along the beach close enough to us that we could try another link-up. We devised a plan over the radio that we would run an air strike between our positions, followed by a mortar barrage from the mortar section that was with his group, and then followed by an assault by Lieutenant Zales' platoon toward the south. A group led by Lt. Dan Hoffman would try to link up with Lieutenant Colonel Austin's command element along the beach area. Tactics training in TBS had taught us that when there was absolutely nothing else to do in a situation—assault. I always thought that seemed pretty stupid, but today it made total sense.

The first order of business was to establish the line between our positions for the air strike. Our battalion air liaison officer, Capt. Barry Cassidy, was with Lieutenant Colonel Austin's command group. We began working together in directing the flyovers until they appeared to have a wingtip over the edge of his group and a wingtip over the edge of our perimeter. Once we felt we had our lines established we had the jets go back on station until we called them in for a hot run.

I then began working with Lt. Joe McMenamin, who commanded the mortar section. He had a limited number of rounds so we couldn't waste many rounds sighting them in. It was also very delicate: he would be firing his mortars directly toward our position and we would suffer casualties from any long round. I had him fire one round into the ocean and gave him an adjustment from there. Based on that adjustment and from what he saw from his position he developed his firing data.

As we prepared to execute the link-up plan, we got a radio call that the helicopters containing reinforcements were returning and would be inbound shortly. It all came together at just the right time.

I called for the air strikes and the aircraft rolled in right on target, dropping their loads. As soon as they cleared, Lieutenant McMenamin's mortars fired for effect. Again, right on target! As soon as his barrage lifted, I gave Lieutenant Zales the order to assault, which he and his platoon did. They quickly routed the Cambodians in front of them, who were taken totally by surprise.

Right behind the assault the choppers began landing with reinforcements from Echo Company and with our badly needed resupply. I remember seeing Lieutenant Colonel Austin coming across the open area of the LZ. I ran up to him to report and he grabbed my helmet, pulled my head to his shoulder, and said, "Good job, kid." I will never forget that moment.

Right after seeing Lieutenant Colonel Austin I got a great surprise. Captain Davis and his Marines had come in with Echo Company. During the initial assault his chopper sustained heavy damage and had to pull out. They limped back to the Thai mainland where the chopper had to put down. They were picked up by a rescue chopper and brought back to Utapao. He and his Marines immediately loaded onto another chopper and flew back to Koh Tang with Echo Company.

I had begun assisting Captain Davis in resetting the perimeter when Lieutenant Colonel Austin called for me. He told me our operations officer, Major Hendricks, had been injured during the link-up and he wanted me to assist Major Hendricks as the operations officer. I told him that, with all due respect, I would rather return to Golf Company and assist Captain Davis. However, because of the varied communication lines I had established during the morning, Lieutenant Colonel Austin was adamant that I remain and assist him with operations.

The situation had greatly changed by then. We were approximately two hundred Marines strong, set in a 180-foot perimeter, with our backs to the ocean. The Khmers had been routed and we had an OV-10 on station, which had taken over coordinating air support. We had a steady stream of air working out in front of us. Life was good.

However, we did not know what we were to do next. We knew that the crew of the Mayaguez had been recovered and it had been directed that all offensive action cease. The problem was that we were on a very small island; there was no place for the Khmers to go, no place for us to go, and we had been trying to kill each other all day.

Lieutenant Colonel Austin radioed for orders. Captain Davis and Golf Company GySgt. Lester McNemar lobbied to continue the attack. I had gotten tired of the whole thing and just wanted to get some sleep. I laid back for a little rest and fell asleep.

I'm not sure how much time passed but I remember when I woke up there was a lot of activity. ABCCC had advised that there were survivors from the crashes on the eastern side of the island and they were sending choppers in to extract them. They also had advised us to prepare for extraction. Lieutenant Colonel Austin very emphatically advised higher headquarters that he would only agree to extraction if he were assured that, once commenced, the extraction would not cease until all Marines were out. He knew that if we stayed the battle would be decided during the night and we were prepared to fight it out. He would not chance diminishing our numbers by an extraction that could not be completed. It was all or nothing.

We prepared for the possibility of extraction by issuing an order for retrograde. It was very simple: As choppers landed in the LZ, the flanks of the perimeter would pull in, Marines would load, and the perimeter would shrink back toward the ocean. This would continue until all Marines were extracted out.

All of a sudden there was a huge explosion and the island shook. Captain Cassidy, our air officer, got on the radio to find out what had happened. He was told that they had just dropped a pallet bomb to blow an emergency LZ for us to use if we got overrun. Nobody knew what a pallet bomb was. We looked up and saw a pallet hanging from a parachute drifting our way. All we thought was, Here comes another one. As it drifted closer and closer we started digging into the sand to get as low as possible. We just knew this was it. We were going to be taken out by our own bomb. It floated over us and went down into the trees about forty or fifty meters in front of us. I thought to myself, "It's a dud. I hope nobody tries to screw with it." We later figured out it was just the pallet the bomb had slid off of. We lived to fight another day.

In the late afternoon radio activity picked up as they began to conduct extractions of survivors on the eastern side of the island. We had never at any point had radio contact with them because they had lost their Marine tactical radio capability early on. I understand that they did have an Air Force radio capability but their situation had never been relayed to us. Had it been, we would have moved to link up with them when we routed the Khmers during our link-up with Lieutenant Colonel Austin.

We got a radio transmission that they were going to cover the eastern side extraction by dropping tear gas and advised us to don gas masks. We put our gas masks on and watched to the north as a chopper flew by spewing a cloud of gas behind it. Good plan. Poor execution. The wind was blowing toward the north and the gas floated harmlessly out to sea.

Finally we got word that the extraction from the eastern side was successful and to prepare for our extraction. Lieutenant Colonel Austin got back on the radio and reiterated his position that we would extract only if he were assured the extraction would continue until all Marines were out. He was given this assurance.

We could see the USS Holt offshore and established radio contact. We were told they would be sending out a gig, call sign Black Velvet-1, with automatic weapon capability to help cover our extraction. We told them to stand by for recovery if things got too hot and we had to hit the water.

Just before dark the first chopper came into the zone. I moved down to the beach area to talk them in and assist in the onloading. The chopper landed in a rocky shoal area just off the beach. During the onload I saw a group of Marines carrying Lance Corporal Loney's body through the knee-deep water to the chopper. I later learned that several of the Marines got hit and his body never made it to the chopper.

The first chopper came in right at dusk, and soon after it departed a moonless night fell. It was so dark you could not see your hand in *front of your face. We began taking heavy fire and tracers lit the sky. It was a pretty spectacular display. We also were taking incoming from mortars. I continued to talk to the inbound choppers as I made my way back to the command group.*

The extraction was moving quickly as choppers came in and the perimeter was closing down as planned. A chopper landed about forty meters to the south of us and Lieutenant Colonel Austin yelled that this one was ours and sent us toward the chopper. I got to the rear of the chopper and Marines were stacking up. We began throwing Marines toward the front as the chopper just stayed there on the ground allowing more Marines to board. Rounds were ricocheting around the chopper and I felt it was a matter of time before it would blow. We finally lifted out, packed with more than fifty combat-loaded Marines. It far exceeded what I believed to be the chopper's load capability. Those pilots and crew had a lot of guts to stay in that LZ for as long as they did to get as many Marines out as they could. We owe them our lives.

We flew off the island, and when we got safely out of range I felt a great sense of relief until I realized that we had a long flight to Utapao and we had received extensive damage. The crew chief began passing out life jackets, of which there were very few. Those went to the Marines who were nonswimmers. After about fifteen or twenty minutes the crew chief motioned to me that we were going down and I felt the chopper begin to lose altitude. I thought to myself "Yeah, this is about right considering how our day has been going. Now we're going swimming." I made my way to the door not far away to see how far up we were from the ocean. It was then I realized that we were not ditching into the ocean but were landing on board the aircraft carrier USS Coral Sea.

Keith completed his tour with the 3d Marine Division in January 1976, leaving Okinawa with the rank of captain and a Silver Star. In June 1980 Keith left the Marine Corps with the rank of major and was sworn in as a special agent of the Federal Bureau of Investigation. During his Bureau career, Special Agent Keith served in the FBI's Mobile, Dallas, New York, Miami, and Tampa field offices.

Capt. Dick Keith being awarded the Silver Star by Maj. Gen. George McFadden Sr., USA, at Ft. Meade, MD, September 1976. Department of Defense

Upon his retirement in April 2004 Supervisory Special Agent Keith accepted a contract position with the Joint Interagency Task Force West (JIATF-West). JIATF-West is a military command based at PACOM [U.S. Pacific Command] headquarters at Camp Smith that has counterdrug responsibility for the Pacific area. He was honored as the first recipient of the United States Interdiction Committee's Award for Personal Achievement. He also was awarded the Distinguished Public Service Award by the United States Coast Guard.

GYSGT. FRANCIS McGOWIN, 2/9 BATTALION S-2

Francis A. McGowin was born on 12 July 1940 in Greenville, Alabama. The son of a forester, McGowin grew up in a variety of rural small towns in southern Alabama and northern Florida, taking his first job at the age of twelve, tallying timber from the back of a mule. He enlisted in the Marines at the age of seventeen, on 31 March 1958.

For the next seventeen years, McGowin served in various capacities in the Corps including machine gunner, military police officer, drill instructor, and a member of the Rifle and Pistol Team, as well as various infantry and intelligence slots. He attended Army Airborne School, Ranger School, Scuba School, and Force Recon training. Additionally, he served two combat tours in Vietnam: with L Company 3/3 Marines (1966–1967) and with the 1st Marine Air Wing (1969–1971) as the SERE (survival, evasion, resistance, and escape) officer.

In February 1975 McGowin, now a gunnery sergeant, reported to Okinawa, assigned to the newly formed 2/9 Marines.

When I reported to the 3d Marine Division, I had just completed a four-year tour as NCOIC [noncommissioned officer in charge] of Marine intelligence at the Fleet Intelligence Center-Europe [FICEUR]. I had a Top Secret clearance with a BI and special access. I was privy to the secrets of the world. Because of this special knowledge and access, I was forbidden to fly in any aircraft that did not have multiple engines, I was not allowed to fly over hostile territory, nor was I allowed to deploy in a hostile situation. Additionally, my spouse and I needed special permission to leave the United States. I brought this knowledge and experience to the 2/9.

I had already successfully completed tours of duty in the majority of leadership positions in a Marine infantry battalion, and as squad leader, platoon sergeant, company gunnery sergeant, S-2 officer, S-3 chief, and operational reconnaissance. My rank at this time was gunnery sergeant and my assigned duties were as the battalion intelligence officer, battalion physical fitness instructor (remedial), headquarters platoon sergeant, and the first surveillance target acquisition platoon leader in the Marine Corps.

The war in Vietnam was over. The 3d Marine Division was tasked with the evacuation of Vietnam, with the exception of 2/9 at Okinawa and 3/3 in Hawai`i. These two battalions were being formed and had just started their training. I should not have been assigned below division level, but the war was over and the U.S. military was standing down.

Life was very good for a gunnery sergeant who knew how to wear his rank. I ran the S-2 and enjoyed the trust and confidence of the CO [commanding officer] and XO [executive officer]. The S-1 and I had served together in force recon. Five days a week, I got the battalion's overweight, weak, or unmotivated Marines for PT [physical training], map and compass training, tactics, and hand-to-hand combat. After six weeks, I had forty well-trained and physically fit Marines. Pain can be a superior motivator.

Around the middle of May, we [the 2/9] received a briefing from the commanding general and his staff on an operation to go into Laos and rescue a group of Americans there. The 3/3 was brought to Okinawa as our back-up. The rest of the division was deployed for the evacuation. The line companies were in the field, training.

A few days later in the early afternoon, I got the word from the battalion CO that we were going. I was to go to Marine Amphibious Force [III MAF] HQ [headquarters] to pick up our intelligence packet and maps. I turned the S-2 section over to the S-2 chief, and the surveillance target acquisition platoon over to the platoon sergeant. After the pick-up and briefing, I was to meet the battalion staff at the airfield.

At MAF-G-2 I received the packet, but no briefing, and was told that the maps would be at the airfield. It was dark when I arrived at the airfield, and there were four or five large boxes of maps on the plane. The troops sat on the deck in their war gear [helmets, rifles, web gear].

We established a CP [command post] forward in the aircraft and I opened the intelligence packet. I learned at that time that we were going to Cambodia, not Laos, and I advised the CO of the change. Opening the map, I learned our objective was Koh Tang and located it on the Joint Operations Graphic [JOG] air map [1:250,000]. We had no tactical maps [1:50,000] in all those boxes. The maps were all of the Cambodian mainland, and thus worthless and of no value for us.

Landing in Thailand, we were billeted in a hangar. The tactical commander, Colonel Johnson, did not bring an S-2 as part of his staff. I was ordered to submit all my essential elements of information [EEIs] and other intelligence requirements [OIRs] to his S-4 supply officer and coordinate with the Air Force intelligence on base. The S-4 had no idea what EEIs or OIRs were or how to get them. The Air Force had no experience with enlisted intelligence officers and had not received my clearance, so their assistance and my access were severely limited.

The last intelligence we received was that there were sixty to eighty militia troops occupying Koh Tang. Having spent the last four years in an environment where we received and analyzed message traffic, moved satellites around, and had photos of everything, I knew what was available, and we were not getting any of it. Additionally, Air Force intelligence was not ground oriented, so there was no inform-ation as to vegetation, water temperature and currents, or indigenous animal life, including reptiles.

Colonel Johnson gave me the impression that he thought we would land two hundred to three hundred Marines by Air Force heli-copters, scare the hell out of the local troops, rescue the crew, and be home for supper with Bronze Stars for all the officers.

There was an overflight of Koh Tang in a small Army plane by the battalion and company commanders, and they took photos with a 35-mm camera, but couldn't get close enough due to hostile fire. The photos showed high trees and thick shrub. We received six 8 x 10 photos that showed the whole island. I put grid lines on them and distributed them: one to the CO, one to the S-3, and two to each line company.

So, armed with intelligence consisting of a JOG 1:125,000 map, six photos, one limited overflight, and two-month-old information from a local who had been on the island, 2/9 went to war. What we didn't receive was intelligence the Air Force had stating that, due to the discovery of oil in the area, the garrison on Koh Tang had been reinforced with six hundred to eight hundred Khmer Rouge veteran combat troops armed with automatic weapons, mortars, and heavy weapons. The resulting action at Koh Tang was what happens when one ignores intelligence, or the lack of it.

I was scheduled to fly in on the second wave with the battalion XO, but there was no second wave. Most of the helicopters were either shot down or severely damaged. My part ended when the first flight departed. I only became important again when a subsequent investigation was launched to lay fault.

I'd kept a log in a personal notebook of everyone I talked with on the subject. It included all my telephone calls (with numbers), my requested EEIs and OIRs, and all my requests to the Air Force, noting names, offices, and times. I was cleared, not court-martialed, and released. They looked for fault higher up in the chain of command. I received orders sending me to photographers school, outside the intelligence field.

One of my young Marines from years before rose to the rank of major in the intelligence field. While at III MAF, he decided to look at the Top Secret Koh Tang file. It no longer exists. Everything, including opinions, conclusions, and blame, has been destroyed.

McGowin retired from the Marines in July 1979 after twenty-one years of service with the rank of master sergeant. In 1990 he was commissioned a first lieutenant in the 444th Infantry Battalion, part of the Alabama Defense Force, a state military unit. He retired as a major in 1999.

OS-2 BEN MICHALSKI, USS *GRIDLEY*

Ben Michalski was born on the east side of Baltimore on 19 September 1953. The son and grandson of sailors, he enlisted in the U.S. Navy in August 1971 shortly after graduating from Mergenthalar High School, in part to avoid the draft.

After boot camp at the Orlando Naval Training Center, and radar training at the Great Lakes Naval Training Center, he reported on board the USS *Kitty Hawk* (CVA-63) as a radarman striker in September 1972. He saw service off the coast of North Vietnam at Yankee Station, a point in the Gulf of Tonkin 190 kilometers due east of Dong Hoi (17 degrees 30 minutes north/108 degrees 30 minutes east) during Operation Linebacker as part of Task Force 77. The operation, which ran from 9 May to 23 October, was an aerial interdiction campaign aimed at disrupting supplies to the invading People's Army of Vietnam [PAVN].

Michalski was on board the *Kitty Hawk* on 11–12 October when a race riot broke out on board ship. Referred to as the *Kitty Hawk* Mutiny, fifty to sixty crew members were injured, three seriously, when one hundred to two hundred black sailors rioted over perceived inequitable treatment along racial lines. Nineteen rioters were convicted in courts-martial, and the incident initiated a congressional investigation into race relations in the Navy. The riot occurred while the ship was off the coast of North Vietnam during combat operations.

The USS *Kitty Hawk* returned to Hunters Point in January 1976 for conversion from a CVA (attack aircraft carrier) to a CV (multi-purpose) carrier. Before the ship was decomisssioned on 12 May 2009 after serving for forty-nine years, it deployed to the Middle East and engaged in the war against terrorism (Iraqi Freedom).

After recovering from dental surgery at Oak Knoll Naval Hospital in Oakland, and a brief period in a transit company at Treasure Island, Michalski, now an E-3, was assigned to the operations intelligence division on board the USS *Gridley* (DLG-21) early in 1974. While on board, he rose to the rank of petty officer second class and was specially trained as part of the guard force that provided security for any tactical nuclear weapons on board ship.

I was an operations specialist second class [OS-2] on board the USS Gridley, a guided missile cruiser, which was the PIRAZ [positive identification and radar advisory zone] station for the entire Mayaguez operation. The PIRAZ is defined by the air search radar coverage of a ship patrolling a designated PIRAZ station. A PIRAZ ship requires a Navy tactical data system [NTDS] to effectively identify and track all aircraft using or anticipated to use zone airspace during combat operations. The NTDS was the primary radar/computer system used to track, link up via computer with other ships, control every weapons system, and simultaneously monitor air, surface, and submarine contacts. It also joined the older conventional radar systems like the SPS-10 (surface) and the SPS-48 (air) with the 55-B Terrier missile launchers and fire-control systems. Those systems were on every Leahy-class guided missile cruiser.

We were the "hard drive" for all ships afloat during the event. We connected everyone with automated data via the NTDS so all data could be displayed in real time for all concerned. Additionally, we were the air traffic control [ATC] and the antisubmarine air controller

[ASAC] for all the Knives [CH-53 helicopters] in the air. We coordinated, identified, tracked, listened to, and logged all the net traffic. We were literally the electronic hub, facilitating the sharing of vital data so that the rest of the attack fleet could do its mission.

We were also the Pri Ci and the U.S. Navy High Command Communications Network [HICOM] connected directly to the White House, and were privy to communications between commands.

We'd been standing off of Sattahip, Thailand, waiting to escort the USS Midway, which was picking up South Vietnamese air force planes, when a commercial ship, a big oil tanker, the SS Saigon Texaco, signaled by flashing light that they had been attacked by gunboats. (Later, one of our P-3s reported being targeted by these same boats.) It caused quite a stir within our command. Captain Straitiff reported directly to a higher command. I thought we were going to destroy the boats. It was piracy in international waters, after all. We had just passed through the Lompoc straits, around midnight, and we had just passed the last command to the other units to form a screening formation for the Midway on the Navy red channel when our orders were countermanded by the USS Coral Sea.

We were ordered to proceed back north at flank speed, but no one would tell us where we were going and the tin cans [destroyers] and the oiler couldn't keep up with us, so they fell behind, leaving just us and the Coral Sea as we steamed north at flank speed. We learned of the seizure of the Mayaguez through monitoring the AP [Associated Press] wire traffic.

I remember a single A-6 mission late at night to blow up some warehouse inland in Cambodia, and preparations being made to recover the ship and crew. My friend OS-1 [operations specialist first class] Jimmy Ramey was one of the watch supervisors during most of the action. He was present in the combat information center [CIC], and told me he remembered hearing the air intercept console [AIC] complaining that the Air Force helicopters were going in too high.

OS-1 Claude McGee was ASAC [associate special agent in charge] for one if not a couple of those Jolly choppers. I was sitting right next to him writing down every radio transmission between the

Gridley, *the chopper pilots, and the rest of the task force, including
the* Holt. *I believe Henry Cohen was also doing communication logs
right behind me in CIC air tracking.*

*I was on the 0400 to 0800 watch, although I stayed on for the
0800 to 1200 watch. Sometime during the first landing of the Marines
we learned the* Mayaguez *crew was not on Koh Tang Island. I was
copying radio transmissions into the log book furiously because the
chatter was like a Hollywood movie. I wrote everything down; I was
particularly good and fast with my CIC radio logbook shorthand.*

*We'd lost a bunch of choppers and a few of them were hit right
out of the gate due to incomplete and inaccurate intelligence. There
had been a flyover of the island the day before to take pictures of who
was supposed to be defending that rock. It didn't go so well.*

*I remember it was only due to the bombing raids that the Cam-
bodians gave in and we picked up a small craft surface contact on the
SPS-10 in combat surface tracking. Then the boat was spotted by one
of our P-3s and it was a small boat flying a white flag. I'm not sure of
this, but I believe the crew was on that boat.*

*Later that evening, I remember hearing a transmission from one
of the pilots talking with McGee, saying that there were a few Marines
who didn't make it back to the LZ, but they were alive, because one of
the Marines said he had seen them. I'm positive I heard someone yell
in the background, "Hargrove and so and so (I can't remember the
other names) were alive and we needed to come back and get them."*

*The next day several of us were called into CIC separately and
signed a document ordering us to keep our mouths shut about what
we had heard, and if we ever talked about what really went down
we'd be sent to Leavenworth. We were told that the whole deal was
considered to be classified Secret.*

*I also remember being told by Chief Gibbons that a rescue mis-
sion was being put together to extract those Marines left behind and
to keep our mouths shut about that whole deal. When we got back
Stateside I remember reading* Time's *and* Newsweek's *accounts: not
a thing was mentioned in them about the Marines who were left behind, and many of the details were left out.*

No rescue mission was ever mounted and most of us had to keep the dirty little secret that those Marines were left to die. They could have been saved. The forces were in place to rescue those Marines but the show was called off when the Mayaguez *was taken back. The call came straight from the White House.*

Michalski left the *Gridley* in April 1976, and was honorably discharged as an E-5.

PFC. FRED MORRIS, WEAPONS PLATOON G COMPANY 2/9 MARINES

Fred Morris was born in Waterloo, Iowa, in December 1955, and enlisted in the Marine Corps in June 1974. By November he was at the MCRD in San Diego as a member of Platoon 3122.

Following advanced infantry and weapons training at Camp Pendleton, California, where he was trained in military occupational specialty (MOS) 0351/antitank assault, he shipped out to Camp Schwab, Okinawa, and was assigned to Weapons Platoon G Company 2/9. He arrived in Okinawa the first week of May 1975.

I arrived on Okinawa about a week before we went on alert for the Mayaguez *rescue. My unit, Golf Company 2/9, had just been on alert because of the evacuation of Saigon, which had begun a couple weeks earlier.*

I arrived at Camp Schwab and went into the field to join my unit. The next day they put us on alert and flew us to Thailand. By the time we got there, we were exhausted. It had been days since I'd had any meaningful sleep. About the time I thought I might get some rest, they decided to start passing out ammo. That was just what I needed to relax. Load me up with live ammo and then tell me to relax for a bit before loading me on board a chopper. The mood changed from exhausted to excited. That's when it became real.

We were told of the situation as they knew it. The island was supposed to be lightly defended, but we were told to be prepared for anything, even though they did not expect heavy resistance.

We were the first bird to land on the island that day; as our CH-53 was coming into the LZ [landing zone], I started to hear some

PFC Fred Morris,
circa 1975.

*different sounds, and it didn't take long to figure out that it was the
sound of rounds [bullets] coming through the fuselage. It seemed to
take forever for our pilot to find a spot to set down. The holes were
appearing all over the place and everyone was bug-eyed. I can't speak
for everyone there, but the word "terrified" comes to mind. He finally
set it down and the side gunner made a motion for us to get out. I
think everyone just looked at him like he was crazy. At about the same
time a round came through and something started to spray inside.
That was the magic moment for me: if that liquid ignited, it would be
safer outside with them shooting at us than inside that helicopter.*

*Sergeant Bernal and Lieutenant McDaniel led the charge and we
ran off into elephant grass and hit the dirt. The chopper was leaving but it was having trouble lifting off. It went out several hundred
yards and then went down in the water. With the noise of the chopper and the surf it was hard to hear. We were under heavy fire as the
next helicopter tried to come in and the jungle came alive with heavy
machine-gun fire and small arms.*

Sergeant Bernal was standing and shouting orders to form a perimeter. About twenty yards away there was a hooch [hut] that eventually ended up being our command post. Al Bailey and I saw some Khmer Rouge soldiers firing at him and we started to lay down covering fire. That was when I learned that I'd been issued an M-16 that didn't work. It was a one-shot wonder! The shell extractor didn't work and each cartridge had to be pried out after every shot.

At this point there were only about twenty-some Marines on the island against a larger-than-estimated Khmer Rouge force. That chopper was rejected [forced to abandon landing] from the LZ a couple of times, as were the next two after it. It was a while before we got more Marines on the ground.

At one point, we located a hut that was built right into the side of a bluff. It turned out to be an ammo depot for the Khmer Rouge. They had about everything we needed. It was almost all U.S. equipment and labeled that way. That's where we got the bandoleers of ammo for the grenade launcher that we were trying to use on them.

Sergeant Hoyles and I were watching the left flank and I looked down to see bits of sand kicking up. It kept happening and finally I said something to Sergeant Hoyles; he couldn't figure out what kind of critter could do kick up the sand, either. So I found a fresh spot and dug down but what I found was a projectile from a gun. With the waves coming in you couldn't hear the shots but when we looked across the cove, about three hundred yards away we could see muzzle flashes. They were shooting at us. We started lobbing grenades from the launcher but they were out of range so we turned an M-60 around and cleared them off the peninsula.

SSgt. Fofo Tuitele went out on a recon to try to find a machine gun that was harassing the choppers as they came in to resupply us and take troops off. We were instructed not to shoot until he returned. There was a huge tree that towered over the island about seventy-five meters out. I saw a half-dressed Cambodian scaling that tree carrying a rifle. I knew it wasn't Tuitele so I asked for permission to shoot him as he was climbing. By the time I convinced them that I knew it wasn't Sergeant Tuitele he was up where I couldn't see him anymore but he was high enough to take pot shots at us. We took an M-60 and just covered the area near the trunk and he and a few more came falling down out of the tree.

Once Captain Davis got there and Colonel Austin's group had reconnected with those of us on the west beach, we knew where all our troops were. We were told to dig in because we might be spending the night there.

As it started to get dark, and with a lot of us still waiting to get off the island, things started to heat up again; you could hear ground fire all around. The rate of fire intensified with each successive chopper that came in to extract more troops. I was asked to take a can of .762 ammunition and go with an M-60 team out to the northeast perimeter. The foliage was so heavy that you couldn't see more than ten feet into the jungle. We were about fifty yards from where the helicopter landed to extract us. Gunny McNemar came around and removed about every other guy as they reduced the perimeter. He then sent a runner around to let us know that the next chopper was it. When the next bird came in, we were to empty the M-60 into the woods and get to the helicopter because it would be the last one out.

The Khmer Rouge were moving around in the bush and we could hear them but the only time we could tell where they were was when we saw their muzzle flashes. I had memorized how many steps it was to the path that led back west to the chopper. When it finally landed, we let loose on where we thought it would do the most damage and then ran like hell. I had only taken about three steps following the rest of the team when there was an explosion to my right.

The blast shattered the hand guard on my M-16, knocking me off my feet. At that point, I was pumped and so focused on what I needed to do that I didn't even slow down. It was total darkness! The jungle was thick and dense, there was no moon, and there was no way we were going to use flashlights. I had lost track of the steps to the path out so was just running toward the sound of the helicopter. "Run to the sound, run to the sound, run to the sound," kept repeating in my mind. Because of the explosion, my hearing wasn't working that well, either.

By the time I made it to the helicopter I still didn't have my wits about me. I must have been half out of it and when I reached the back of the helicopter at full speed, my left foot hit the ramp but my right foot missed and I slammed my head into the side of the chopper. Gunny McNemar, Captain Davis, and TSgt. Wayne Fisk dragged me onto the already fully loaded aircraft. Shortly afterwards, we tried to take off.

As the pilot attempted to get us out of there the chopper began vibrating violently. One of the air crew, TSgt. Wayne Fisk, had forgotten to lock the rear ramp and was sliding out of the back. Gunny McNemar and Captain Davis grabbed him and literally tossed him back into the chopper right onto our laps in the back of the bird.

Once we got off and were out far enough that we knew we were out of range, smiles started to go around along with cheers and hugs. It was a major relief, to say the least. I looked out a window and could see we were moving, then we seemed to stop. We weren't very far off the water and the chopper got real noisy, vibrating, and seemed to be struggling. I could tell we were gaining altitude but still not moving. About then there was a bright red light that at the time I thought were tracers and braced myself, but as it turned out we were setting down on the USS Coral Sea.

After finishing his tour in Okinawa, Morris returned to the States, and was assigned as an S-3 clerk at battalion headquarters, 2/6 Marines at Camp Lejeune, North Carolina. He was honorably discharged as a corporal/E-4 on 30 October 1976.

PO1 THOMAS NOBLE, BLACK VELVET-1, USS *WILSON*

Thomas Noble was born in Jamestown, Kentucky, in 1947, and enlisted in the U.S. Navy four days after graduating from high school. After boot camp and radar technician training at the Great Lakes Naval Training Center in Illinois, he was assigned on board the carrier USS *Kearsarge* (CVS-33) out of Long Beach, California. He volunteered for duty in Vietnam, and received orders for swift boat training while on his second WESTPAC [Western Pacific] deployment. His five deployments off the coast of Vietnam included time on board the USS *Juneau* (LPD-10) and the USS *Bronstein* (DE-1037), as well as a year on board swift boats. In

January 1973, now a first class petty officer, Noble was assigned on board the USS *Henry B. Wilson* (DDG-7), a guided missile destroyer. In February 1975 the ship deployed to WESTPAC.

On board the Henry B. Wilson *was my close friend, John Ellis, whom I'd served with in Vietnam. The* Wilson *had a new captain, Cdr. J. Michael Rodgers, and the crew was still unsure about him. As the events of the next three months unfolded, Captain Rodgers earned the respect not only of the crew, but of the entire Seventh Fleet. He was the finest commanding officer that I served with in my twenty-four years of naval service.*

We left Pearl Harbor and steamed to Subic Bay in the Philippines for what was scheduled to be a ten-day stay. Our first day in Subic we were informed that Cambodia was in a complete state of turmoil and that Americans were being evacuated from Phnom Penh. Cambodian evacuees were fleeing to a small island named Phu Quoc, which is on the border between Vietnam and Cambodia. The United States was attempting to evacuate these people to Guam. The Henry B. Wilson *would refuel and immediately steam for Phu Quoc Island and assist in the evacuation. We were there for thirty-one days until all were evacuated. We received orders to proceed back to Subic.*

About four hours into our transit toward Subic Bay, we were ordered to proceed to a position off Saigon because Saigon was under siege by the Communists; we were told that we had an even larger evacuation problem. We arrived off Saigon on 7 April 1975; for the next thirty days we assisted in the evacuation of Saigon. Both John and I were constantly busy interpreting for the countless refugees, along with our normal duties.

On 30 April Saigon fell and we were ordered to proceed to Kaohsiung, China, for a well-deserved five-day rest. On 9 May we departed Kaohsiung for Subic and were scheduled to arrive on 13 May. I awoke at approximately 0600 on 13 May and immediately realized that the ship was steaming at flank speed, which did not make sense since we were supposed to be arriving at Subic and so should have been steaming at about ten knots. I ran up to the combat information center [CIC] and was informed that Captain Rodgers had received re-

Lt. Cdr. Tom Noble, USN.
Tom Noble collection

ports that a U.S.-flagged merchant ship had been seized by gunboats of the Khmer Rouge, and it was believed the crew was being held on the small island of Koh Tang. In the early afternoon the ship refueled and headed southwest toward Koh Tang, which was approximately 1,200 miles away.

The plan was for the USS Harold E. Holt *to come alongside the* Mayaguez, *which was anchored to the northwest of the island, and her Marines would board from the deck of the* Harold E. Holt. *Captain Rodgers decided that he would bring the* Henry B. Wilson *from the opposite side of the island. During the evacuation of Phnom Penh and Saigon, Captain Rodgers had seen the need for small-arms weapons teams to be stationed on areas of the ship in case a gunboat got inside the minimum firing range of our 5-inch guns. Therefore, Captain Rodgers made the decision to arm two fire teams with M-60 machine guns, M-14 rifles, and even hand grenades. John Ellis was the team leader for his thirteen-man team on the main deck and I was the team leader for the second thirteen-man team positioned on the signal bridge.*

As dawn broke on 15 May, we were approximately twenty miles from Koh Tang to the southeast. We could see from the radar presentation that the Harold E. Holt *was making its approach on the* Mayaguez. *At 0600 Captain Rodgers sent the ship to general quarters [battle stations]. I was on the signal bridge with my fire team manning an M-60 machine gun. By now it was full light; as we approached the island I could see the* Harold E. Holt *alongside the* Mayaguez; *I could see heavy smoke. After a closer look I could see two HH-53 Air Force helicopters that had been shot down on the east side of the northernmost tip of the island.*

Captain Rodgers took the ship to about a thousand yards from the northern tip of the island. We now could clearly see that the Harold E. Holt *was alongside the* Mayaguez *but there was no gunfire coming from the* Mayaguez. *USAF aircraft were strafing and bombing enemy positions in support of the Marines ashore. At approximately 0720 a ship's lookout who was standing right above me shouted that he saw people in the water.*

The ship's executive officer [XO], Lt. Cdr. Tom Furgeson, ordered me to get a gig crew together. The gig is a twenty-six-foot boat used to ferry the captain and is not designed in any way as a combat vessel. John Ellis and I took our M-60s, a coxswain, a corpsman, and a young ensign as an officer in charge. Along with three others, we launched the gig immediately. Three groups of people had been sighted swimming away from the island.

We picked up two of the groups with the gig and Captain Rodgers brought the ship alongside the third group; sailors from the ship dove into the sea and assisted the personnel. I was on the bow of the gig, which was about three square feet, with my M-60 and two canisters of ammunition. We were about 150 yards from the beach and I was concentrating on the tree line trying to identify the friendly and enemy lines. We picked up three in the first group; as we came alongside the second group, I saw this Marine [SSgt. Robert Pruitt] with a .38 caliber revolver getting ready to point it at me. I yelled, "You stupid son-of-a-bitch. What are you doing?" He yelled back, "I thought you guys were Russians, and I wasn't going to be captured." I had never

USS Wilson *gig* Black Velvet-1 *shown rescuing Marines and returning fire on enemy ashore.* Wayne K. Stewart collection

thought about people not knowing that we were Americans. In all we picked up thirteen Marine and Air Force personnel.

The Wilson *recovered the gig and was in close proximity to the* Harold E. Holt *and the* Mayaguez *when a P-3 patrol aircraft reported that there was an enemy gun boat headed toward Koh Tang from mainland Cambodia (about twenty-five miles east). The P-3 then reported that it was in fact a fishing boat and that it appeared that it was flying "white flags," and that it looked like there were Americans on board. The officer of the deck [OOD] then took the* Henry B. Wilson *alongside the fishing boat for inspection.*

Once they were identified as the Mayaguez *crew, ship personnel tied the fishing boat up to the side of the* Henry B. Wilson *and our fire teams stood easy on station as the forty members of the* Mayaguez *crew were brought on board, along with five fishermen from Thailand that had been held as prisoners by the Cambodians for several months.*

The Wilson *headed back to Koh Tang, and the crew of the* Mayaguez *was then transferred back to their ship by the* Henry B. Wilson's

*gig, after which we proceeded toward the northern tip of Koh Tang.
As we passed close to the northern tip of the island an enemy gun
position opened fire on the ship. After about five rounds of 5-inch
shells from our guns, however, we received no more fire from that
position. Captain Rodgers took up a position approximately a thousand yards off Koh Tang and received a call for naval gunfire support from an airborne command spotter against several enemy gun
emplacements that were firing at the Marines on the beach. As we did
our gunfire missions the ship was fired on several times but the fire
was not accurate and would cease as soon as we returned fire. Additionally, the* Henry B. Wilson *sank one former U.S. Navy swift boat
that had fired on a U.S. Air Force helicopter.*

*At approximately 1515 Captain Rodgers sent word for John Ellis
and me to report to the bridge. When we arrived Captain Rodgers explained that we had to find a way to get these Marines and Air Force
personnel on the island extracted before dark. In coordination with
the other commanders, he made the decision to arm the gig and send
it close to the beach to draw fire away from the recovery helicopters,
suppress hostile fire, and destroy enemy gun positions; to act as a
rescue boat for any helicopters that might be shot down; and to stand
ready to pick up anyone who made a dash for the water.*

*We had many volunteers for the mission, but Captain Rodgers let
Ellis and me pick our gig crew. Our crew consisted of John, myself,
GM2 Don Moore, and RD3 Mike Williams all manning M-60 machine
guns. RM2 Eddie (EJ) Oswalt would act as radio operator and man
an M-14, EN2 Greg (Bubba) Elam would serve as boat engineer and
man an M-14, and the best boat driver in the Navy, BM1 Jesse Hoffman, would serve as coxswain. Lt. (jg) Larry Hall was assigned as
officer in charge. The radio call sign of the* Henry B. Wilson *was Black
Velvet, therefore the gig was given the call sign Black Velvet-1.*

*At approximately 1620 the gig was launched and we headed for
the east beach. Our initial orders were to beach the boat and attempt
to get as many people on the boat as possible. I say without reserva-
tion that had we done this we would have lost a lot more people.
While en route to east beach our orders were changed and we were
told to stand off and provide fire support for the HH-53s. We posi-*

Jolly-42 passes over USS Wilson *with Marines on board.* U.S. Air Force

tioned ourselves about seventy-five to one hundred yards from the landing zone [LZ]. The Air Force then laid down a barrage of fire and two HH-53s flew over us into the LZ.

An HH-53 [piloted by Don Backlund] approached the LZ, and fire from enemy machine guns and recoilless rifles from the jungle was extremely intense. While this heavy fire was going on, he flew his heli-copter to within twenty-five yards of the enemy fire and set it down to take the Marines on board. He then started receiving even heavier fire from three different directions.

I heard John tell Jesse to bring the boat to "All stop." I saw the look on the face of a couple people as they looked at John, like, "Are you nuts?" I then told them that that was the last thing that the enemy would expect and that you cannot direct fire from a speeding boat. At this same time I opened fire on the position to the west of the HH-53 and immediately realized that no one else was firing. Jesse Hoffman tapped me on the back and yelled that no one knew where the fire was coming from. I stopped firing for a second and told everyone where the enemy position was. We then opened up with all weapons on the

Black Velvet-1 from the USS Wilson *stands off Koh Tang and provides fire support for HH-53 helicopters extracting Marines off the island.* U.S. Naval Institute Photo Archive

western position. Almost immediately two of the three enemy posi-
tions opened up on the gig. I had been in more than my share of fire
fights in Vietnam and this one was right up there. Initially the enemy
fire was machine-gun and AK-47 fire, but then we took a 75-mm
recoilless rifle round that exploded within twenty yards of the boat.

Once the Marines were extracted, the gig proceeded to the west
side of the island and repeated the action of running cover fire for the
CH-53 helicopters that were extracting Marines on that side of the
island. After the heavy action on the east side, the Air Force made
the decision to drop a fifteen thousand–pound [daisy cutter] bomb on
the enemy positions to the south of friendly lines. We were not sure
what was happening until EJ Oswalt received a radio transmission
telling us to clear away from the island to about five hundred yards.
It was quite a sight seeing the parachute with that huge bomb com-

ing down. It looked almost peaceful until it exploded and the whole island shook like there had been a violent earthquake.

At approximately 1915 EJ Oswalt received a message over the radio that there was a missing lieutenant, possibly inside a downed helicopter; we were requested to go back to the east side, send some of us ashore, and rescue this guy. John, EJ, and I were discussing the situation; we decided that John would climb up on top of the HH-53, which was lying on its side, and get the guy out while EJ and I maintained cover fire. I can tell you without a doubt that if we had done that you would not be reading this account. Just as we were beaching the boat, EJ got another call over the radio stating that there was no one in the helicopter, and the missing man was alive and well on the USS Coral Sea. He had been in the "head" when they were taking muster.

We proceeded back to the west side and ran cover fire for the remaining extraction helicopters. At approximately 2030 a helicopter flew over the gig twice and we realized that he was trying to identify us. On the third pass it dropped an illumination round. If not for the superb boat-handling skills of Jesse Hoffman, it would have landed in the boat, which had ammunition lying all over the deck. I have talked to several of the Air Force pilots in recent years and all swear that none of the helicopters had illumination rounds on board. I know of eight sailors on Black Velvet-1 who would tell a different story. The last CH-53 left the island at approximately 2100.

At approximately 2230 the XO contacted John Ellis and me and told us that we might have to go back the next morning. We were told that there were three Marines unaccounted for. We did not have quite the number of volunteers this time as we did earlier, so we got started rearming the gig and getting us a complete crew. At approximately 2340 we were informed that the gig run the next day would not be needed, and that it was believed that everyone was either accounted for or dead.

On 16 May, after fueling was completed, the Wilson steamed back to the vicinity of Koh Tang; at first light it made an observation run on the island as close as possible, with many people looking through high-power binoculars. I cannot remember for sure but I

believe we also "hailed" to anyone who could hear over the ship's
topside loud speakers. No Americans were sighted. After completing
the observation run we onloaded all the Marines from the Harold E.
Holt *[approximately eighty-five] on board the* Henry B. Wilson *and*
steamed toward Subic Bay in the Philippines.

Promoted to chief petty officer fifteen days after Koh Tang, Noble was
then assigned as an instructor in the CIC officers course at Fleet Combat
Training Center, San Diego. In April 1977 he was commissioned an ensign
in the limited duty officer (LDO) program and assigned to the USS *Con-*
stellation (CV-64) as electronic warfare officer (EWO).

After twenty-four years of service, Noble retired as a lieutenant commander. His awards include the Bronze Star (with V for valor), three Navy
Commendation Medals, and five Navy Achievement Medals.

LCPL. SCOTT STANDFAST, 3D PLATOON E COMPANY 2/9 MARINES

(John) Scott Standfast was born in Mineola, New York, on 16 May 1956.
He enlisted in the U.S. Marine Corps on 26 January 1974 at age seventeen. The son of a father who served with the Marines in the Pacific during
World War II and the grandson of a Marine who served at Belleau Woods
during World War I, Standfast grew up knowing he'd also be a Marine.

Standfast went through boot camp at Marine Corps Recruit Depot
(MCRD)-Parris Island, South Carolina, as part of Platoon #354, then attended infantry training school at Camp Pendleton, California. He arrived
in Okinawa just after Christmas, on 26 December 1974, as a newly minted
eighteen-year-old private first class assigned to 3d Platoon 2/9 Marines.

I was assigned as the squad leader for 3rd Squad, 3rd Platoon of Echo
Company. I was responsible for twelve men. These twelve brave and
disciplined men were the crucial element in the final disengagement of
the Marines and other U.S. armed forces from Koh Tang.

After we heard three whistle blasts, I sent the MG [machine-gun]
team of Marshall, Hall, and Hargrove back to the extraction beach
with two security personnel. I then went from right to left, water to
inland, checking each of my squad's positions to direct each pair of men

to withdraw, and checking their positions. All men were accounted for on my assigned perimeter, including the MG team of Marshall, Hall, and Hargrove. I followed the last pair of men down [inland to water], again checking the vacant positions, then made my way north to the LZ [landing zone].

Arriving at the LZ, I went from man to man to ensure all my people were there. Someone ordered me to get down. I continued to do my job. We were under fire, and I returned fire and directed fire when necessary. All of my men were accounted for, including the MG team of Marshall, Hall, and Hargrove. None of my squad or the MG team of Marshall, Hall, and Hargrove were at the primary, original, all-day-long perimeter. I clearly recall Marshall, Hall, and Hargrove on the beach about three to five men down to my right. We were in a tight 180-degree perimeter.

I heard someone call for a "MG team to the left" and I heard people running behind me from right to left. I looked over my left shoulder at the helicopter and saw people falling down in the water. I tried my best to see if anyone was moving past the helicopter on the beach heading north.

The birds [helicopters] were turning on their lights, which blinded us and drew fire. The helicopter departed and those in charge started yelling that the next helicopter would be the last. There was a lull in firing and it was easy to hear this communication, that this [incoming] helicopter would be the last bird and everyone had to get on.

The enemy knew we'd been reduced to a small element and as that last helicopter began its approach inbound we were told to fire off all our ammunition, similar to a final protective fire. I was one of the last on board. There was a mixture of Echo and Golf Company Marines. The helicopter was so crowded that I had to crawl over people to get on board.

Within the perimeter that had been assigned to my squad, I had assigned sectors of fire to all squad members, including the MG team of Marshall, Hall, and Hargrove. The MG team sector of fire and principal direction of fire was narrow due to the terrain inland and my squad's fighting positions to their left. Their principal direction of fire was down the avenue of approach to the south along the beach.

I was already familiar with this area, having returned from an earlier patrol to the south along that same beach.

I clearly recall that I went back to the old perimeter and checked each position again. I called out their names and shouted, "Is anyone there who speaks English? If so, let's go!" No one else came. Why? Because no one was there or left in my assigned sector!

During the debrief on Okinawa in May 1975, I told the person asking questions about an MG team being called to the left and about people falling down in the water. I never heard anything more.

In 1996, I was asked to accompany the JTF-FA and return to Koh-Tang Island to help find remains of the missing Americans. I was totally prepared and did all that I was asked to do, but was later taken off the manifest. I was never provided any explanation why. I think I provided them too much information concerning the who, what, where, when, and why.

In 1996, my platoon commander (now a lieutenant colonel) told me that the MG team of Marshall, Hall, and Hargrove was never assigned to 3rd Platoon. But I believe in the old saying, "Possession is nine-tenths of the law." I was responsible for them. I will never forget their faces or their names. They are on my mind every day and are in my prayers daily, including their families.

A year later while at sea in the Mediterranean, in a ceremony on board the USS *Iwo Jima*, Standfast was promoted to sergeant and awarded the Bronze Star with Combat Distinguishing Device (V) for his actions on Koh Tang.

His citation credits him with leading his squad "on two patrols into a heavily sniper-infested, thickly vegetated jungle area. With complete disregard for his own personal safety, he exposed himself to heavy arms and mortar fire while placing himself in the most advantageous positions to direct and control his squad. He was instrumental in destroying or capturing large quantities of enemy's ammunition, food supplies, and fighting positions."

"Later, despite almost nine hours of close combat, he led his squad in covering the remainder of his company to secondary positions to prepare for final extraction from the island. As he directed the final disengagement of his own squad, he advanced forward to the then-exposed and abandoned perimeter to personally ensure that all members of his squad had withdrawn."

Following Koh Tang, Standfast served with the 3/2 Marines, as a drill instructor at Parris Island, with the 2d Force Reconnaissance Company, and as gunny for an intelligence company. He finished his career as a sergeant major before retiring in 2004.

SSGT. FOFO TUITELE, 2D PLATOON G COMPANY 2/9 MARINES

Fofo T. Tuitele was born on New Year's Eve, 31 December 1947, in the village of Vailoatai, American Samoa. He attended Belmont High School in Los Angeles before he decided to enlist in the Marine Corps. He arrived at the MCRD [Marine Corps Recruit Depot] in San Diego on 12 April 1966.

After boot camp and advanced infantry training, where he excelled in marksmanship, he was sent to sniper school at Camp Horno, Camp Pendleton, California. Upon graduation he was assigned to headquarters, 5th Marine Regiment, 1st Marine Division at Camp Pendleton.

The regiment shipped out for Vietnam, arriving in March 1967. Assigned as a scout-sniper, he was credited with eighteen confirmed kills and was awarded his first Navy Commendation Medal with Combat V for participation in more than twenty major combat operations. After attending NCO [noncommissioned officer] school on Okinawa, he returned to Vietnam for a second tour, this time with a line company, L Company 3/5. On 10 August 1968, while assigned as a squad leader, Lance Corporal Tuitele rescued a pinned-down and wounded Marine under fire and carried him to safety, actions for which he was awarded the Bronze Star.

On 13 May 1975 Staff Sergeant Tuitele was in the field on maneuvers with the newly minted Marines of the 2/9 Marines. He was one of the few combat veterans assigned to the unit.

On 13 May 1975 I was on a tactical field training exercise in the Northern Training Area of Okinawa with Golf Company, 2/9 Marines. We had been out there for several days and nights, practicing company-sized movements, especially at night. I remember how the terrain on

Okinawa was nothing but rolling small hills that went on and on. The weather was miserable, raining on and off, more on than off, and it was hard to stay clean and dry in the wet and muddy terrain. Morale was down due to long hours of training and lack of sleep. We were all wet as we bedded down on the evening of 14 May. As usual, it was raining hard and it was dark, so all anybody could do was put away what they could and try to stay warm.

When the alarm sounded, everybody got the word, passed down from higher up, to pack up and get ready to move back to the base camp at Camp Schwab. In the dark and rain we fumbled around to find our gear and get it together.

We gathered together at the rally point and waited for the 6 x 6 trucks or busses to take us back. I believe we were transported out in 6 x 6s due to the bad condition the roads were in. We had a meeting of platoon sergeants before we boarded the trucks, and we were told we'd have fifteen minutes when we got back to get inside the squad bay and inventory all our belongings and box them up. In the meantime, there was no word as to what the hell was going on. There were all sorts of rumors, and many believed we were headed to Vietnam again.

Another meeting was held in the company office as all the troops, now fully geared and with weapons, waited in formation on the street. At the meeting, we were told to make sure we had all our weapons checked out from the armory and to make sure every billet was filled. This was between midnight and six in the morning. We got on the buses and headed south to Camp Hague, lined up for chow, and loaded back on the buses that took us to Kadena Air Force Base. We still had no word regarding what was going on as we all got off the bus, put our name on the manifest list, and boarded the C-5 aircraft. Seven hours later, we landed at Utapao Air Force Base in Thailand. They herded us into a hangar with cots already set up; while in formation, we were advised that there would be a briefing later in the day.

We started planning small unit logistics for ammo, water, and chow for one day. After noon chow, our company gunny started passing out C-rations and ammo. I took extra .45 and 5.56 ammo since I also carried an M-16. Late that afternoon they finally called a meeting with all the platoon commanders inside the hangar, and we finally were told why we were there. The company commander, Captain Davis, had just returned from a reconnaissance trip high above Koh Tang Island. A merchant marine vessel had been hijacked by the Cambodian Khmer Rouge and we were there to take back the ship and rescue the crew. There were no maps of this island available, only the black-and-white photo taken from an OV-10 (Bronco) high above the island.

Intelligence said there were only supposed to be a few, lightly armed Khmer Rouge on the island. We got the word to break down into helicopter teams and to keep platoon integrity. Before daylight on the morning of 15 May, I found myself on a different chopper from my platoon's. In my chopper were the first sergeant and XO [executive officer] and a few of the command group from Golf Company and a couple of corpsmen.

I was assigned to a chopper (Knife-32) in the second wave. We had an Army interpreter with us in our chopper. As we took off, it was still night and we had been in the air for what seemed a long time when daylight broke. There was a tension inside the chopper and I just stared at the ceiling until one of the crewmen got my attention and pointed out the window. I noticed a billow of black smoke from an island below. The XO was on the radio talking to somebody to get the scoop on what was going on before we went in. We were told that the first couple of choppers that had gone in had been shot down and we would have to circle until we got clearance to come in. This was my first indication that it was not going to be an easy day.

The original LZ [landing zone] where we were supposed to land was closed and we were diverted to a secondary LZ. There were a couple of choppers ahead of us trying to land but they couldn't because of the high volume of incoming small-arms fire; the Cambodians were dropping mortar rounds into the LZ. The LZ was a very small stretch of sand and there was lots of uneven coral and small reef like potholes all over in the water. The chopper in front of us finally got down and unloaded its Marines and it was our turn to come in.

We went in and the LZ was very hot with intense enemy fire. The pilot decided to abort the landing and try again. The second time, the crew told us the chopper would hover low and slowly move in. We would have to jump off from the ramp as the chopper approached low, moving left to right to avoid making an easy target. As the word was passed to jump, you could hear bullets flying and mortar rounds landing all around the chopper. All of us finally jumped out, except for the Army interpreter, who refused to dismount the chopper.

As we got out of the chopper, all hell broke loose; as soon as it flew off, everything went quiet again. I calmed down and got my bearings. My platoon and the platoon commander were in the chopper in front of us, and they couldn't land. It had been shot up so bad it had to return to Utapao, but I never knew this until afterwards. I quickly surveyed the area. To my left about 150 meters away was a hut. Behind that there was an eighty-foot cliff of jungle. You couldn't see fifty feet to the front; as I moved forward and inland, I found about ten Marines all huddled up. They were not moving for anything. I just yelled at them to "get the hell up and follow me." I finally saw Staff Sergeant Bernal coming from the right side of the beach. Staff Sergeant Bernal was also a combat veteran of Vietnam. I told him to secure the right side of the beach and I'd take the left.

We moved and positioned whoever we found on the beach. A corpsman found a little hut and set up a makeshift dispensary with the platoon command group as they were setting up. I was busy positioning whoever I could find and put them into position. After that was done I told everyone that when the next chopper came in for landing they were to fire into the tree line and pop some M-79s out there to keep the enemy busy as the chopper came in.

After we cleared out the area and pushed inland, we found lots of ammo, supplies, and the Khmer Rouge's morning breakfast of rice still on the fire. We were without communications until a couple hours later when our platoon commander, Lieutenant Zales, finally arrived with some of the platoon. We were told to get ready to sweep up the road to the opposite side of the island where the first wave had been shot down.

We moved out on line and had started to quietly move forward when I heard my platoon commander screaming out commands. I just backed up and stopped. He looked at me and I told him to shut up and just point and move, each man keeping in visual sight of the person near him. Our intelligence briefing described the island as brush and low trees, but the reality was that the island was covered with jungle and overgrown trees, the canopy so thick that if you looked up you couldn't see the sky.

After we hacked our way about 150 meters, we came upon a clearing about one hundred meters wide; at the far side more trees hid what seemed to [be] a trail leading east. I thought to myself this was an ideal setting for an ambush and I passed the word that nobody was to cross into the open area. Everyone was to stay low with weapons ready and keep their eyes forward on the tree line. After a while, we got the word to move back to the beach.

We pulled back to the perimeter and started positioning ourselves for a possible night defensive, because there were rumors we'd be staying overnight. During this time the Khmer Rouge continued to lob mortar rounds into our position. The only weapon we had to counter their high angle fire was the M-79 grenade launcher. I collected all the seventy-nine rounds I could find and waited. The Cambodians seemed to open up only as the choppers came in, so I instructed my Marines that when the choppers came in, they were to open up, firing into the tree line to suppress the Khmer Rouge. After two choppers, everything quieted down and we heard this fast mover [jet] pass overhead. The next thing we knew, the jet opened up, firing his 20-mm cannons on the beach within fifty feet of us, and so close we got hit by the sand that the impact of his rounds threw up. I was furious and cussing up a storm. I ran over to the lieutenant who was talking on the radio, I believe it was McDaniel, and I yelled, "Goddamn it, he's shooting at us! Stop firing! Stop firing!" He got the message. I remember having a couple of color panels [signal devices] I always carried with me inside my helmet and I took them off and I told the lieutenant to pass the word to the fast mover about the marking. I had two that I snapped together and staked it down close to the water. Finally he quit, but it was some scary shit.

Night was about to fall and we still didn't know what the plan was, whether we'd extract or remain, so we just waited and waited. Finally the word was passed down that the extraction by helicopter would start soon. We were told to be aware of our men's positions, keep the perimeter manned, and only abandon it and withdraw when we were ready to load on the chopper.

As night fell, the first chopper came in; Marines were pulled from the line and the Khmer Rouge continued to pour on intense fire as each chopper came in. There seemed to be nothing we could do to stop the incoming fire, so we just dashed for the chopper. Due to the volume of incoming mortars, the choppers didn't land but hovered, and so what everybody did was to take a running jump up onto the ramp of the chopper while the guys inside pulled them in. Our turn came to load the chopper but as we raced toward it, it slowly moved away from us, skipping on the water. The uneven reef under the water made it hard to step and jump in.

I tried one time and had to hang onto the ramp as the chopper lifted off with me hanging there. After about a minute, the crewmen pulled me in and onto the ramp. My heart was beating like crazy but I quickly got myself together and tried to relax. I was safe and off that damn island. We landed, barely, on the helipad of the USS Holt. Our units were landing everywhere, so we took muster in the galley, turned in all leftover ammo, and secured most of the weapons. Then we tried to get some rest. It had been a long couple of days.

A couple of days later, we pulled into port at Subic Bay, Philippines, and caught a connecting flight back to Camp Schwab, Okinawa.

Master Sergeant Tuitele finished his career as an infantry unit leader (0369) with the historic 2nd Battalion 1st Marines at Camp Pendleton. He retired from the Marine Corps on 29 January 1989, after almost twenty-three years of service that included combat in Vietnam and Cambodia.

He was awarded a second Navy Commendation Medal with Combat V for his actions at Koh Tang. The citation credits Tuitele with leading his platoon under "intense enemy fire" to secure a perimeter immediately after landing, while "routinely exposing himself to enemy fire" as he distributed captured ammunition and hand grenades along the line.

AT1 ALAN ZACK, USCG CUBI POINT, SUBIC BAY, PHILIPPINES

Alan Zack was born in 1942 and enlisted in the United States Coast Guard following his graduation from high school in 1960. After boot camp at Coast Guard Island, Alameda, California, Zack was trained in aviation electronics.

USCG aviation electronics technicians repair all electronic equipment on the ground, and also fly as crew members on board a variety of USCG aircraft. Zack began his career as a radioman on board HU16-Es and C-130s.

He served at USCG air stations at San Francisco; Kodiak and Annette, Alaska; and Elizabeth City, North Carolina. His first deployment to Vietnam was in October 1969. The Coast Guard was setting up a chain of LORAN [LOng RAnge Navigation] stations between Vietnam and Thailand. During that thirty-day deployment, they landed at every operational airfield in Vietnam and Thailand.

In April 1975, with the North Vietnamese overrunning the south, Zack was deployed to the Naval Air Station (NAS) Cubi Point in the Philippines, assigned as a navigator on board a Coast Guard C-130. Their mission was to fly daily patrols searching for the so-called boat people fleeing the Communists, and report their position to surface craft so the refugees could be assisted.

On 15 May 1975 the mission changed.

On 15 May 1975 we were awakened at 0200 and ordered to report to the operations center at Cubi Point. We were given a secret mission: to fly to a point offshore of Koh Tang Island and act as a communications relay for Marine helicopters flying from the USN aircraft carrier USS Coral Sea. *We were supplied with radio frequencies for the mission and directed to maintain radio contact and provide navigational support. Because we orbited higher than the helicopters, we could act as a communications relay point; in addition, our air-to-air tactical air navigation [TACAN] could assist their navigation.*

We arrived and remained in position, circling for more than eight hours, providing communication and navigation assistance to the Marine helicopters. We could observe the helicopters below on our

radar. After we were released, we returned to Cubi Point. The next
day, we were back searching for boat people.

Many people are unaware that the Coast Guard was involved in
the Koh Tang mission. Our contribution was not that heroic, but we
were there.

Promoted to chief petty officer then CWO, Zack retired from the
USCG Chicago in 1985.

2ND LT. RICHARD ZALES, 2D PLATOON LEADER, G COMPANY 2/9 MARINES

Born in Erie, Pennsylvania, on 13 March 1949, and raised there, Richard
Zales decided to join the Marine Corps flight program. Restricted from
the flight program because of his eyesight, he entered officer candidate
school on a ground officer contract and was commissioned a second lieutenant in March 1974. After completion of The Basic School in August
1974, his first duty assignment as a second lieutenant was to 2/9 3d Marine Division, which was located in Okinawa.

Upon arrival at Camp Schwab, Okinawa, I was immediately assigned
as a Rifle Platoon commander with G Company. Within several
weeks our company was fully formed and we were ready to begin our
predeployment training package. This consisted of a number of small
unit training exercises, field problems, and live fire exercises. On 13
May 1975 our company was in the field practicing night company de-
fensive operations. I can vividly remember this because our company
commander, Capt. Jim Davis, commented to me that the defensive
positions I employed in my sector were too far apart and created gaps
where the enemy could infiltrate during a night assault. Little did I
realize that this advice was going to be put to good use in a combat
situation in less than forty-eight hours!

We knew something out of the ordinary was occurring because
late that night we heard an unusual amount of air traffic heading into
Kadena AFB. Shortly after that we were called up to the command
tent by our CO [commanding officer] and told to immediately pack
up our gear and get our platoons out to the staging area and await

transport back to our camp area. We returned to Camp Schwab to close up our company area, and then we were then transported to Kadena, where we boarded aircraft and eventually landed at Utapao AFB in Thailand.

The Air Force had prepared cots for us in a large aircraft hangar. We were told to get some rest and stand by for further orders. I'm not sure if any of the officers got any rest during the flight over to Thailand. I know I didn't sleep much that next night. At this point we were told that an American merchant ship had been hijacked by the Cambodians and we were going in to rescue the American crew. That was the sum total of all of the information I was given until early the next morning.

Captain Davis called the officers together and gave us our five-paragraph battle order. In it, as I recall, we were informed that the objective was an island off the Cambodian coast called Koh Tang. We were told that the crew was sighted there a day or so ago and that the island was lightly defended. Because the island was small and the exact location of the crew on the island was unknown, there was not going to be any preassault prep fire of any kind prior to our landing. We were counting on the element of surprise and our superior numbers and fire power to get the job done. Up to this point, all of this sounded pretty good to me. I was confident that we would land on that island and get the crew back in short order. I'm not sure if my confident attitude was due to arrogance or ignorance, but my opinion on the degree of difficulty of this mission changed a short time later.

After our briefing, we were issued live ammunition and two frag-mentation grenades. We formed up on the tarmac in our boarding sequence behind the helicopters we were assigned. At that point, Captain Davis called the officers back for a revision of the battle order. Apparently, new intelligence had just been received that indicated that the "enemy situation" was not as originally reported. Now we were told that there was at least a reinforced company on the island equipped with heavy machine guns and mortars. We were also told to expect hot LZs [landing zones]. Finally, Captain Davis left it up for us to decide what we would tell our men about the revised enemy threat. I immediately called my platoon sergeant and squad leaders together

*and told them about what we were facing. We all experienced a huge
attitude adjustment.*

*The helicopter ride over to the island seemed to take forever. I
was in the second wave of helos to land on the island. As we approached, the tail gunner pointed down and told me to take a look.
I was shocked to see that we were circling the island. I could see a
helicopter burning in the water very close to the shore on the eastern
side of the island. Then I saw another helo that was flying away from
the island at a very low altitude tip and somersault into the ocean. I
really couldn't believe my eyes. Here I was watching all of this unfold
beneath me like some kind of tourist.*

*I asked the tail gunner to check with the pilot to determine if any
Marines had made it to the beach. I did not have headphone communication with the pilot. The gunner informed me that there were
Marines on the ground. At that point, I became very agitated and told
the tail gunner I was going to go up to the cockpit to tell the pilot to
get us down now! I'm not sure what the tail gunner told the pilot but
he stopped me from going to the cockpit and told me the pilot would
attempt to land us.*

*We started the approach to our LZ but the pilot was coming in
rather high and we circled at treetop level and took small-arms fire
until we were out of range. This occurred several more times before I
again asked what the problem was. This time I was told that the pilot
was waiting for the LZ to be secured. Now, a hot LZ is by definition
not secure. This made no sense to me and frankly I was tired of being
shot at in that damn helicopter. It was a miracle that no one on board
was hit by enemy fire. I then asked the pilot to get us as close as
possible and let us off. We approached our LZ and briefly touched
down before we began taking mortar and automatic small-arms fire.
The pilot lifted off as my men were disembarking; a couple of them
jumped several feet to the ground and several men couldn't get out.
They went back to Utapao with the helicopter and never landed on
the island. I relay this story not to denigrate the Air Force pilots. They
were pros and every bit as courageous as the troops on the ground.
It was simply the result of different tactical doctrines and mission
requirements.*

Once on the ground I met up with 1st Lt. Dick Keith and asked him where he wanted my men deployed. He was trying to coordinate the air assets and link up with the command group that had landed to the south of our LZ. He was talking into two radios, one in each hand. He looked up at me and made a sweeping gesture with one of the radio handsets. I positioned my men on both sides of the thin beachhead he had established and prepared for the link-up and push forward to find the crew.

We dug in just inside the tree line only a few meters from the water. Shortly after my platoon dug in, my platoon guide, Cpl. Nephtali Rivera, approached me to let me know the men were in place but they were not pleased about our location in the perimeter. It was infested with large red ants that inflicted a painful burning sting. From time to time, I could hear Marines slapping themselves and cursing at them. Thankfully, the ant threat diminished as darkness fell.

Throughout the early part of the day we took small arms and mortar fire. At one point, a squad of Cambodians attempted to flank us on our right, north along the water's edge. I called in our own mortar support and we drove them back into the jungle. I later learned that the mortars were with the command group and that they were in a very exposed position but chose to assist with mortar support, putting their own group at great risk.

Later that afternoon we linked up with the command group and the rest of G Company. Elements of E Company also arrived later that day and took up positions on our extreme right flank. At some point during the day, Lieutenant Colonel Austin informed me that the crew was not on the island and that we would be evacuated after dark.

The only officer on the east LZ was Lt. Mike Cicere. Mike and I were very good friends during that period and I remember asking Captain Davis if I could lead a rescue party to retrieve him and the cut-off Marines from the opposite side of the island. My request was denied because the decision to leave the island was already in the planning stages and a cross-island rescue was not an option.

Late in the afternoon, I approached Captain Davis and requested a water resupply. Lieutenant Colonel Austin, who was within earshot, answered me directly, informing me that a resupply was unnecessary because we were being evacuated after dark. This information lifted everyone's spirits.

As darkness approached, we began shrinking our perimeter in preparation for the extraction. I recall sending out one of my squad leaders, Cpl. Kee Chief, to check to ensure that all of our men got the word to pull back to the beach. He came back and told me there were men in our old fighting positions but they were not speaking English! I boarded the third or fourth extract helicopter along with the last elements of my platoon.

We disembarked on the Harold E. Holt, *a destroyer escort. The Navy officers were amazed that the CH-53 helicopter could touch down in such a small space to offload us. That was a remarkable piece of flying.*

On board the Holt *we stowed our combat gear and turned in all unused ordnance. There were endless head counts to verify exactly who was on board. It was clear that although the extraction went as well as could be expected under the circumstances, Marines were scattered and units separated. I had an extremely difficult time getting an accurate count of the Marines on board because they immediately got some hot food and went to sleep anywhere they could find enough room to stretch out. There really wasn't enough room to get everyone together in one spot to muster even if we had wanted to. Over the course of the next day or so, we were never sure if we were going back to Koh Tang Island to retrieve our dead and missing fellow Marines. Ultimately, the decision was made not to do so. How unfortunate.*

It seems ironic to me that the Mayaguez *crew was ultimately released by the Cambodian government as a direct result of military action by U.S. forces, yet we abandoned some of those same forces that were responsible for their release.*

Zales retired as a full colonel in June 2004 with slightly more than thirty years active service.

Appendix A

U.S. Helicopter Aircrews and Transport of Marines and Other Personnel
(Military Sealift Command, Navy, U.S. Air Force, and Army)

INSERTION ONTO THE USS *HOLT* (15 MAY 0605 HOURS LOCAL TIME)
Jolly Green-11

1st Lt. Backlund, Donald R.	Aircraft Commander
1st Lt. Weikel, Gary L.	Copilot
SSgt. Cash, Harry W.	Flight Mechanic
MSgt. Eldridge, John J.	Pararescueman
Sgt. Stanaland, Joseph S.	Pararescueman
A1C Marx, Brad E.	Pararescueman
1st Lt. Rand, Ronald T.	Photographer

Jolly Green-12

Capt. Jacobs, Paul L.	Aircraft Commander
Capt. Nickerson, Martin A.	Copilot
SSgt. Kaiser, Joseph L.	Flight Mechanic
MSgt. Gray, David L.	Pararescueman
Sgt. Cook, Burt W., Jr.	Pararescueman

Jolly Green-13

1st Lt. Greer, Charles R.	Aircraft Commander
1st Lt. Brown, Charles D.	Copilot
SSgt. King, Milas L.	Flight Mechanic
SSgt. Froehlich, Karl J.	Pararescueman

Sgt. Lundregan, Ronald A.   Pararescueman
Sgt. Lemminn, Stephen W.   Pararescueman

Collectively inserted fifty-seven Marines, six MSC civilian volunteers, two USAF EOD, two USN corpsmen, and one U.S. Army linguist onto the USS *Holt*.

INSERTION ONTO KOH TANG ISLAND—1ST WAVE
(0555–1010 HOURS LOCAL TIME)
Knife-21 (0555 hours local time): Marines inserted: 20
Lt. Col. Denham, John H.   Aircraft Commander
1st Lt. Poulson, Karl W.   Copilot
TSgt. Boissannault, Robert A.   Flight Mechanic
SSgt. Rumbaugh, Elwood E. (KIA)   Flight Mechanic

Knife-22 (0600 hours local time): Marines inserted: none
Capt. Ohlemeier, Terry D.   Aircraft Commander
2nd Lt. Greer, David W.   Copilot
SSgt. Wilson, Michael C.   Flight Mechanic
Sgt. Paul, Norman A.   Flight Mechanic

Knife-23 (0600 hours local time): Marines inserted: 20
1st Lt. Schramm, John H.   Aircraft Commander
1st Lt. Lucas, John P.   Copilot
SSgt. Gross, Ronald A. (WIA)   Flight Mechanic
AIC Arrieta, Eduardo E.   Flight Mechanic
SSgt. Barschow, James M.   Photographer

Only troops inserted onto east beach—Lieutenant Cicere's third platoon.

Knife-31 (0600 hours local time): Marines inserted: none
Maj. Corson, Howard A. (WIA)   Aircraft Commander
2nd Lt. Vandegeer, Richard (KIA)   Copilot
SSgt. Harston, Jon D. (WIA)   Flight Mechanic
Sgt. Hoffmaster, Randy L.   Flight Mechanic

Aborted landing on east beach. Thirteen KIA, thirteen rescued by USS *Wilson*.

Knife-32 (0640 hours local time): Marines inserted: 13

1st Lt. Lackey, Michael B.	Aircraft Commander
2nd Lt. Wachs, Calvin O.	Copilot
TSgt. Olsen, Michael B.	Flight Mechanic
SSgt. Morales, Nick (WIA)	Flight Mechanic

Recovered three surviving crew members of Knife-21.

Jolly Green-42 (0720 hours local time): Marines inserted: 27

1st Lt. Pacini, Phillip M.	Aircraft Commander
1st Lt. Dube, Robert C.	Copilot
TSgt. Straughn, Andrew, Jr.	Flight Mechanic
SSgt. Jablonski, Martin M.	Flight Mechanic
SSgt. Brown, Michael A.	Pararescueman
AIC Dunham, Lewis L., III	Pararescueman
SSgt. Martin Cavalos	Photographer

Jolly Green-43 (0720 hours local time): Marines inserted: 29

Capt. Purser, Roland W.	Aircraft Commander
1st Lt. Gradle, Robert P.	Copilot
TSgt. Willingham, Billy D.	Flight Mechanic
TSgt. Harding, Peter S.	Pararescueman
Sgt. Bateson, Thomas J. (WIA)	Pararescueman
A1C McKiver, Dennis W.	Pararescueman

Jolly Green-41 (1010 hours local time): Marines inserted: 22

1st Lt. Cooper, Thomas D.	Aircraft Commander
1st Lt. Keith, David W.	Copilot
TSgt. Little, Rhornell	Flight Mechanic
SSgt. Donovan, Jeffrey	Flight Mechanic
SSgt. Beranek, Thomas E.	Pararescueman
A1C Ferris, John E.	Pararescueman

Additionally, Jolly Green-13 (Greer) made an *unsuccessful* attempt to extract the Marines from the east beach at 0815 hours and sustained sufficient battle damage to remove it from service.

Total Marines inserted: 131 (not including five USAF crew members)

REINFORCEMENT KOH TANG ISLAND, 2ND WAVE
(1130–1230 HOURS LOCAL TIME)

In addition to Jolly Green-11, Jolly Green-12, and Jolly Green-42, two additional helicopters were involved in the effort to reinforce Marines already on the Island: Knife-52 and Knife-51.

Knife-52 (1150 hours local time): Marines inserted: none

1st Lt. Rakitis, Robert E.	Aircraft Commander
2nd Lt. Lykens, David J.	Copilot
SSgt. McDowell, Donald R.	Flight Mechanic
TSgt. Dunbar, William R.	Flight Mechanic

Attempted without success to reinforce the east beach. Emergency landing on coast of Thailand.

Knife-51 (1155 hours local time): Marines inserted: 19

1st Lt. Brims, Richard C.	Aircraft Commander
2nd Lt. Danielson, Dennis L.	Copilot
SSgt. Riley, Marion L.	Flight Mechanic
A1C Pack, Phillip A.	Flight Mechanic
TSgt. Fisk, Wayne L.	Pararescueman
Sgt. Cooper, Roland A., Jr.	Pararescueman

Jolly Green-42 (-43) (1155 hours local time): Marines inserted: 28
Jolly Green-11 (1200 hours local time): Marines inserted: 27
Jolly Green-12 (1200 hours local time): Marines inserted: 26

Additionally, Jolly Green-42 (-43) attempted to extract Cicere's Marines on the east beach at 1435 hours.

Total Marines inserted: 100 Marines
Total on island: 211 Marines/ West Beach—20 Marines, 5 USAF/ East Beach

EXTRACTION OF KOH TANG ISLAND—(1800–2010 HOURS LOCAL TIME)

Even with the return to service of Jolly Green-42 (-43) and the arrival of Jolly Green-44 from Thailand, only five helicopters remained available to extract 236 U.S. service personnel as darkness rapidly approached. Jolly Green-12 flew with a new crew.

Jolly Green-11 (1815 hours local time): Marines extracted: 20

Jolly Green-12 (1830 hours local time): Marines extracted: None

Capt. Walls, Barry R.	Aircraft Commander
2nd Lt. Comer, Richard L.	Copilot
Sgt. DeJesus, Jesus P. (WIA)	Flight Mechanic
SSgt. Cash, Harry H.	Flight Mechanic
TSgt. Patterson, David L.	Pararescueman
Sgt. Styer, Randy H.	Pararescueman
A1C Rhinehart, Frederick	Pararescueman

Extensive battle damage, returned to USS *Coral Sea.*

Knife-51 (brims) (1850 hours local time): Marines extracted: 41

Jolly Green-42 (-43) (purser) (1854 hours local time): Marines extracted: 54

Jolly Green-44 (1857 hours local time): Marines extracted: 34

1st Lt. Blough, Robert D.	Aircraft Commander
1st Lt. Mason, Henry M.	Copilot
SSgt. Bounds, Robert G.	Flight Mechanic
SSgt. Howell, Jimmy F.	Flight Mechanic
Sgt. Daly, Bruce M.	Pararescueman
A1C Ash, David D.	Pararescueman

Jolly Green-44 (1930 hours local time): Marines extracted: 40

By offloading his Marines on board the USS *Holt*, Blough was able to cut turnaround time in half and quickly return to the island.

Knife-51 (brims) (2110 hours local time): Marines extracted: 29

Total of 218 Marines extracted from Koh Tang (some wounded extracted during 2nd wave).

ADDITIONAL PERSONNEL

OV-10 pilots

Maj. Undorf, Robert	Nail-68
Capt. Roehrkasse, Rick	Nail-47
Capt. Wilson, Gregory	Nail-69
1st Lt. Carroll, William	Nail-51

AC-130 gunships
2nd Lt. Raatz, Donald   Spectre-11

EC-130 ABCCC aircraft   Cricket

Appendix B

U.S. Military Dead

The following is a list of servicemen who gave their "last full measure of devotion" during operations to recover the SS *Mayaguez* and her crew from Cambodia in May 1975.

On 13 May a CH-53 helicopter crashed while transporting eighteen members of the 56th SPS from Nakhon Phanom to Utapao, to serve as a contingency security force during the mission. All five crew members and eighteen SP were killed.

56th SPS killed in crash

Sgt. Jimmy Black
Sgt. Bobby Collums
SSgt. Gerald Coyle
Sgt. Thomas Dwyer
Sgt. Bob Ford
Sgt. Gerald Fritz
TSgt. Jackie Glenn
Sgt. Darrell Hamlin
Sgt. Gregory Hankamer
Sgt. David Higgs
SSgt. Faleagafulu Ilaoa
Sgt. Michael Lane
Sgt. Dennis London

Sgt. Robert Mathias
Sgt. William McKelvey
Airman Edgar Moran
Sgt. Tommy Nealis
Sgt. Robert Ross

Crew of CH-53C tail # 68-10933

Capt. James G. Kayes
1st Lt. Lawrence E. Frohlich
TSgt. George E. McMullen
Sgt. Paul J. Raber
Sgt. Robert P. Weldon

On 15 May ten Marines, two Navy corpsmen, and an Air Force pilot were killed when their helicopter, Knife-31, was damaged by enemy fire on Koh Tang Island and crashed into the ocean.

2nd Lt. Richard Vandegeer USAF**

HM2 Bernard Gause USN**

HM Ronald J. Manning USN**

Pfc. Daniel A Benedeir USMC

Pfc. Lynn Blessing USMC*

Pfc. Walter Boyd USMC*

LCpl. Gregory Copenhaver USMC*

LCpl. Andres Garcia USMC*

Pfc. James Jacques USMC*

Pfc. James R. Maxwell USMC*

Pfc. Richard W. Rivenburgh USMC*

Pfc. Antonio R. Sandoval USMC*

Pfc. Keimn R. Turner USMC*

*   Remains identified by DNA tests on 8 May 2000.
** Remains identified by DNA tests on 23 June 2000.

Additionally, four Marines were killed on the west beach of Koh Tang Island and one airman was killed assisting wounded from a downed helicopter, Knife-21.

LCpl. Ashton Loney USMC

Pfc. Gary Hall USMC

Pfc. Joseph N. Hargrove USMC

Pvt. Danny G. Marshall USMC

SSgt. Elwood E. Rumbaugh USAF

In total, forty-one U.S. service personnel gave their lives in the *Mayaguez* rescue operation.

Appendix C

Partial List of Marines Wounded

The following is a partial list of Marines wounded or injured during the *Mayaguez* operation, as provided by the reference branch of the Marine Corps History Division.

Capt. James H. Davis

2nd Lt. James McDaniel

SSgt. Dennis R. Davis

Sgt. Victor Salinas

Cpl. James H. Jones Jr.

Cpl. Ricardo Rodriguez

LCpl. Ronald Hughes

LCpl. Gilbert C. Lutz

LCpl. Charles L. Mitchell

LCpl. Lee W. Smiley

LCpl. Alan D. Wyatt

Pfc. Walter W. Akerly

Pfc. Daniel M. Carrasco

Pfc. Michael S. Cooper

Pfc. Mark Dick

Pfc. Tex E. Duke

Pfc. Kendrick E. Deckard

Pfc. David L. Fowler

Pfc. Kenneth J. Fry

Pfc. Mark A Mears

Pfc. Steven T. Morgan

Pfc. Timothy W. Trebil

Pfc. Herman Walton Jr.

Pfc. Jerome N. Wemitt

Pfc. Larry D. Yerg

Pvt. David R. Gibbs

Pvt. MacArthur Leonce

Pvt. Charles F. Lunsford

Awards of the Purple Heart have continued to be presented to qualified veterans who are able to document their wounds or injuries. Most recently, on 6 June 2009, Pfc. Allen Bailey was awarded the Purple Heart, to date the last Purple Heart of the Vietnam War.

Appendix D

U.S. Military Personnel Decorations

Awards for *Mayaguez* Rescue:

USMC

Navy Cross
2nd Lt. James V. McDaniel

Silver Star
Lt. Col. Randall W. Austin
1st Lt. Michael S. Eustis
1st Lt. James D. Keith
1st Lt. Terry L. Tonkin

Bronze Star
Col. John M. Johnson
Maj. John B. Hendricks
Capt. James H. Davis
Capt. Mykle E. Stahl
2nd Lt. Michael A. Cicere
2nd Lt. James W. Davis Jr.
2nd Lt. Daniel J. Hoffman
2nd Lt. Robert E. King
2nd Lt. Joseph J. McMenamin

USAF

Air Force Cross
Capt Rowland W. Purser
1st Lt. Donald R. Backlund
1st Lt. Richard C. Brims
SSgt. Jon D. Harston

Silver Star
Lt. Col. John H. Denham
Maj. Howard A. Corson Jr.
Maj. Robert W. Undorf
Capt. Terry D. Ohlemeier
Capt. Barry R. Walls
1st Lt. Robert D. Blough
1st Lt. Thomas D. Cooper Jr.
1st Lt. Robert P. Gradle
1st Lt. Charles R. Greer
MSgt. John J. Eldridge
TSgt. Wayne L. Fisk
SSgt. Joseph S. Stanaland

2nd Lt. Richard H. Zales
1st Sgt. Lawrence L. Funk
GySgt. Lester A. McNemar
SSgt. Seferino Bernal Jr.
Sgt. Gilbert C. Lutz
LCpl. Ashton N. Loney**
LCpl. Robert L. Sheldon
LCpl. John S. Standfast

Sgt. Thomas J. Bateson
A1C Brad E. Marx

Distinguished Flying Cross
1st Lt. Ronald T. Rand

USN
Silver Star
Cmdr. J. Michael Rodgers
    Commanding Officer of the *Henry B. Wilson* DDG-7
Lt. (jg) Larry Hall
    Officer in Charge of Second Black Velvet-1 Mission*

Bronze Star

RD1 Thomas K. Noble Jr.	(M-60 Machine Gunner)*
GM1 Alvin (John) K. Ellis	(M-60 Machine Gunner)*
RD3 Michael Williams	(M-60 Machine Gunner)*
GM2 Donald Moore	(M-60 Machine Gunner)*
RM2 Eddie J. Oswalt	(Radio Operator M-14 Rifleman)*
EN2 Greg Elam	(Engineer and M14 Rifleman)*
BM1 Jesse Hoffman	(Coxswain)*

*   Crew of Black Velvet-1
** Posthumous Award
All Marines were also awarded the Combat Action Ribbon.

Notes

Part 2. The Capture of the SS *Mayaguez*

1. George R. Dunham and David A. Quinlan, "U.S. Marines in Vietnam, 1973–1975: The Bitter End," History and Museums Division, HQ USMC, Washington, DC (1990), http://ehistory.osu.edu/vietnam/books/end/0238.cfm.
2. *Seized at Sea: Situation Critical*, Discovery Channel documentary (Arlington, VA: Henninger Productions, 2000).
3. CINCPAC Command History 1975, Appendix VI, The SS *Mayaguez* Incident, Command History Branch, HQ CINCPAC (San Francisco, 1976).
4. *Seized at Sea*, Discovery Channel.
5. Ibid.
6. Dunham and Quinlan, "U.S. Marines in Vietnam, 1973–1975."
7. David R. Mets, *Last Flight from Koh Tang: The* Mayaguez *Incident a Generation Later* (Joint Force Quarterly National Defense University Press Issue #45, 2nd Qtr 2007).
8. Interview with Randall W. Austin, 12 December 2009.

Part 3. First Casualties

1. Dunham and Quinlan, "U.S. Marines in Vietnam, 1973–1975."
2. Don Poss, *SS* Mayaguez *56th SPS—NKP, Call Sign Knife*, Vietnam SP Association Website, http://www.vspa.com/nkp-56th-sps-mayaguez-1975.htm.
3. "23 GIs Die in Thailand Helo Crash," *Pacific Stars and Stripes*, 15 May 1975; "The Truth About the *Mayaguez* Incident," *Bangkok Post*, 21 May 1975.
4. Ralph Wetterhahn, *The Last Battle: The* Mayaguez *Incident and the End of the Vietnam War* (New York: Carroll and Graf Publishers, 2001).

5. Interview with Dan Hoffman, 25 October 2008.
6. Dunham and Quinlan, "U.S. Marines in Vietnam, 1973–1975."
7. Wetterhahn, *The Last Battle*.
8. Mets, *Last Flight from Koh Tang*.
9. *Seized at Sea*, Discovery Channel.
10. Capt. John B. Taylor, "Air Mission: *Mayaguez*," *Airman Magazine*, February 1976.

Part 4. President Ford Orders Military Action
1. CINCPAC Command History 1975, Appendix VI.
2. Dunham and Quinlan, "U.S. Marines in Vietnam, 1973–1975."
3. Ibid.
4. Walter J. Wood, *Mayday for the* Mayaguez, U.S. Naval Institute Proceedings, November 1976.
5. Ibid.
6. Interview with Francis McGowin, 15 November 2008.

Part 5. Operation Plan
1. Interview with Randall W. Austin, 12 December 2009.
2. Robert A. Peterson, *Mayday for the* Mayaguez, U.S. Naval Institute Proceedings, November 1976.
3. "Official Records of the Union and Confederate Navies in the War of the Rebellion by United States Naval War Records Office," U.S. Office of Naval Records and Library (Washington, DC: U.S. GPO, 1897).
4. Dunham and Quinlan, "U.S. Marines in Vietnam, 1973–1975."
5. Ibid.
6. Peterson, *Mayday for the* Mayaguez.

Part 6. Marine "Boots on the Ground" on Koh Tang
1. Taylor, "Air Mission: *Mayaguez*."
2. Interview with Fred B. Morris, 12 September 2008.
3. Ibid.
4. Interview with Al Bailey, 5 September 2008.
5. *Seized at Sea*, Discovery Channel.
6. Interview with Fred B. Morris, 12 September 2008.
7. Interview with Al Bailey, 5 September 2008.
8. Mike McKinney and Mike Ryan, *Chariots of the Damned: Helicopter Special Operations from Vietnam to Kosovo* (New York: Thomas Dunne Books, 2002).
9. Interview with Al Bailey, 5 September, 2008.
10. McKinney and Ryan, *Chariots of the Damned*.

11. Silver Star Citations, *Mayaguez* Incident, www.Homeofheroes.com.
12. Air Force Cross citation for SSgt. Jon D. Harston, USAF Special Orders GB-583, dated 14 July 1975.
13. *Seized at Sea*, Discovery Channel.
14. Dunham and Quinlan, "U.S. Marines in Vietnam, 1973–1975."
15. Wetterhahn, *The Last Battle*.
16. Ibid.
17. Letter to Gen. P. K. Carlton from Gen. Louis L. Wilson Jr., USAF Office of the CINCPAC Air Forces, dated 25 June 1975.
18. John B. Hendricks, *Mayday for the* Mayaguez, U.S. Naval Institute Proceedings, November 1976.
19. Letter to Gen. P. K. Carlton from Gen. Louis L Wilson Jr., 25 June 1975.
20. Greg Wilson, *The* Mayaguez *Incident*, http://www.kohtang.com/growth.htm.
21. J. Michael Rodgers, *Mayday for the* Mayaguez, U.S. Naval Institute Proceedings, November 1976.
22. Interview with Tom Noble, 10 October 2008.
23. Rodgers, *Mayday for the* Mayaguez.
24. Interview with Jim Beck, November 2009.
25. Robb Rowan, *The Four Days of* Mayaguez (New York: W. W. Norton, 1975).
26. Ibid.
27. Wetterhahn, *The Last Battle*.
28. Letter home of 2nd Lt. James McDaniel, dated 16–17 May 1975.
29. Ibid.
30. Interview with Al Bailey, 5 September 2008.
31. Interview with James McDaniel, 9 November 2008.
32. Interview with Al Bailey, 5 September 2008.
33. Interview with James McDaniel, 9 November 2008.
34. Interview with Al Bailey, 5 September 2008.
35. Interview with James McDaniel, 9 November 2008.
36. Ibid.
37. Dunham and Quinlan, "U.S. Marines in Vietnam, 1973–1975."
38. Interview with Dan Hoffman, 22 December 2008.
39. Interview with James McDaniel, 9 November 2008.

Part 7. Extraction
1. Wetterhahn, *The Last Battle*.
2. McKinney and Ryan, *Chariots of the Damned*.
3. Letter to Gen. P. K. Carlton from Gen. Louis L. Wilson Jr., 25 June 1975.
4. Wetterhahn, *The Last Battle*.

5. "Nail" was the call sign for the OV-10 Bronco, a two-seat twin-turbo-prop observation aircraft used to identify and mark targets for the fast-moving fighter aircraft.

6. Interview with Randall W. Austin, 12 December 2009.

7. McKinney and Ryan, *Chariots of the Damned.*

8. Interview with Tom Noble, 10 October 2008.

9. Ibid.

10. Interview with Randall W. Austin, 12 December 2009.

11. Hendricks, *Mayday for the* Mayaguez.

12. Interview with Randall W. Austin, 12 December 2009.

13. Wetterhahn, *The Last Battle.*

14. John F. Guilmartin, *A Very Short War: The* Mayaguez *and the Battle of Koh Tang* (College Station, TX: Texas A&M University Press, 1995).

15. Wetterhahn, *The Last Battle.*

16. Guilmartin, *A Very Short War.*

Part 8. The Fate of the Missing Marines

1. Maj. Peter Brown, "Investigation to Inquire into the Circumstances Surrounding the Missing in Action Status in the Case of Private First Class Gary Hall, Lance Corporal Joseph Hargrove and Private Danny Marshall," Headquarters, 3d Marine Division, FMF (Fleet Marine Force), 7 June 1975.

2. "A Military Mission Gone Wrong: A New Look At The *Mayaguez* Incident," *CBS News Online,* 24 January 2001.

3. "Two Men, Two Schools," *Organizing for America,* http://my.barack obama.com/page/community/post/billboth/gG5hhY.

4. Brown, "Investigation to Inquire Into the Circumstances Surrounding the Missing in Action Status."

5. Ibid.

6. Interview with Scott Standfast, October 2008.

7. Brown, "Investigation to Inquire into the Circumstances Surrounding the Missing in Action Status."

8. Ibid.

Part 9. After the Battle

1. William Shawcross, *Side Show: Kissinger, Nixon and the Destruction of Cambodia* (New York: Simon & Schuster, 1979), 433n–34n.

2. Gerald R. Ford, *A Time to Heal* (New York: Harper & Row, 1979), 284.

3. Douglas Brinkley, *Gerald R. Ford* (New York: Henry Holt, 2007), 104.

4. Ibid.

5. U.S. Marine Corps Report 1/PCB/lek, 5520/0535, dated 7 June 1975, Subject: Investigation to Inquire into the Circumstances Surrounding the Missing in Action Status in the Case of Pfc. Gary C. Hall, USMC, LCpl. Joseph N. Hargrove, USMC, and Pvt. Danny G. Marshall, USMC.
6. Joint POW/MIA Accounting Command (JPAC), www.jpac.pacom.mil /index.php?page=mission_overview&size=100&ind=0.

Part 10. Return to Koh Tang
1. Wetterhahn, *The Last Battle*.
2. Molly K. Dewitt (Staff Columnist), "Time to Bring Joseph Home," *Jacksonville North Carolina Daily News*, 13 April 2009.
3. Telephone interview, Duplin County, North Carolina, Commissioner Cary Turner by James E. Wise Jr., 13 January 2010.

Sources
Awards Database, Home of Heroes Website, www.homeofheroes.com/valor.

Index

Page numbers in **bold** indicate personal recollections. Page numbers in *italics* indicate photographs.

About the Authors

James E. Wise Jr., a former naval aviator, intelligence officer, and Vietnam veteran, retired from the U.S. Navy in 1975 as a captain. He became a naval aviator in 1953 following graduation from Northwestern University. He served as an intelligence officer on board the USS *America* and later as the commanding officer of various naval intelligence units. Since his retirement, Captain Wise has held several senior executive posts in private sector companies. His many other books include *The Silver Star, The Navy Cross, Stars in Blue,* and *U-505: The Final Journey.* He is also the author of many historical articles in naval and maritime journals. Captain Wise lives in the Washington, DC, metropolitan area.

Scott Baron, a U.S. Army veteran of the Vietnam War and former law enforcement officer in California, is the author of *They Also Served: Military Biographies of Uncommon Americans* and coauthor, with James Wise, of *Women at War: World War II to Iraqi Freedom, International Stars at War, Soldiers Lost at Sea: A Chronicle of Troopship Disasters in Wartime, The Navy Cross,* and *The Silver Star,* all from the Naval Institute Press.

The **Naval Institute Press** is the book-publishing arm of the U.S. Naval Institute, a private, nonprofit, membership society for sea service professionals and others who share an interest in naval and maritime affairs. Established in 1873 at the U.S. Naval Academy in Annapolis, Maryland, where its offices remain today, the Naval Institute has members worldwide.

Members of the Naval Institute support the education programs of the society and receive the influential monthly magazine *Proceedings* or the colorful bimonthly magazine *Naval History* and discounts on fine nautical prints and on ship and aircraft photos. They also have access to the transcripts of the Institute's Oral History Program and get discounted admission to any of the Institute-sponsored seminars offered around the country.

The Naval Institute's book-publishing program, begun in 1898 with basic guides to naval practices, has broadened its scope to include books of more general interest. Now the Naval Institute Press publishes about seventy titles each year, ranging from how-to books on boating and navigation to battle histories, biographies, ship and aircraft guides, and novels. Institute members receive significant discounts on the more than eight hundred Press books in print.

Full-time students are eligible for special half-price membership rates. Life memberships are also available.

For a free catalog describing Naval Institute Press books currently available, and for further information about joining the U.S. Naval Institute, please write to:

Member Services
U.S. NAVAL INSTITUTE
291 Wood Road
Annapolis, MD 21402-5034
Telephone: (800) 233-8764
Fax: (410) 571-1703
Web address: www.usni.org